W9-CJC-903

FAMILY
OF
SHADOWS

FAMILY OF SHADOWS

A Century of
Murder, Memory, and the
Armenian American Dream

GARIN K. HOVANNISIAN

HARPER
An Imprint of HarperCollins*Publishers*
www.harpercollins.com

FIRST EDITION

Designed by William Ruoto

Library of Congress Cataloging-in-Publication Data

    Hovannisian, Garin.
      Family of shadows : a century of murder, memory, and the
    Armenian American dream / Garin Hovannisian.
        p.   cm.
      ISBN 978-0-06-179208-3
      1. Armenian-Americans—History. 2. American
    Dream. 3. Armenian massacres, 1915–1923. I. Title.
    E184.A7H685   2010
    956.6'20154—dc22   2010007874

(Hovannisian) No B
10 11 12 13 14 ID/RRD 10 9 8 7 6 5 4 3 2 1

TO VARTITER AND TAKOUHI

And on the seventeenth day of the seventh month the ark came to rest on the mountains of Ararat.

—Genesis 8:4

You mistake the shadows of the mountains for men.

—Judges 9:36

CONTENTS

Black Sea

Constantinople

Izmit

Brusa

Angora

TURKEY

Smyrna

Aflon – Karahisar

CILICIAN

Mediterranean
Sea

Jerusalem

EGYPT

Cairo

0   100   200
          miles

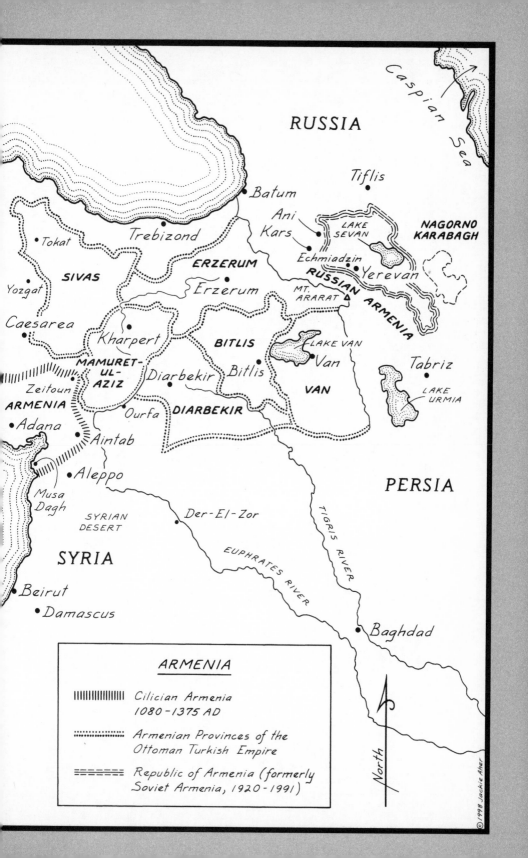

RUSSIA

Caspian Sea

Tiflis

Batum

Ani

Kars

NAGORNO
KARABAGH

LAKE
SEVAN

Trebizond

Tokat

ERZERUM

Echmiadzin

Yerevan

SIVAS

Erzerum

RUSSIAN
ARMENIA

Yozgat

MT.
ARARAT △

Caesarea

Kharpert

BITLIS

LAKE VAN

Tabriz

MAMURET-
UL-
AZIZ

Diarbekir

Bitlis

Van

LAKE
URMIA

Zeitoun

ARMENIA

Ourfa

DIARBEKIR

VAN

Adana

Aintab

PERSIA

Aleppo

Musa
Dagh

SYRIAN
DESERT

Der-El-Zor

TIGRIS RIVER

SYRIA

EUPHRATES RIVER

Beirut

Damascus

Baghdad

North

© 1998 Jackie Aher

ARMENIA

||||||||||||||| Cilician Armenia
1080–1375 AD

:::::::::::::: Armenian Provinces of the
Ottoman Turkish Empire

======= Republic of Armenia (formerly
Soviet Armenia, 1920–1991)

PROLOGUE

On the evening of December 7, 1988, in a quiet home at the end of Terryhill Place, a television was illuminated with strange images. I could not appreciate the horror of it all, the fallen buildings and frozen bodies—what the 6.9 number on the Richter scale meant for a country made of cards. Only from the panic spread upon my father's face did I realize that something extraordinary was happening to our homeland.

"Hayastane ufig e," I said in my first voice. "Armenia is hurting."

My mother marveled at that infant phrase, but my father did not share the moment with her. He was already gone into the storm of telephone calls that was connecting all the major cities of the Armenian diaspora: Boston, New York, Detroit, Montreal, Paris, Moscow, Beirut, Aleppo, Jerusalem, Tehran, Athens, Sydney, and Buenos Aires. We were in Los Angeles, the command center.

The phone rang all through the night, delivering the burning voices of priests, editors, and doctors to the ears of my father, a rising community leader—but still, inescapably, the son of the famous professor. Reports were already suggesting that more than fifty thousand people, residents of Soviet Armenia's northwestern towns and villages, were dead.

It was all wrong. This was supposed to be a good day. Only a few hours earlier, at United Nations headquarters in New York, Ronald Reagan and Mikhail Gorbachev had been negotiating the close of a long and cold war. At the same time, on the stage of the Shrine Auditorium in Los Angeles, my mother had been sworn in as an attorney at law. She had raised her right hand and pledged to defend the Constitution of the United States. "Against all enemies," she had said, glowing in the American dream, "foreign and domestic."

And just then, seven thousand miles away, the jealous earth had moved under Armenia.

I WOULD BE PLEASED TO recall for you the more glorious moments of our national history, how Tigran the Great once ruled over an Armenian empire stretching from the Mediterranean to the Caspian seas. But that was in the first century B.C., and the truth is that history was not so kind to the Armenians. For millennia they suffocated between Roman and Persian, Byzantine and Arab empires. They lost their kingdoms, their independence, and then their unity.

The Armenian saga unraveled into modernity on separate stages: Turkish Armenia to the west and Russian Armenia to the east. This is a tale of two homelands.

In 1915, under the cover of world war, the ultranationalist Young Turk government erased the Turkish Armenian homeland; a million and a half Armenians were murdered, and a million more escaped to create diasporas of memory around the world. That is where my great-grandparents came from—Turkish, or Western, Armenia.

Russian, or Eastern, Armenia was exempted from the annihilation. As the tsar's Petrograd combusted in a Bolshevik revolution, the Armenians of his empire seized an opening in history and declared in 1918 the independent Republic of Armenia. But only two years later, caught between the forces of Turkish nationalism and

Russian Bolshevism, the republic's leaders were forced to choose their surrender.

In 1920 the Armenians submitted to the promises of a new government in Moscow. They did not know that in 1923 Joseph Stalin, the people's commissar for nationalities, would seal the transfer of Mountainous Karabagh (in Russian, Nagorno-Karabagh) and other Armenian lands to neighboring Soviet Azerbaijan—that Armenia, shredded and sovietized, would be shredded again and stuffed into a humiliating thirty thousand square kilometers in the South Caucasus.

It was there, in the Armenian Soviet Socialist Republic, that the Eastern Armenians lived for decades, waiting through Malenkov, Khrushchev, and Brezhnev.

"*Glasnost y perestroika,*" Mikhail Gorbachev declared from Moscow, "openness and restructuring"—and the Armenians thought they had been waiting for him. In February 1988 half a million Armenians converged on the streets of Yerevan, their capital city. They appealed to "Mikhail the Savior" to reunite Mountainous Karabagh with Armenia, and Gorbachev responded a few months later by banning all demonstrations.

In the fall of 1988 the Armenians returned to their homes— thinking about their cousins in Mountainous Karabagh and wondering, for the first time, what democracy felt like. Meeting in candlelight, the Armenians sought their fortunes in coffee cups and told stories of freedom in the night.

"*Gar u chgar.*" The Armenian fairytales always began with those mysterious words. "There was and there was not . . ."

THE AMERICAN TRANS AIR BOEING 727 was carrying six crew members, twenty-one passengers, and more than fifty thousand pounds of medical equipment, food, and blankets. This was an emergency charter flight of the Department of State, yet there they were, Raffi and Vartiter Hovannisian, that curious son-and-mother team, racing to the fatherland.

They were on the same airplane, but Raffi and Vartiter were embarking on two very different journeys. Raffi, a lawyer and activist, was on a mission of hope to the land of his dreams. Vartiter, a doctor, was on a pilgrimage of grief to the Soviet nightmare she had renounced long ago. Her name means "rose petal," but occupying her narrow frame—under graying hair and behind precision lenses—was something thornier, more complicated than that.

Raffi had been to the Yerevan airport before, most recently in May, when he had come to participate in the last demonstrations against the Kremlin, before the ban. Upon each arrival, the Russian colonel at customs had searched and questioned the dark, bearded American with the Armenian name. But today there were no questions, only utter confusion among Soviet airport officials who had no choice but to accept the planeloads of foreigners and goodwill that were flooding into their empire.

But then the trees—naked and dead—on the road to the hotel. Then the potholes. Then the frozen fields. Then the city, untouched by the earthquake: rectangular cars parked by rectangular buildings. Then the Soviet tanks, soldiers on the streets. The opera house, the scene of the demonstrations, looked to be a hostile military encampment. Citizens walked their capital in silence—out of sorrow or fear, it was their choice. The wrath of heaven and earth had fallen upon the Armenians.

And then Raffi saw them, the great white mountains—the lesser and greater peaks of Mount Ararat—glowing vast and eternal just beyond the city, as if they had been freshly painted upon a bleak canvas. Those awesome mountains, where Noah's Ark is said to have landed, had once served as the symbol of a unified homeland. But today, rising through fog and blizzard, Ararat stood as the behemoth boundary between two homelands: a broken Soviet state on one side and the memory of a murdered civilization on the other—reality and dream. Ararat itself was part of the dream. It stood in Turkey, on the other side of the border.

Raffi and Vartiter stayed at the Armenia Hotel, a sprawling nine-story building that followed a pink and gold procession of government ministries, museums, clock towers, archways, and statues around an oval called Lenin Square. The scowling deity himself stood there, enforcing the evening curfew.

Rescue workers were already back from Spitak and Leninakan and the ruins of the northwest, and the bar of the Armenia Hotel was filling with the languages of the world: the native Armenian, the official Russian, but also the English and Spanish and French that had been banished from the Soviet Union more than a half century before. There were doctors, diplomats, and the three classes of confidence men that trail diplomats everywhere: journalists, sycophants, and spies.

Sitting at the bar, amid the smoke of the world's cigarettes, Raffi drank down a one-dollar Coca-Cola and smiled. He could not help but smile at this spectacle—a serendipitous meeting, in his very own homeland, of enemy civilizations.

THE SIGNPOST OF A SECURITY agency stood in the grass by the door, but my grandfather's house, just across the street from the University of California, Los Angeles, had never been wired with an alarm. The door was unlocked, so I let myself in and dashed through a creaky corridor to the professor's office. The books and papers were piled so high, the classical music so loud, the clanging of his typewriter so passionate, that my grandfather did not notice me.

"*Hairig!* Father!" I yelled, having heard my mother call him that. And here my grandfather emerged from his grumpiness, his serious, scholarly features rearranging themselves into a jolly smile. For a moment, he could leave his life's ongoing work—a four-volume history of the Republic of Armenia, 1918 to 1920—in his typewriter and turn to his first grandchild.

My mother soon appeared at the sliding doors. She smiled sweetly at my grandfather and asked if he had any news from Raffi or Mama Vart. "No news," he said, and my mother, always the observant daughter-in-law, concealed her anxiety. She walked back through the corridor and began to tidy the professor's house.

Sometimes when she came across a newspaper headline about the earthquake, my mother paused to read. The *Washington Post*: "In Spitak, the living are searching for the dead. . . ." She imagined Raffi amid the destruction: a pair of brown eyes and a white knit sweater, the one he had worn when she fell in love with him.

THE TORTUOUS ROAD WAS NOT a new one for Raffi, or for the Soviet Kamaz truck crushing the morning ice as it made its way to Spitak. The last time Raffi visited this northern town, he had found schools, chapels, and factories. There was no warning that Spitak would be different this time. Along the road from Yerevan, the same white fields unfurled, the same cattle grazed, the same Kurdish village appeared and then disappeared in the fog.

But when the Kamaz pulled into Spitak, Raffi found no city, just rocks and twisted metal and rasping Soviet cranes. Some buildings had lost only their facades, their inner lives suspended in the air, like dollhouses. Pictures hung on walls. Coffee cups were overturned on kitchen tables.

When Raffi arrived at the soccer stadium, he saw what he had feared: thousands of corpses stacked upon the bleachers and grass. His heart shuddered. He knew that he was seeing what his grandfather Kaspar had once seen. Only that was in 1915, on the other side of Mount Ararat.

Outside the stadium, survivors and volunteers were digging for life. Raffi joined them, but that morning he exhumed only corpses. Horrified and dizzy, he staggered through the rubble, a video camera in one hand and a bag filled with sweaters in the other. Soon the sweaters had all been given away, but the beggars did not stop coming. So Raffi, helpless in snow and sorrow, took off his white knit sweater and passed it to a stranger. Then he moved on.

That is what you did in Spitak. You helped, then moved on.

"In Spitak, the living are searching for the dead." Those words, which appeared on the front page of the *Washington Post* on December 15, 1988, were written on a $600 Tandy TRS–80 computer in a room of the Armenia Hotel. The author, David Remnick, was among the journalists—Ann Cooper of National Public Radio, Bill Keller of the *New York Times*, and many others—who were charged with making sense of a tragedy so great that Mikhail Gorbachev, after completing his tour of sympathy in Soviet Armenia, confessed never before to have "seen one one-thousandth of its suffering."

But the earthquake had not solved Gorbachev's political problems. Bloody but unbowed, the survivors in the northwest had renewed their demands: for the unification of Armenia and Mountainous Karabagh, for visible democratic reforms in the Soviet Union. They had bought Gorbachev's attention with blood, and they would not squander it in lamentation.

One day they would achieve the top offices at the *New Yorker* and the *New York Times*, but for now David Remnick and Bill Keller were on the Soviet beat, reporting from the ruins. Remnick wrote:

> Mikhail Gorbachev is a superstar around the world and in most
> parts of the Soviet Union, yet when he came here the other day to

survey the damage and console the people, the townspeople just
stared at him, like family members turning in their pews trying to
figure out this curious guest at the funeral.

Meanwhile, Keller observed Armenian earthquake victims "jeer-
ing, whistling and spitting on the ground" in front of Gorbachev.

The Soviet leader had trouble masking his wrath, and he cracked
out of his grief to condemn the popular movement, calling it a project
of "demagogues" and "dishonest people" who were lusting for power.
On the eve of his departure from Armenia, Gorbachev ordered the
arrest of the Armenian leaders, a group of intellectuals known as the
Karabagh Committee.

The obedient Communist media did not report on Gorbachev's
rage, but even they slowly joined in subtle acts of insubordination.
Keller took note:

> The Soviet press has played up the Western donations as the great-
> est example of East-West comity since Soviet and American troops
> met at the Elbe River in 1945. Nightly features on the television
> news and daily articles in the newspapers have doted on French,
> American, German and even Israeli contributions, often stressing
> the superior mobility and readiness of Western teams.

Remnick, in his turn, proclaimed a "sea change"—the arrival in
Moscow of the first swallows of self-criticism.

IN LENINAKAN, HISTORIC ALEXANDROPOL, THOUSANDS of wooden
coffins were piled in the central square. Tents were pitched, and bon-
fires were crackling. Raffi looked up at the town clock, which towered above the square. It had stopped ticking at 11:41 on the morning
of December 7, 1988. Thousands of clocks buried under a fallen city,

all of them stopped at 11:41—this must have been some madman's vision of the apocalypse.

Many survivors had fled, but most had stayed in Leninakan. With bleeding, frostbitten hands, unshaven fathers and shivering mothers were searching desperately for an entire generation of missing children. The earthquake had struck just before students were to be released for the noon recess.

In the afternoon Raffi found a few dead bodies, and once a boy drawing his final breaths. He yelled for doctors, and his voice echoed about the vacant city. The destruction was endless, and here there was no hope. So from time to time Raffi got down on his knees and cried into the debris of his fatherland.

Raffi spent the freezing night in Leninakan, walking from bonfire to bonfire. The survivors gathered around to share stories, theories. Many Armenians claimed to have seen a bright light on the horizon the morning of December 7. They said that the earthquake had been detonated by the Soviet military.

The following morning Raffi returned to the capital on a road teeming with Zhigulis, Nivas, and Volgas that were making special deliveries to Yerevan hospitals and orphanages. Raffi was being delivered to an emptying hotel. Rescue workers and journalists were slowly leaving Armenia in search of newer tragedies.

Raffi was disappointed, even hurt, yet he knew that the story of his life and his nation was only now beginning. At the Armenia Hotel, a new cast of characters was already checking in: Andrei Sakharov, Soviet dissident and Nobel Peace Prize laureate; Margaret Thatcher, prime minister of Great Britain; and the many foreign masterminds who were finding in Armenia the chance for the ultimate democratic struggle.

That Christmas 1988 Raffi spent in the service of John Ellis "Jeb" Bush and George Prescott Bush, the son and grandson of President-elect George H. W. Bush. He led them through the malodorous wards of Yerevan hospitals, and twelve-year-old George handed out candy and teddy bears to the orphans. At the Holy See of Etchmiadzin, the headquarters of the Armenian Apostolic Church, Raffi joined the Americans in a prayer for national salvation.

On the morning of December 28, Raffi and Vartiter emerged from the Armenia Hotel. For the past ten days, Vartiter had been a featherweight soul floating about the republic, drifting to any corner where her languages—English, Armenian, Russian, and German— or her medical expertise was needed. But for this mission, she had reconnected with her son.

They were carrying cardboard boxes filled with the papers of the Armenian Assembly of America, a pillar organization of the Western diaspora, so Vartiter and Raffi walked cautiously through Lenin Square. The few blocks felt like football fields, and Raffi recalled the words of Mr. Kahn, his P.E. teacher at Paul Revere Junior High School in Los Angeles: "Stand tall! Feel tall! Think tall! You *are* tall!" They walked tall, mother and son, walked confidently as the Soviet soldiers stared at their boxes, loaded with flammable ideas.

Vartiter and Raffi reached the water fountains near the National Gallery and then, just before the intersection of Abovyan and Pushkin, the grilled doors of a hulking gray building. Raffi produced a golden key. He was about to open in Soviet Yerevan the first embassy of democracy—the embassy, though he did not realize it, of return.

On New Year's Eve 1988, we waited for the travelers at baggage claim. I noticed the roses in my grandfather's hands—I had never seen him with flowers before—and the worry in my mother's eyes. And then, in the distance, I made out the two familiar figures. I dashed toward them. My father kneeled and stretched his arms wide, and I launched into his embrace. My grandmother reached over to pull at my hair. I did not know why she liked hurting me.

The next morning, tucked between my father and mother, I awoke to the New Year's messages of Presidents Reagan and Gorbachev. This was the last time the two leaders would appear together on television. In fact, this was the last time Reagan, as president, would address the public. He spoke first:

> In your country and mine, the New Year is a time of hope and renewal. Never have these qualities of the spirit been more necessary than now, as Soviet Armenia begins to heal from its wounds.

You must understand what a miracle that was. Until that exact moment, our Armenian identity had never really been proclaimed to the American world. We had kept our language and ritual mostly to ourselves. It had become our custom, at movie theaters in Los Angeles, to wait through the concluding credits and to cheer at the sight of an Armenian last name, the iconic *-ian* or *-yan* ending. We must have seemed like lunatics to the Americans around us, but that was one of the ways we kept our identity in this land.

And now, on international television, Mikhail Gorbachev was saying:

> Armenia's tragedy has evoked great sympathy throughout the world. We are grateful to the American people and to all peoples who have come to our aid. Seeing all this, one cannot help thinking that all people who live on this Earth, all of us, however different, are really one family.

My father was astonished by these sentiments, and he knew then that the Armenian earthquake of December 7, 1988, had been the groundbreaking event of Soviet-American relations. The East had crumbled and the West had rushed to its aid. Soviets and Americans had recognized, in the rubble of Armenia, their different sins and common values. At the fault line of history, Raffi had seen the end of the Soviet Union.

Now he was back in his Los Angeles office, trying to reinvest himself in the law. But he could not do that. Sometimes after work Raffi drove alone to the nearby hospital where a few child survivors of the earthquake had been brought for advanced surgery. Mostly he played with Greta, a little girl with no legs, who lay on a board with wheels and used her hands to move across the floor. Chasing Raffi around the room, Greta was the giggling phantom of a past that was quickly catching up to the lawyer of Terryhill Place.

In the early days of their marriage, my father and mother had often talked of returning with children to the forbidden land of Western Armenia, where their grandparents had once lived. But after the earthquake it was increasingly Eastern Armenia that consumed their imagination. Armenians actually lived there, between a history of horror with Turkey and the anticipation of war with Azerbaijan— waiting in a Soviet dungeon.

But after seven decades in stagnation, history was moving again. The earthquake had ripped open the fatherland, and the passions once buried underground had been liberated before the world. The Armenians were pushing the Kremlin for reforms, and the Kremlin was punishing the Armenians. A popular movement was growing to match the Kremlin's wrath. It was clear, finally, that the Armenians were ready for freedom and fated for independence. It was the dream of my father to share in that fate.

I, too, inherited my father's dreams, though I realized them in my own way. "Look," I would say, stacking my wooden blocks on the living room floor, "I'm building homes and schools." And then I would smash the blocks with my fist. "Look," I would say, "the Turks broke Armenia. But don't worry. We'll get them back."

Of course the Turks had nothing to do with the earthquake. But my young mind could not distinguish between the natural disaster of Eastern Armenia in 1988 and the planned catastrophe of Western Armenia in 1915. I did not know that my father spoke about one from experience and the other from stories he himself was told as a child— the stories of his grandfather Kaspar, who once lived in another Armenia, on the other side of the mountain.

I don't remember exactly when it was, but not too long after the earthquake I learned my first poem. Around the dinner table, my family and its many friends would toast me and say, *"Anunit dere tarnas"*—"May you live up to your name." I would stand tall on my chair and begin to recite. The words tasted sweet in my mouth, yet I did not understand them. To me, they were only syllables, still without meaning or destiny:

> *Herve heru garod em kez,*
> *Ov im anush hairenik.*
> *Voch vok grna sirdes hanel*
> *Surp anunt, hairenik.*
> *Or me bidi jampa iynam,*
> *Ev kirgt kam, hairenik.*
> *Ev al kezme ch'heranam,*
> *Im anushig hairenik.*

> From afar I long for you,
> My sweet fatherland.
> No one can take from my heart
> Your holy name, fatherland.
> One day I will set out for you,
> And come to your lap, fatherland.
> And never again shall I leave you,
> My sweet fatherland.

FAMILY
OF
SHADOWS

Chapter One

WASTELAND

The bells of Bazmashen tolled at noon, and Kaspar looked anxiously toward the church. All across the Golden Plain, women hurried home, red jugs of water balanced on their shoulders. Their husbands returned from the fields, where a new generation of red wheat was being sown into dry soil. The elders, who had been debating war and grapes on the street corner, called out to their grandchildren. And now all three thousand Armenians walked on the narrow dirt paths leading to the church, a stack of stones in the village of Bazmashen, in the province of Kharpert, in the eastern reaches of the Ottoman Empire.

The villagers gathered in the church called Surp Mariam Asdvadzadzin—Holy Mary, Mother of God. Kaspar stood in line with the children, all of them barefoot. He was fourteen years old, maybe just a little too old for this. His mother, Heghnar, holding a baby boy in her arms, observed from a distance, and so did Kaspar's grandparents, and the Gavroians and the Der Sarkisians, and the whole congregation of Armenians among whom there were no strangers that spring afternoon. The priest knelt at the altar, and the service began. It was Maundy Thursday 1915, and the Christian minorities of a Muslim empire were commemorating, toward the end of Holy Week, Jesus' Last Supper and his betrayal by Judas Iscariot.

The priest dipped his hand into the vat by his side and sprinkled water on Kaspar's feet. They were rough, dark feet—not like the feet of children from Kharpert and Mezre, the more sophisticated Armenian towns to the east. They were feet of the earth. They were feet that had been raising dust and mischief for fourteen years. Today they were washed.

"*Ev chur arial dzarayapar / Vodkere lvanayir ashagerdatsn,*" the believers sang. "And like a servant He took the water / And washed the feet of His disciples."

After the purification, the villagers channeled out of the church and vanished into their homes. There were more than three hundred homes in Bazmashen (the name itself meant "place of many homes"), mostly one or two stories high, and all of them packed with the same coterie of grandfathers and cousins and brides, the same pastoral sensibilities—and, on this occasion, the same basket of eggs.

But Kaspar's home was different.

Construction had begun two years earlier, shortly after a handsome, blue-eyed man who was Kaspar's father arrived in Bazmashen. Hovhannes Gavroian had been saving money to build a new house since the early 1900s, when he had consigned his wife and infant son to relatives and left his village for a chance at the American dream. Heghnar's brother, Manoug, had moved even earlier to the San Joaquin Valley of California, and together Hovhannes and Manoug had ventured into the business of buying vineyards—until the vineyards, and their relationship, soured. Hovhannes returned to Western Armenia in 1912, embittered by America and determined to plant anew family foundations in the thirsty soil of Bazmashen.

There could not have been a worse time for this. Hovhannes had been back in the village for just two years when the Ottoman Empire entered a world war and called on him, and many Armenians like him, to join the campaign of the Central Powers, led by the German and Austro-Hungarian empires. That is how he came to leave Heghnar and Kaspar a second time. Except this time Kaspar had a brother, Gabriel, and Heghnar the secret of life inside her.

Holy Week gave mother and son the opportunity to lose their sorrows in ritual. Those eggs, for example—Maundy Thursday was devoted to preparing them. Heghnar and Kaspar would boil the eggs in a pot with red onion skins to achieve the coloring of Jesus' blood. On Good Friday the family would mark the crucifixion. And on Holy Saturday, in the courtyard of the church, all village children would hold out their eggs and strike them against each other. Some children hit hard, others gently. They did not know that their strategies were futile, that it did not actually matter how they struck: a weak egg would never beat a strong egg.

The most magnificent day was Easter, when the great feast was set on the fields of Bazmashen. *"Kristos hariav i merelots,"* one villager said to the other. "Christ is risen from the dead." They kissed each other, once on each cheek. *"Orhnial e harutiune Kristosi,"* the other villager responded. "Blessed is the resurrection of Christ." And then the men began to sing, the women assembled into a circle dance, and the children ran through the open fields, chasing the bees.

Then the festivities ended. The villagers stepped back into the furrows of daily life. But those red eggs, boiled and painted in multitudes, lasted a while longer, only slowly disappearing from baskets all across the Armenian plains.

EVER SINCE THE SECULAR YOUNG Turks ousted Sultan Abdul Hamid II from Constantinople and restored a liberal constitution in 1908, the Armenians of the Ottoman Empire had enjoyed some hope for freedom. Their six provinces—Erzerum, Bitlis, Van, Dikranagerd, Sepastia, and Kharpert—had broken loose from the tyrant's grip. For a time the Armenians were even allowed to bear arms, which kept nomadic Kurds from plundering their villages. They had overwhelmingly supported the revolution and, in the euphoric aftermath, even invited the Young Turks into the meetings of their own political societies. Armenians and Turks had exchanged toasts to liberty, equality, and justice.

That is how the new Turkish authorities acquired the membership rosters, and that is how they knew exactly whom they wanted to take from Bazmashen. Of course they phrased it more pleasantly than that. Chatter about reforms was all right, they said, but the Ottoman Empire recently had entered a great war, and the village people of Bazmashen and all Armenian people were expected to fight. Nearly a hundred thousand Armenians, including Hovhannes Gavroian, were already wearing the Turkish uniform.

Bazmashen was without its men, but spring flourished all the same, the hills blossoming with their first violets. In the afternoons the children of the small Protestant and Catholic schools and the academy of the Armenian Apostolic Church ran out to pick them.

But Kaspar did not play with these children. Since the enlistment of his father, Kaspar had been promoted to an early manhood—the responsibility of cultivating the family crops and appeasing the Kurdish and Turkish *aghas*. These were the dreaded feudal landlords who would arrive every few months from Mezre to collect tribute and a 35 percent production tax.

Kaspar knew the politics of his town; he recognized the peculiar names whispered on the street corners. The newly created Sahmanatir Ramgavar (Constitutional Democrat) Party offered a liberal, evolutionary agenda for Armenian politics within the boundaries of the Ottoman Empire. The Social Democrat Hunchakian Party and the Hai Heghapokhakan Dashnaktsutiun (Armenian Revolutionary Federation, ARF), by contrast, were older establishments, and more ambitious. They both dreamed of an emancipated Armenian state, and they were bold enough to believe that this awful world war might finally make room for it.

Many in Bazmashen, including Kaspar's family, shared the ARF's vision. They did not suspect that a very different plan for the Armenians was being drafted in Constantinople by the ruling triumvirate—the minister of war, Ismail Enver; the minister of interior, Mehmet Talaat; and the minister of the navy, Ahmed Jemal. It was in Constantinople on April 24, 1915, that Ottoman police arrested hundreds of Armenian intellectuals, clergymen, and community leaders.

But the plan, whatever it was, had been approved before April 24. Thousands of Armenians in Van and Zeitun had already been murdered. Tens of thousands across the empire already had been locked in jail cells and torture chambers. Sometimes there was an explanation—most often a charge of treason—and sometimes there was not.

There was no explanation offered at the beginning of May, when a Turkish commander and ten soldiers, known as gendarmes, arrived in Bazmashen. They were looking for guns, they said. Kaspar hid and watched as the gendarmes entered the homes, emerging sometimes with rifles, sometimes with trembling villagers. The few remaining men of Bazmashen were shoved into their church—the makeshift interrogation room.

Kaspar could hear the midnight screams and pleas of these men. A few of them ultimately confessed. Others borrowed money so that they could buy rifles and turn them in as their own.

The gendarmes were pleased. Having confiscated the guns and terrorized the women and children, they left the village. They took with them the insubordinate souls and the photographs of the collected weapons. These snapshots would be used as precious evidence that the Armenians of the Ottoman Empire were organizing a rebellion.

Kaspar tended the family gardens through the summer, while the sun roasted the countryside. Some nights, when he could not bear the heat, he slept on the roof, where the breeze drifting from the nearby mountains would cool him. The breeze was sweet, but not the news that daily followed it to Bazmashen.

"If they take you from the village, do not go with them," warned a sick refugee woman who hobbled one day into town. "Die in the village if you can, but do not go."

Kaspar paid no heed to the woman. But a few days later he heard that the men of Bazmashen, those who were taken from the village by the gendarmes, had been butchered in the mountains.

For those remaining in the village, their fate was delivered in June, and nailed—appropriately, for such a great reformation—on the church door. They would soon be relocated, not to return until the end of the war.

It was in this way that an Armenian village founded in 1165 prepared to shut down. The streets of Bazmashen transformed into an open-air bazaar. Whatever could not be roped onto a single donkey was sold at preposterous prices to Kurds who descended eagerly from the mountains. And so Bazmashen was liquidated. Some money was hidden underground, stashed in walls, or entrusted to the foreign consulates in nearby Mezre. There was, apparently, some hope of returning.

DURING THE FALL HARVEST OF 1892—or was it earlier? The villagers never did agree—a cool wind arrived in Bazmashen to announce the coming of winter. The wind was modest, yet by some special power it proceeded to topple the immense white *khachkar*, or cross-stone, of the village. The cross itself had been carved by Greek monks in the seventh century. At least that is what the villagers believed. But the villagers believed all sorts of things. They believed, for instance, that the crash of the *khachkar* was an omen.

That was not mere peasant prophecy, and its jurisdiction reached far beyond Bazmashen. The curse made itself known first to the villagers of Sasun, who in 1894 stood up to their violent Kurdish chieftains. A battle raged, and eventually the exhausted Sasunites agreed to trade their rifles for amnesty. After the rifles had been collected, the Kurds, joined by army regulars, massacred the village population—and this with such efficiency that Sultan Abdul Hamid II, the Ottoman ruler, organized the Kurdish fighters into semiregular Hamidiye regiments and charged them with carrying out similar massacres in all Armenian provinces of his empire. Between 1894 and 1896, two hundred thousand Armenians were killed in Western Armenia—their villages, including Bazmashen, pillaged and burned. The European powers did not intervene.

It was in protest against both Ottoman slaughter and international silence that in the early afternoon of August 26, 1896, a team of twenty-six Armenians armed with guns, grenades, and dynamite entered the Ottoman Bank in Constantinople. Led by seventeen-year-old Papken Suni, the radicals of the Armenian Revolutionary Federation gained control of the bank, its staff and clientele, for fourteen hours. They had no interest in the bank's vault, only a list of demands: appointment of a European diplomat as high commissioner for Turkish Armenia, withdrawal of the gendarmerie from Armenian villages, guarantee of rights to free speech and conscience, and a general amnesty for Armenians condemned under political charges.

Ottoman forces endeavored to recapture the bank, and Suni died upon a grenade. But as evening settled upon Constantinople, Turkish authorities realized that they had no option but to negotiate. Eventually they promised to respond to Armenian grievances. The Armenians, consumed by hunger and by grief for the death of their leader, accepted the Ottoman guarantees. The bank was cleared and the surviving warriors were on a boat sailing to Marseilles—and into the mythology of the Armenian revolutionary movement.

Instead of implementing the promised reforms, however, the Turkish government authorized a vendetta so swift and effective that many wondered if it had not already been planned, if the sultan had not known about the Armenian plot. For the next few days, Turkish theological students roamed the streets of Constantinople, where, according to a *New York Times* report, they "looted shops and residences and murdered everybody whom they suspected of being an Armenian or a sympathizer with the Armenians." In Constantinople six thousand Armenian men, women, and children were killed.

This was the context in which the Armenians of the Ottoman Empire enrolled in the revolutionary movements—both the Armenian movement, headed by the ARF and the Hunchakian Party, and the Turkish movement, being organized by the progressive and secular Young Turks. This is why Armenians rejoiced when the Young Turks took power in 1908. The rising regime might have been nationalistic, but it was not a clerical government.

What the Armenians of the Ottoman Empire did not understand was that a religious dictatorship at least had a god to answer to. But an oligarchy rooted in a pure, secular Turkish nationalism—headed by the human triumvirate of Enver, Talaat, and Jemal—was the creator and judge of its own conscience.

IN THE SUMMER OF 1915 the Armenians began to walk. They followed the gendarmes southward, in the direction of Malatia and the river Euphrates. For a brief moment, the Armenians were allowed to stop by the village fountain, where Bazmashen's singing women once had filled their red jugs. They drank the water one last time and, as they turned to leave, a few women began to wail, as if they just now realized that something astonishing was happening to them.

As they walked, Kaspar looked back at his village. Its homes, gardens, and churches were fading into the summer sky.

"*Krge indzi,*" the young children cried, pleading to be carried. But the mothers were already carrying their even younger siblings. And what could they do but speak madness into children's ears?

"Stop crying," they whispered. "If you cry, the Turks will kill you."

Actually, those words were not so mad, because soon the Turks

and the Armenians were all alone in the world. Beneath a brutal, un-
blinking sun, Ottoman tempers were scalding.

At first the violence had some logic. The gendarmes shot only the
weak, the sick, and the elderly straggling at the end of the caravan.
They were merely keeping order. But soon they found new reasons
for cruelty. *"Giavur!"* the gendarmes shouted. "Infidel!"

The people of Bazmashen spent the first night in the fields of
southern Kharpert. Gendarmes yelled at the villagers, as village dogs
had once barked at their sheep. They did not yet know the name or
nature of this conspiracy, but the Turks and the Armenians were
perfect for their roles. The Turks amused themselves by tormenting
the Armenians; the Armenians simply pretended to sleep. A crescent
moon reigned in the sky.

By the morning, when the Armenians began to walk again, faith
in survival had expired. The only question on this dry yellow road
was when they would die.

Bare feet burned on scorching earth. Children could not walk,
and when their mothers found a patch of shade under a tree, sometimes they left them there. *"Hos getsir. Ertam kezi chur perem,"* they
said. "You stay here. I will bring you some water." Heghnar clung
to Gabriel, her gaze set sorrowfully upon Kaspar—his brown eyes,
bushy brows, round nose.

Kaspar was horrified by what he saw on the banks of the Euphrates River. Thousands of Armenians were congregated there, and
as they waited for their turn to cross, they prayed for an exit. The
prayers were answered for many Armenian women, but not in the
way they had hoped. Turks and Kurds wandered through the masses,
searching for wives and concubines.

A Kurd with a thin mustache and a turban was looking for a boy
who could work, and he found one standing next to Heghnar Gavroian.

Kaspar's mother trembled. *"Hayir,"* she said in Turkish. "No."

But "no" meant nothing at the end of the world, and the women huddled around Heghnar told her that this was Kaspar's last chance. They had heard that boys above the age of twelve would soon be separated from the group.

Gunshots blasted in the distance, and the Kurd told Heghnar that he would save her son's life. She knew what had to be done. She wrapped her arms around Kaspar.

"Vay, mairig, vay!" Kaspar cried. "Oh, Mother, oh!"

Heghnar and Kaspar cried together, and around them cried the Gavroians and Der Sarkisians and the Chiloyans and an uncle hiding in a woman's dress. Only Gabriel, blessed with incomprehension, was quiet.

The Kurd tugged at Kaspar, and Kaspar broke away from his mother's grasp.

Following the Kurd along the riverbank, Kaspar could still hear his pregnant mother's screams. He looked back and, through his tears, he saw her and his baby brother in her arms. He would not know him. He would never see his mother again.

Kaspar continued to walk forward, look backward. And then he walked more and looked less until he wasn't looking at all, until he had no will or consciousness, until Kaspar was not a villager or an Armenian or even a boy anymore, only a breathless series of movements, *left-right-left-right-left-right*, dragging left and right through the wastelands of history and fate.

KASPAR BEGAN HIS NEW LIFE as a serf in a settlement on the outskirts of Izol, which had received, in the previous weeks, an influx of young laborers and brides. As he led his master's goats through the fields, Kaspar often thought of his own fields, and of his mother and Gabriel, who were perhaps still walking, and of his father, who was perhaps still fighting on the Turkish front lines.

At dusk Kaspar returned the goats to his master. They were stuffed and satisfied, but the boy himself was kept hungry. So one night Kaspar sneaked into his master's pantry and stole two loaves of bread and a jar of mulberry jam. He did this the following night, too, and the night after that, but one night he found the pantry door bolted.

The next morning Kaspar heard that a mischievous Kurdish boy called Osman had been beaten for stealing from his master. Kaspar said nothing.

Toward the end of summer, Turkish gendarmes marched into the Kurdish settlement and demanded the surrender of all Armenian boys. This time there would be no exceptions.

Compassion now visited Kaspar's master. He refused to give up his boy to the gendarmes, and instead took him to Izol, where he pleaded for Kaspar's freedom with the local Turkish administrator.

"He's only a boy," the Kurd muttered.

The Turk shook his head. "They will kill you, too," he said.

Then the Turk astounded Kaspar. He reached into his drawer and brought out a handful of sugar cubes. He smiled and offered them to the boy. "No," the Armenian said proudly. And then he began to bawl.

Back in the Kurdish settlement, Kaspar waited for the gendarmes, who would soon return for him. But the Turks were not his most immediate problem. A Kurdish girl, intoxicated by her power, pestered Kaspar. "Your father's mustache is dirty!" That was her baffling and harmless insult, yet she said it so often and with such malice that Kaspar decided to punish the girl. The next time she delivered her line, the boy answered, *"Your* mustache is dirty!"

The girl ran away and returned with her older brothers. They stripped off Kaspar's clothes and beat him to the ground.

Cold and bleeding, Kaspar thought how strange it was that he had challenged the Kurdish girl. This gave him some strength, and he stood up. Slowly he walked toward the mountains of Izol, fanta-sizing. Maybe there were Armenians in the mountains, he thought. Maybe they would save him. Maybe the troops of brave Antranig were searching for him.

Kaspar began to sing for them. He sang the Armenian revolution-ary songs he had heard his father sing. His voice echoed in the moun-tains:

> *Antranige kach, ir engernerov,*
> *Guze baderazm, ge sbase karnan.*

> Antranig the brave, warriors at his side,
> He waits for spring, aching for a fight.

KASPAR EMERGED FROM THE BLACK-AND-WHITE horrors of his sleep and waited for reality to be restored to his senses. He discovered who he was—orphan and slave—and it occurred to him that he was sup-posed to be watching over his master's goats. He jumped to his feet and dashed across the field, but there were no goats in sight. They had fled, and Kaspar knew that his master would not forgive him. He would have to escape.

He left the settlement by night and headed northeast, in the direc-tion of Bazmashen, and on the way he encountered Kurds who beat him, who warned him, who consoled him. Everywhere he found the rotting corpses of children. They were scattered lavishly about the *ergir*, the homeland. It was the autumn of 1915.

Kaspar continued walking through fields and rivers. In the eve-nings, when he was soaking wet, the wind pounded the cold into his bones.

For days Kaspar had gone without food, and so when he saw a vil-lage quivering on the horizon, he hastened toward it. He had resolved to offer himself to chance. But as he approached the village, he heard the barking of dogs. Then, just off the main road, he stumbled upon more corpses.

Maybe they asked for bread, Kaspar thought.

Kaspar obeyed his fears. He found a boulder in the fields and sat against it, shivering. An early winter had settled over Kharpert. The boy coughed into the cold. What happened next might not actually have happened, but Kaspar could swear that he saw before him a gray wolf, howling and gnashing its teeth. He rubbed his eyes. His mind was freezing, tingling, fainting . . .

Kaspar awoke under a thick blanket of morning fog. Another day of walking was ahead, and the boy started for the mountains. He believed that Bazmashen was on the other side. As he climbed, the fog grew thicker. His foot slipped and he plummeted into an abyss.

It could have been the end of Kaspar, but he had survived too long to die so absurdly. He landed safely in a stew of flesh and blood.

Kaspar did not scream. Somewhere in this vast nightmare, he had shed his fear of death. With the calmness of a practiced survivor, he shook himself free of the bodies. He clasped at the grass and weeds of the hillside and pulled himself out of the gorge.

A reward was waiting for him on the trail—a colony of white roses, which Kaspar recognized from his childhood. He was not so far from it. He stuffed his mouth with the sweet petals and continued to walk.

Soon the fog thinned and the mountains fell onto golden fields. Kaspar could already see in the distance a family of scarlet and gold dresses fluttering in the breeze, and beside them a silhouette he recognized.

"Zachariah!" Kaspar yelled. "Zachariah!"

He dashed toward the phantom in the fields, but it was not his friend. He looked at the Armenian dresses, and he saw that Kurdish women were wearing them. *"Giavur!"* they yelled. The word stung

Kaspar, and he kept running, now toward the other end of the plain, where a monster of a windmill was growling.

The owner of the windmill, a compassionate Kurd who had done business with Hovhannes Gavroian, invited the boy to spend the night at his home. He prepared a hot meal and brought in a cot. For the first time in months Kaspar fell asleep in peace.

But that night, memory screamed from the depths of sleep. "Don't beat me!" Kaspar cried. "Don't beat me! Don't beat me! Don't beat me!"

The voice of horror haunted the Kurd, and in the morning he asked the boy to stay with him. Kaspar refused. He said that he was going home.

KASPAR SHUDDERED AT THE SIGHT of Bazmashen. Turkish police roamed the quiet roads, and Kurdish peasants emerged so casually from Armenian homes that you would think they had lived there for a thousand years. The village crops were now ready for harvest, but the men who had sown them in the spring were now dead.

The boy walked through a landscape of memories. He passed a barn, which had been his church, and the dust and stones scattered at his address. Kaspar was searching for the home of his uncle, who had been exempted from the deportations.

Mikael Chiloyan was a powerful man. When in the sultan's time Kurdish brigands had descended on Bazmashen, he had fought heroically. He had made it into the village folklore and the village government. But now, at the sight of his nephew, Mikael began to cry.

"I'm sorry you have to see me like this," he said.

Life had broken Mikael. It had silenced the revolutionary songs in him.

Kaspar did not know the true source of Mikael's tears, but he knew the salt of shame was in them. He sat beside his uncle and listened to a hero confess: about his conversion to Islam, the humiliating circumcision; about the death of his family and friends; how he had chosen not to die with them. For the next few weeks, Mikael and Kaspar cried together. They did not understand why they were alive.

Then, one day, Mikael found his death waiting for him at the end of a gun in the mountains near Bazmashen, where he had been summoned for a meeting. The Kurdish leaders of the village had been taken by the paranoid thought that the surviving Armenians were plotting to return to Bazmashen.

Kaspar was not surprised by the news of his uncle's murder. He did not curse God, for that would require faith in Him. The vestiges of hope and humanity had been torn from the boy. He was down to his naked soul and his final instinct, which was to walk away, to walk—though it seemed impossible—forward in time.

Kaspar walked toward Mezre, where his mother had entrusted some money to the consulate of the United States of America.

A NATIVE OF PORT JEFFERSON, New York, the man with the white mustache and a three-piece suit had gathered his diplomatic credentials at Cornell University and the George Washington University School of Law. But in the fall of 1914 Leslie Davis was deep into the deserted world. He was an educated man among mostly peasant Armenians, nomadic Kurds, and nationalistic Turks in a remote parcel of Ottoman hinterland. When Davis had taken up his post as the U.S. consul in Kharpert, he did not know that he would be spending his term in hell.

The road to hell was paved swiftly. In October 1914 the Young Turk leaders repealed the Capitulations, the corpus of regulations that had given legal privileges to foreign powers and their subjects. In March 1915 the Armenian schools of Kharpert, including the prestigious American-sponsored Euphrates College, were closed. In April intellectuals and clergymen in Constantinople were rounded up and ultimately killed. The rumor was that Turkish police were uncovering guns and ammunition hidden in homes across the six Armenian provinces. Davis believed that much of the weaponry was planted by the police. But to concoct what charge and to seek what punishment, he still did not know.

And then, on May 30, 1915, came the decisive law: the Temporary Law of Deportation, which authorized Ottoman military personnel to deport from towns and villages those people "whom they suspect of being guilty of treason or espionage." From one end of the empire to the other, the mass relocation of Armenian populations was suddenly enforced. In an official report to the Department of State, dated June 30, 1915, Davis wrote:

> The full meaning of such an order can scarcely be imagined by those who are not familiar with the peculiar conditions of this isolated region. A massacre, however horrible the word may sound, would be human in comparison with it. In a massacre many escape, but a wholesale deportation of this kind in this country means a lingering and perhaps even more dreadful death for nearly everyone.

In the next few months, Davis watched as his predictions were realized: the bodies of thousands floating in Lake Dzovk (Golchuk), piles of charred and naked corpses. He wrote of these to Henry Morgenthau, the American ambassador in Constantinople, who was himself recording the massacres of the Armenians, and together they appealed to the Department of State for intervention, for aid, for advice.

But office men in Washington did not respond with adequate passion; they could not possibly understand what was happening. They instructed the Americans to avoid the impression that they were tampering with Ottoman sovereignty. So Leslie Davis ceased being a diplomat. His days consisted now of saving Armenians, who were lining up by the hundreds to beg for Western mercy. He found them shelter and kept their monies in American safes. But he also realized that his efforts were ultimately futile, that he could not prevent these un-coined crimes against humanity—what Davis called "the most thoroughly organized and effective massacre this country has ever seen."

"I do not believe it possible for one in a hundred to survive," the consul wrote, "perhaps not one in a thousand."

KASPAR WAS ONE IN A thousand, but he did not know why he had been chosen. He was nobody, except that his number had turned up in some satanic lottery. But that was an altogether different issue. For many men and women who began walking in the summer of 1915, God was a traitor. He had deserted His believers in the killing fields of Armenia. He had stood by and ignored the slaughter of a nation. He had played deaf to Armenian prayers.

Many Armenians quit praying. Others prayed louder.

Kaspar knew that prayer was no currency in Kharpert. Prayer had done nothing for him. The American consul had kept his mother's money from him. "You'll get killed," he had said.

So Kaspar did not pray. He decided, by reason more than faith, that he would leave his godforsaken fatherland forever. By 1916 the Russians had overtaken parts of Turkish Armenia from the north, and it was rumored that Tsar Nicholas II was exercising some compassion toward the Armenians. In fact, several Armenian volunteer units, one of them headed by the legendary warrior Antranig, had been attached to the Russian army.

Kaspar would make a run for it, and he was not the only one. Local Kurdish "tourist agencies" all across Western Armenia were now in the lucrative business of smuggling Armenians across the Ottoman-Russian border. One of these, a group of women who pretended to be net weavers, was soon to leave from Mezre.

With a fez on his head and a single bag of bread and clothes, Kaspar followed some thirty Armenians toward the northern bend of the Euphrates and the lands of Eastern Armenia beyond. They walked by night and slept by day. Some time in the fall of 1916, they reached the river.

The Armenians spent the afternoon in a shed on the banks. The men stooped over wooden planks and began to toil. It took a few hours for something like a raft to take shape and then just a few heartbeats for the Armenians to make a final dash for the river. But there was the outstanding question of who would go first. There was a squabble on the riverbank. The raft crossed and returned several times, and then Kaspar stepped on.

The raft wobbled off into the water.

Kaspar was on the Euphrates now, that blue-green boundary between the Ottoman Empire and the Russian army just beyond, between fear and promise. And this was strange, because only two years and some kilometers downstream, this very Euphrates had served as an altogether different boundary. Those who had crossed it southward in the summer of 1915—Heghnar and Gabriel—had done so not by will but by force. The Euphrates River had been the entrance to the nightmares of the Syrian desert. It was a river that had, for those terrible days, turned red from the blood of the Armenian women and children who were butchered there.

But those bloody waters had long ago spilled into the Persian Gulf. These were fresh waters, waters without memory, and they were delivering Kaspar to new and fearless beginnings in Russian Armenia.

Chapter Two

———✖———

ARMY OF ORPHANS

G rumbling through the bitter winter of 1916, the frosty freight train pulled at last into the station at Alexandropol. The doors were unbolted and out fell Kaspar, fifteen years old, a coughing bundle of shiver and sweat. *A Turk must have poisoned me along the way,* he thought. *They could have put something in my food.* The Turks were not the cause of his fever, but even so, Kaspar was relieved to reach Alexandropol, the historic city of Giumri, safely sprawled inside Eastern, or Russian, Armenia.

After Tiflis and Baku, Armenian Alexandropol was the principal trade city of the Caucasus. Even in the forbidding depths of this severe winter, its merchants, carpenters, blacksmiths, and painters were casually going about their business. Kaspar had no business yet, but he was hopeful that a job and some version of peace could be found in the city. He took this thought to a café and settled into a warm seat. He looked out at the white city, its hurrying Armenians, its majestic churches, its Russian soldiers—the subjects of Tsar Nicholas II.

Kaspar dissolved his worries in a cup of tea and observed the Armenians making conversation around him. They were different, these Armenians. They spoke fast and loud, their lips turning up coarse and incomprehensible syllables, their features twisting in foreign patterns. They spoke of the endless war, of the blossoming hope of socialism, and of a bold new scientific theory called "relativity." They spoke also about the slaughter of their brethren across the border in Western Armenia, but they were not worried. To the Eastern Armenians, the Ottoman Empire was a dying monster that had no appetite for their lands.

Kaspar was not so sure. He knew the beast from inside its belly.

Kaspar found a job looking after the animals of a local butcher, a kind man who removed the lice from Kaspar's hair and gave him some clothes, and after a few months rewarded him with a pair of shoes. With care, Kaspar's cough subsided. And as winter melted into spring, the red stone factories, black stone churches, and green lawns were animated again. But spring also revealed something more sinister about the city—something winter had disguised. Alexandropol was covered with graves.

It was in that spring of 1917 that Kaspar's lucky journey into Eastern Armenia came to its end. The butcher's daughter inexplicably turned against Kaspar and one afternoon whispered lies into her father's ear. The hen had laid eggs that morning, she said, but the eggs had disappeared. Almost two years before, Kaspar had stolen bread and jam from his Kurdish master. He had stood silent as another boy was beaten for his crime.

And so, once again, Kaspar left. He hid amid the cargo of a cold westbound train and waited for Kars, then Sarikamish, then Erzerum—known by Armenians as Garin. That was the end of the line, the heart of Western Armenia, where Kaspar had unfinished business with history.

KASPAR LAY STIFF ON A hospital bed, forced into solitude with his memories, which boiled inside him. "Typhoid fever," Dr. Tushian announced, and those were not benign words in 1917 Garin, where medicine was more art than science. Yet it was the immobility, not the fever, that distressed Kaspar. Fever burned the body but immobility petrified the soul, made it surrender, made the brave boy think that most shameful thought: *I hope someone, somewhere, knows I'm here.* Kaspar had no prospects beyond the hospital walls, but when the typhoid signaled its first retreat, his restlessness became unbearable. He threw off his covers, tiptoed through the wards, and emerged on the streets of Garin.

The city was unlike any other Kaspar had seen. It had none of the rustic comforts of Bazmashen or the urban bustle of Alexandropol. Surrounded by walls, then mountains, and replenished by the headwaters of the Euphrates just beyond, Garin was a city made not to impress but to endure. Over the past decades, it had sustained the massacres of Sultan Abdul Hamid II and then of the Young Turks.

In Garin, Kaspar lived with a few thousand Christian Armenians amid Muslim Turks under Russian military occupation. He gazed upon its churches—Apostolic, Catholic, and Protestant—which had endeavored, each in its own style, to revamp faith among a race of people that had great need but little evidence for it. He found the famous Sanasarian Academy, which had attracted an intellectual climate to a city that, by tradition and instinct, preferred the fight.

After 1915, it was the fight that enchanted the thousands of loose teenage souls that wandered about Garin. It was the fight that gave meaning to the city, and the city that gave the fight its first anthem. In the 1890s, during the massacres under Abdul Hamid, it was in Garin that the national struggle found melody and rhyme:

> *Tsayn me hnchets Erzerumi hayots lerneren,*
> *Tunt tunt elan hayots srder zenki shachiunen.*
> *Hai kiughatsin taruts iver sur, zenk cher desadz.*
> *Tashde toghuts, sur hratsan pahi deghn arav.*

> A sound echoed in the Armenian mountains of Garin,
> Armenian hearts awoke from the blast of guns.
> For centuries, the Armenian villager had seen no weapon.
> Now he left his field—in shovel's stead, a sword and rifle held.

For the time being, though, Kaspar held neither sword nor rifle. In Garin, luck ran thin and living was a full-time job. The Turks were troublemakers, and the Russians, it turned out, were no saints, either. To each according to his ability—that was the crude, unwritten code of survival in Garin, and it happened to describe the ideal setting for the development of entrepreneurial talent. Kaspar now entered the labor market, offering himself to anybody who looked to need a day's or even an hour's worth of work.

One day—it is not clear how—an envelope found Kaspar. It carried a hundred-dollar bill from a town called Tulare in golden California. The sender was Manoug Der Sarkisian. Kaspar remembered that name. It was the name of his mother's brother, the name that had been spoken in 1902 when his father left Bazmashen, the name that had been yelled when he returned in 1912. Kaspar accepted the expensive apology. He took the money to the bazaar of Garin. He bargained for a miniature kerosene heater and a pot, his first investments, and he began boiling *jigars*, lamb livers. Kaspar was seventeen years old.

THE WALLED FORTRESS CITY OF Garin had been among the iconic cities of Western Armenia. In 1915 its residents, too, had been deported and exterminated behind the curtain of world war. Those who chanced to escape vowed never to return, but they soon had cause to reconsider. In 1916 Tsar Nicholas II moved to capture Garin from the Turks, presumably to integrate it into his empire and to guarantee there the rights of his Armenian subjects.

By 1917, when consecutive revolutions in Petrograd upended the royal Russian government, thousands of Armenians had already returned to Garin. The tsar overthrown, a peculiar messianic leader named Vladimir Ilyich Lenin marched into the ruins of Russian history and encouraged, in the name of brotherhood among nations, the withdrawal of Russian troops from the Western Armenian cities.

It did not take long for the Russian soldiers to desert Garin. "Down with the war!" they chanted on the retreat, leaving the Armenians to the rebounding Ottoman armies. But the Armenians did not lose hope, not yet, because there were rumors that a great general was on his way to organize a defense.

As they waited, the Armenians prayed and told stories—stories that began with a man or a woman in Garin or Kharpert or Sepastia or Van and ended at the bottom of the Euphrates or in the dunes of the Syrian deserts or in a million ashes scattered about the killing fields of Western Armenia. The stories could be told in sorrow or in rage, but all of them were populated by helpless characters who were caught up in the violent throes of history. And the storytellers—they, too, were characters in an epic tragedy from which they could not escape.

At the Euphrates boys over twelve were separated from their mothers. They were marched upstream and killed. The younger children and the women did not hear of these killings. They waited for their turn to cross the river and, as they did, Kurdish and Turkish men came to collect the pretty ones. Some of the women gave in without a fight. Others refused and jumped into the river. The river meant many things to many people in Western Armenia, but for the Armenian children and women who crossed it southward in the summer of 1915, it meant one thing: the gates of an even greater hell. They marched toward the Syrian deserts. Hunger became unbearable, and in some groups the Armenians began to eat their dead. A few weeks before, they had been eating Christ's flesh and drinking Christ's blood in their churches.

The children and women kept walking. They looked like skeletons. More and more often now children were left behind and women collapsed and died en route to death. At nights, when the Armenians slept on open fields, the Turkish gendarmes teamed with local Kurds to rob and rape the women. Sometimes when the gendarmes stripped off the Armenian dresses, they found the naked bodies of men. They killed them. But pregnant women made them especially happy. "Boy or girl?" one asked the other. "Girl," said the other, and made a wager. Then the first gendarme drew his sword and sliced open the woman's belly. As the mother screamed her immutable agony, the gendarme pierced his sword into the skull of the unborn and lifted it from the womb. He held out his bloody sword as the gamblers of the desert laughed and clattered their coins.

IN GARIN, KASPAR LISTENED CAREFULLY to the stories of his brothers in blood. They were all orphans who had survived the great Armenian annihilation, only to be condemned to live in its memory. But now, with the Bolshevik Revolution in Russia and Lenin's retreat from the Caucasus, the hope for an autonomous Armenian homeland was renewed. There was only one problem: the Ottoman army had overtaken Erzinga (Erzinjan) in February 1918 and was marching for the walls of Garin.

So it was that an army of orphans was born—an untrained, emotional army tasked with defending the front lines of Armenian history. Hovagim Kotcholosian, a twenty-two-year-old survivor from the nearby village of Tsitogh, surveyed the boisterous Armenians who were supposed to protect Garin. He was suspicious of those young and vengeful faces, but one of them, at least, he would learn to trust. He would see that face again, years and hemispheres away, in a distant, unfathomable future.

Kaspar was not trained for war, but war had come to him. He sold his kerosene heater and the last of his boiled *jigars* and enlisted in the corps of fighters that were preparing to defend Garin. Kaspar picked up his first weapon: a Mosin-Nagant rifle that had belonged to a long-gone tsarist soldier. He gripped the rifle and became a part of the song that was being sung often in March 1918: *"Govgasi kacher, khmper gazmetsek / Kach Antranigin oknutian hasek."* Fighting words: "Braves of the Caucasus, organize your bands / Go to the aid of courageous Antranig." The boys sang and waited for the general:

> *Kach Antranige, anvakh sur aradz,*
> *Hayastan knal vaghuts er ukhdadz,*
> *Ach u tsakh chartel Turk zinvornerin,*
> *Kurderits madagh perel vankerin.*

> Brave Antranig, fearless, with sword in hand,
> An Armenian pilgrimage he had long begun,
> To crush, right and left, the Turkish soldiers,
> To bring Kurdish offerings to our churches.

Songs were sustenance for Kaspar. He never tired of singing them—of sharing in a struggle greater than himself. The fact was, however, that Kaspar was not in this for a hypothetical struggle. This battle was about memories of a village: a father who would not see another harvest, a mother who would not bear the child in her womb, a church that would never echo with another prayer. And these songs, these revolutionary songs, had a way of translating memories into a terrible ache for revenge.

ON THE EVENING OF MARCH 3, 1918, Kaspar rushed to the gates of Garin, where the Armenians were gathering to welcome a legend in the flesh. Rumors of General Antranig's imminent arrival in the fortress city had inspired true hope among the Armenians. No one there knew, of course, that just hours before, in a distant place called Brest-Litovsk, Russian officials had signed more than a million and a half square kilometers of their land, including all of Western Armenia, to the rule of the Ottoman Empire.

The Turks of Garin hurried home and locked their doors that night, for Antranig was a frightful man. When leaders of his Armenian Revolutionary Federation denied him the use of capital punishment in his battalion, Antranig had spat on them. And if he had done that, if he had spat on his superiors, there was no telling what he would do to the Turks.

"Getse Antranige! Getse Antranige!" The chant for Antranig grew louder in the cold night, and Kaspar's heart galloped in excitement. A brigade of horses materialized from the distance, and soon Kaspar saw him: the general with a mustache and a karakul cap.

The crowd whistled and applauded, but the man who entered through the gates was silent. From his horse, he looked down into the glistening eyes of Armenians. He did not share their hope. He was not flattered by their chants. Antranig's voice thundered in the night: "Do not clap for me, but listen to my words. Let every man immediately depart for the arsenal, then for the battlefield tonight. Now that would be the beautiful and useful version of applause."

The chants dissolved into nervous whispers, and Antranig passed through the crowd. Kaspar and several other young men followed the general to the trenches. Most others left for their homes.

The city fell silent; in the inns and bunkers of Garin, the plans of war were being debated. Too many plans. Antranig cabled his fury to the headquarters of the Armenian National Council in Tiflis: "Chaos! Complete chaos, in the truest sense of the word! General Odishelidze commands, the National Council commands, Military Union boss Aghamalian commands, the ARF representative commands. There is no one left for me to command."

In the next few days, as the Ottoman forces advanced and the whiff of war reached the fortress city, the fighters grew anxious. Many Eastern Armenians who had no direct experience of 1915 began to desert. "This is not our country!" they yelled.

Each morning Kaspar awoke to find the trenches emptier than ever. By the second week of March, only a few thousands fighters remained.

Commanders begged their general not to fight, but Antranig refused to surrender. The war was ending, he said. Germany, Turkey's senior ally, was exhausted. An armistice was imminent. Antranig had been dissuaded once before. In July 1915, he had been leading a volunteer unit of the tsarist army to the Western Armenian cities of Bitlis and Mush, where Armenian populations were trapped by their Ottoman executioners. Just as Antranig's detachment reached the western shore of Lake Van, the Russian commander ordered him to withdraw. Obedience had come at a price: the blood of a hundred thousand Armenians.

For years this blood had been marinating in Antranig's conscience. That is what Kaspar did not know about the general. It was shame—nothing else could so completely numb a man's sense of fear—that owned him on the snowy morning of March 11, when he ordered his men to charge the Turkish front line just outside Garin. But the offensive had hardly been launched when news of sedition reached Antranig. Apparently Colonel Bejanbekov, the commander of the central offensive, had instructed his men to stand down.

Antranig was furious, and now the legend himself charged for the Turks. Along the way, at the village of Kez, he encountered Bejanbekov's men. Terror swept their cold, red faces. "To the front lines!" Antranig yelled, but the general's order was overruled by the crackling gunfire. "We won't fight here," the men said.

The general was quick to retort: "If you don't fight here, you won't fight anywhere!"

Antranig would go alone if he had to. As Kaspar and the orphans watched, the hero from the song hurled his cap away and drew his sword. Alone with his horse, he turned his back on them and raced across the field to meet the enemy.

Distant silhouettes began to twitch.

"Will he come back?" the Armenians whispered to each other as they watched Antranig move closer and closer to his finish. "Is he testing us?" The general was testing no one but himself. He did not look back.

Swayed by shame more than duty, hundreds of orphans soon began to follow Antranig. Already the Turks were within a shouted insult of the general, and the general was within the sight of their rifles. But the bullets hissed by Antranig, piercing the snow-white carpet that unfurled before Garin.

On the battlefield, fears vanished. Myth and song ruled the teenage souls. Bullets were flashing through the winter air, and Kaspar held firm to his rifle. He walked forward, shooting at the faceless Turks. *Load. Shoot. Reload. Shoot. Reload.*

The reloading was a necessary inconvenience of a bolt-action rifle, but it served to keep Kaspar always conscious of the power and responsibility of the shot. It was an indemnity against the conscience of any Armenian boy who might later want to plead ignorance or passion. But the clanks and blasts of other rifles were contagious, and soon a mad symphony of clanks and blasts was echoing in the mountains of Garin. Turks and Armenians were falling all around Kaspar, red puddles bubbling in the snow.

Was it God's grace that brought a Turkish soldier to his knees at the tip of Kaspar's rifle? The Turk's own rifle had been lost, and its owner begged the Armenian for his life. Kaspar examined the strange, dark creature kneeling before him. Just a moment before the Turk had been a tyrant in uniform—eyebrows furled, loathing in his eyes. He had been all too ready to kill Kaspar. But now, on account of a lost rifle, he had fallen to his knees.

Kaspar aimed the rifle at the Turk. His whole life had been winding up to this moment. The Turk begged for mercy, but Kaspar did not hear him. The sounds of the battlefield had long been muted to the deafening memories: the death marches, the cries of abandoned children along the Euphrates, the final sight of a wailing mother.

Suddenly Kaspar snapped into the present. Inhabiting his own body again, he looked at the begging Turk and saw in him the killer of his family.

A sound echoed in the Armenian mountains of Garin.

THE MORNING'S BATTLE ENDED IN a draw, which stunned the Ottoman army and awakened some optimism in Antranig's men. If rationed wisely, the general thought, the city's food and ammunition could fuel the defense for another year. The moment's cheer could evolve into actual morale. It was Antranig's public belief that the Armenian people would soon celebrate a decisive national victory in Garin. The city could not be conquered; if Garin was lost, it would be lost by the incompetence, cowardice, and treachery of the Armenians themselves.

So it was. No sooner had the fighters returned from the battlefield on March 11 than the city's defense unraveled. A few Armenian men, bought or coerced by the Ottoman forces, began to destroy the rails of the Garin-Kars railway. Another group of Armenians raided the city's treasury and escaped with its gold. One of Antranig's subordinates, assigned to the city's arsenal, defected to the Turks. Kaspar knew that the battle was shamefully, scandalously over.

In the morning, the Armenians awoke in an undefended city. Most made a run for the eastern gates. Kaspar and a few hundred men stayed a short while longer. Following the general's instructions, they dug through the snow and soil of Garin. Then they helped Antranig descend into the city. *"Ov hayots lernashkharhi Garin pertakaghak: menk aysor ge toghunk kezi, payts ku dzotsi mech ge toghunk piuravor hai naha-dagneru shirimnere!*" Antranig declared from the heart of Armenia. "O Garin, fortress city of mountainous Armenia: today we leave you, but in your embrace we leave the graves of countless Armenian martyrs!"

Antranig took a pinch of the earth and sprinkled the grains into his handkerchief. "I know that I shall have to die in exile, with great yearning for the fatherland," Antranig said. "Let those who bury me take this soil and scatter it upon me, so that I may rest in peace in the earth." Satisfied with these words, Antranig climbed out of the pit. He saddled his horse and led his men out of Garin.

As they withdrew, the Armenians killed many of their Turkish captives and torched several villages. When they reached Sarika-mish, just inside Russian Armenia, they established a new front line. Antranig continued to fight, but no longer as an officer. "Being surrounded by traitors, I resign as general of Armenia's territorial army," he telegraphed the leadership of the ARF. Antranig took off his general's uniform. He put on a common tunic and tucked a revolver into his leather belt.

Within a few weeks, Turkish soldiers drove the Armenians from Sarikamish, then surged into Eastern Armenia. The Turks overtook Kars on April 25, and on May 15, defying the terms of the Treaty of Brest-Litovsk, they marched into Alexandropol. Turkish troops now stood within 125 kilometers of Yerevan and 250 kilometers of Tiflis.

Panic plagued the Armenian highlands. The Armenian resistance disbanded. Its fighters, sparse and demoralized, fled as far from the chaos as their kopeks would take them. Kaspar looked north to Tiflis. He could not know that it was to the south, in Yerevan, that a sensational era of Armenian history was about to dawn.

THE TURKISH ARMIES HAD SWALLOWED up Garin and then Kars and Alexandropol—two major cities of Russian Armenia—but these victories had only piqued the Ottoman appetite. On May 21, 1918, Turkish forces moved toward Yerevan, the only Armenian city they did not control. Then the unimaginable happened. On May 26 at Sardarabad, forty kilometers west of Yerevan, the pathetic, disjointed Armenian battalions repelled the army of the Ottoman Empire.

On the same day Georgia, with support from Germany, declared its independence. Azerbaijan, with support from the Ottoman Empire, followed on May 27. And on May 28, 1918, with support from no one, the Armenian National Council declared the independent Republic of Armenia. Soon, upon a black stone building in the center of Yerevan, a new flag waved: red, blue, and orange.

Democracy did not grow easily on this sliver of Eastern Armenia, a rocky and mountainous hinterland tyrannized for centuries. Famine and disease competed for human life. Muslim minorities did not accept the new order. The Armenian parties that had opposed independence in favor of a Russian guardianship found themselves in an awkward position before the Armenian Revolutionary Federation. The party itself cracked into factions. Antranig, for example, repudiated the republic, blaming the loss of Western Armenia on the incompetence of its leaders, his former comrades.

Yet the republic endured. Inspired by founding father Aram Manukian, prime ministers Hovhannes Khachaznuni and Alexandre Khatisian invited non-ARF leaders into their cabinets. Territorial expansions soon followed. By mid-1919, the republic had almost quadrupled in size and regained most of its Eastern Armenian lands. And General Antranig was on the rim of Mountainous Karabagh when he was persuaded by the Allied powers to stand down. The Central Powers had surrendered, he was told. The Ottoman Empire was finished.

At the Paris Peace Conference of 1919, Prime Minister David Lloyd George of Great Britain vowed that Armenian lands would never again fall to the "blasting tyranny of the Turk," and President Woodrow Wilson of the United States, encouraged by the powerful

American Committee for the Independence of Armenia in Washington, proposed an American mandate for Armenia. But the idea of a united Armenian homeland was doomed. An isolationist American Congress officially rejected the mandate in May 1920.

Woodrow Wilson did not forget the Armenians. The Treaty of Sèvres, signed in August by the Allies and the Ottoman Empire, Armenia, and other states, authorized President Wilson to draw the borders of the independent Armenian homeland and to issue a binding arbitral award. And he did so with great care and responsibility, granting the Armenians not only Eastern Armenia but also most of the Western Armenian provinces of Van, Bitlis, and Garin, together with an outlet on the Black Sea.

There was one problem. The Treaty of Sèvres, that glorious document for the Armenians, had been signed by the sultan's government. Yet it was not the sultan in Constantinople, but rather an army officer with a following in Ankara, who now claimed to speak for the Turkish people. His name was Mustafa Kemal, and he refused to believe that the West had won the war.

AFTER ANTRANIG'S FIGHTERS DISPERSED, KASPAR wandered through the North Caucasus, living from freight train to freight train, searching for work but finding only war—most recently the civil war between the Bolshevik Red Army and anti-Bolshevik White Army, which was most violent from 1918 to 1920.

Kaspar continued to wander, trying to find his future in various Russian cities. He peddled cigarettes and lived in hostels and jail cells. By 1920 there was no place left to go. In an absurd turn against destiny, Kaspar decided to move to the very place where the blueprints of his family's murder had been drafted: Constantinople.

The city was different now, he had heard. Since the Allied armies had occupied it in November 1918, the sultan had returned to power and the Young Turks—the authors of the Armenian extermination—had been expelled. A Turkish court-martial went so far in 1919 as to condemn to death the wartime triumvirate of Enver, Talaat, and Jemal, who had fled the country in anticipation of the ruling. A community of more than a hundred thousand Armenians had reconstituted in the Ottoman capital.

But there was also bad news for the Armenians, and it concerned the new nationalism that was brewing in Ankara. Sustained by resentment of the Western occupiers, Mustafa Kemal's vision of national resistance was winning converts in Constantinople, too.

In this complicated city, Kaspar led a complicated life. His heart slowly lost its simplicity, his conscience its youth. In Turkish bordellos, Kaspar became a man. He was a victim, but his thoughts never drifted far from the cold day on the plains of Garin when he had killed a weak, kneeling Turk. With that shot Kaspar had rejected his role as subject—some unmoving thing to be acted upon by a gendarme, a tribal chieftain, or another courier of history—and had dared to be an actor, a mover, a changer of history.

Kaspar's conscience had been forced to absorb that fundamental act of revenge. But his heart, it seemed, would never fully recover from the Turkish boy's final, ageless expression of doom. Regrets possessed Kaspar, and he could not cleanse himself of them—not here, anyway, in a country finally possessed by Kemal's ultranationalist philosophy. In April 1920, Kemal opened the Turkish Grand National Assembly in Ankara, setting into motion an extraordinary plan: to overthrow the sultan, expel the Allied soldiers, and create a new nationalist government in Turkey.

Within weeks of the good feelings at Sèvres, the Turkish movement represented by Mustafa Kemal entered into a new partnership with Soviet Russia against the Western "colonizers." The Bolshevik-Kemalist compact rejected the Treaty of Sèvres and empowered Kemal in the fall of 1920 to send his armies to destroy what he called "the imperialist Armenian government." As Turkish soldiers marched deeper into the Armenian republic, Yerevan was left with only two options: to surrender to the crescent of the Turks or to the hammer and sickle of the Soviet Empire.

There was not much debate. And so it fell to the republic's last prime minister, Simon Vratzian, to arrange for the sovietization of Armenia. On December 2, 1920, the Armenian government officially closed down. After a thirty-month residency in Armenia, democracy was evicted and the Armenian homeland yielded once again to a foreign ruler. There was one consolation, for those who wished to see it. It was an announcement by Joseph Stalin in the December 4, 1920, issue of *Pravda*:

> Soviet Azerbaijan is willingly turning over to Soviet Armenia Zangezur, Nakhichevan, and Mountainous Karabagh. . . . The centuries-old animosity between Armenia and the surrounding Muslims was solved by one stroke, by the establishment of brotherly harmony among the proletariats of Armenia, Azerbaijan, and Turkey.

The news of Kemal's ascendancy sent chills through the Armenian community of Constantinople. Thousands quickly arranged to abandon the city. Kaspar, too, decided to leave. There was no future in Constantinople. There was no future in Kemal-occupied Western Armenia, either, or in a fragile Eastern Armenia. So in early August 1920, Kaspar fled westward to Le Havre, the port city of northwestern France. There he boarded a narrow two-masted ship, the SS *La Savoie*.

As the ship broke into the blue Atlantic, Kaspar's mind was awash in the ancient rituals of rebirth. All alone among the crowd, he thought often about his past—the cracked red eggs of Easter week, the gendarmes, Antranig, the bullet of redemption and guilt, the great rituals and countless useless details of a failed existence. Kaspar wished the past would not follow him to the New World. He resented his memories. He resented his name, Gavroian. He would change it. Kaspar would change everything once he arrived in America, where, he had been assured, it was men who defined history and not the other way around.

Chapter Three

—◦◦◦—

HAPPY GO LUCKY

W hen he arrived at Ellis Island on August 30, 1920, the man who had been traveling alone was asked to identify himself. He said he was an Armenian, though he had been born in Kharpert, Turkey. A workman, he called himself. He was not sure of his age. The exact date of birth would have been recorded in the margins of his family Bible, which, along with the family, along with the town, along with the civilization, had disappeared. "Twenty years old," he said. "Kaspar Hovannisian." And that was a remarkable change, from Gavroian to Hovannisian, revealing as it did Kaspar's seasick emotions: the desire to forget the past and the instinct to honor it. Hovhannes had been his father's name.

Kaspar found the first figments of his American dream in a shoe factory in Chelsea, a manufacturing town that looked enviously across the Mystic River to Boston. It was in the dust of American industry that he toiled, in the dank of boardinghouses that he lived, and in the dim of speakeasies that he drank, but Kaspar did not hide from history. More and more frequently, Kaspar would take the bus to nearby Watertown and Whitinsville, where thousands of Armenian refugees—among them a young artist named Arshile Gorky—had been settling into communities, building churches, and reopening the political parties of the old country: the Hunchakian, the Ramgavar, but most often the Dashnaktsakan, the Armenian Revolutionary Federation. That was Hovhannes's party, the party of the deceased republic.

Kaspar saluted the party's red flag. He recognized the quill, the sword, and the spade pictured there—once the instruments of revolutionary longing, now mere relics of a shared national memory. Quills were abundant in New England; the ARF newspaper *Hairenik*, or *Fatherland*, was daily filled with the forecasts and brainstorms of an emerging diaspora. But there were many Armenians who favored braver strategies of struggle: the sword. From the political underground of the 1920s, they were conjuring up an astonishing plan.

The code name was Operation Nemesis, and its trademark mission remains the centerpiece of Armenia's revolutionary canon:

> *On March 15, 1921, a twenty-three-year-old Armenian man appeared on the streets of Berlin and began to follow a larger man with a cane. A few times the Armenian appeared to hesitate. He crossed the street and walked briskly ahead, turning for a clean view of the man on the opposing sidewalk. The mustache was unmistakable; it was the Turk. The Armenian crossed the street again and, when he was within two meters of the man, he pulled out a pistol and shot him in the head. The man fell on his face; blood splashed onto the sidewalk. The assassin dipped the tip of his shoe in the blood. Then he ran off into the daylight, yelling: "He was a foreigner! I am a foreigner! This has nothing to do with you!" The Armenian was Soghomon Tehlirian, a member of the ARF and a witness, eight years earlier in Garin, of the rape and murder of his mother and sister. The dead man was Talaat, the Turkish minister of interior who had masterminded the entire program of rape and murder across Western Armenia in 1915.*

Kaspar followed the trial of Soghomon Tehlirian. He knew that the jury in Berlin was about to judge not only the guilt or innocence of one man but also the salvation of all Armenian men who had sought to avenge the deaths of their mothers and sisters. The verdict, issued in the summer of 1921, was exhilarating; the legal justification was thin. Temporary insanity, the jury reasoned, but it had not been swayed by legal logic. The Germans had been moved by sympathy for Tehlirian and disgust for Talaat's extraordinary plot to kill a whole race of people.

Kaspar had little money, but he had enough, apparently, to buy himself a brown three-piece suit and a session at a photo studio in Boston. The result is a portrait that is so implausible and staged that it says exactly nothing about the man he was and much about the man he wanted to be. Kaspar wears the suit with a white collared shirt and slender cream tie. His hair, thin and receding despite his youth, is combed back, and it reveals a full, serious face with brown eyes. Those eyes do not look at the camera. They try to be indifferent to it, and only the first insinuation of a grin betrays that the subject might not be so comfortable as he looks. Kaspar crosses his arms decisively. We are expected to notice the contents of his breast pocket: a thick black Parker pen.

The pen and the pose were for posterity, but in real life Kaspar was still a lost and broken soul, a stranger in the promised land. He left the shoe factory for a barbershop, where he swept floors, washed razor blades, and eventually gained a chair of his own. As his English tongue loosened, Kaspar made conversation with his customers, finding his first channel into the private lives of everyday Americans.

By the twenty-fifth year of his life and of the twentieth century, Kaspar had mastered the sensibilities of the New World. Yet the smoke and grunge of Chelsea had only aroused his nostalgia for the simpler rural life of his youth. That was the very life that was being reinvented in a small town thousands of miles away, in the Central Valley of California. That was the town where Kaspar's father had lived and worked years before, the town where his uncle Manoug Der Sarkisian still lived. It was Manoug, in fact, who now summoned Kaspar to Tulare. Some two dozen Armenian families had settled there, he explained, most of them refugees from the extinct village of Bazmashen. Hagop Gavroian, Kaspar's cousin, was living there, too.

"Tulare is like Kharpert," Manoug said.

AS THE NATION DEBATED THE Scopes "monkey trial," Kaspar reached by train the modest farming community where most people were hoping for the conviction of the young teacher of evolution. From the passenger seat of a Model T Ford, Kaspar studied the rotund, clean-shaven man at the wheel. Manoug Der Sarkisian wore a suit, and already he had found occasion to flaunt the roll of cash he kept in his trouser pocket. He was something of a showman and something of a cheat— Kaspar knew why his father had returned early to Bazmashen—but Der Sarkis, as his uncle preferred to be called, was his host.

Midway between Los Angeles in the south and San Francisco in the north, Tulare was a town emblematic of California's San Joaquin Valley. Simplicity was its pride, and most every travel brochure mentioned something about the good country people who lived there:

> I like to live in a friendly town
> Where the trees meet across the street,
> Where you wave your hand and say "Hello"
> To everyone you meet.
> I like to stand for a moment
> Outside the grocery store,
> And listen to the friendly gossip of
> The folks that live next door.

Tulare was a friendly town indeed. Its hundred or so Armenians were free of the racial prejudice that suffocated their cousins in Fresno, the big town forty-five miles north on Highway 99. Among common folk and Portuguese immigrants from the Azore Islands, the Armenians slowly acquired stock in the destiny of Tulare. Some worked as shoemakers, clothiers, and cleaners downtown. Most others, including Der Sarkis, owned farms. A mile to the east, along the Lindsay and Visalia highways, the vineyards and orchards of the Armenians unfolded, twenty acres apiece, toward a pure blue sky.

The Armenians were at peace. Piffles of internal politics had been silenced by the great catastrophe of 1915, and the refugee communities taking shape in Boston, Beirut, and elsewhere in the world were engaged now in a collective therapy of goodwill. In Tulare, for example, rival groups had worked together to purchase a small social hall, where all Armenians could gather for banquets and religious services. There was no Armenian church in Tulare, but every month an itinerant priest would come down from Fresno, where a more substantial number of Armenian expatriates, including Kaspar's old general Antranig, had settled.

Even so, politics did not entirely vanish from the California landscape; they survived as repressed animosities and grapevine gossip. And each Armenian farm Kaspar passed on the Lindsay highway could be reduced by Der Sarkis to a surname—Ametjian, Choboian, Assadourian, Aronian—and a whispered judgment. *"Mer goghmen,"* Der Sarkis would say, or *"mius goghmen"*—"from our side" or "from the other side." "Our side" meant the ARF, those who viewed the Soviet Union as an illegal occupant of an independent Armenian homeland. "The other side" meant the Ramgavar and the Hunchakian, those who accepted Soviet Armenia as their homeland. Der Sarkis's Tulare was a patchwork of friends and other friends who were potential enemies, because no one knew what would come when the tears of the people dried.

The twenty-acre farms along the Lindsay highway appeared and then disappeared, and soon the Ford Model T turned left onto the Visalia highway, which serviced the Nalbandian and Arakelian farms, and pulled into the driveway of the largest farm of them all. Its size had provoked some envy among the Armenians, but pity, too, for those who appreciated the reason. Manoug's wife, Ester, was unable to bear children.

Kaspar moved into his uncle's farmhouse, and he was pleased to discover that everyone and his daughter gathered there for weekend festivities. Apparently Der Sarkis was the godfather of the local Armenian community, and he was eager to use his influence to find a wife for his nephew. This was not difficult. Kaspar was engaged in no time, but then in no time also separated, because he was suddenly taken by another woman—a girl, actually, whom he had seen at Der Sarkis's parties. Her hair was curled and she had a cherubic smile.

She was only sixteen in 1926, a student at Tulare Union High School, but Siroon Nalbandian was perfect for Kaspar. She was a child of the ARF and a child of Kharpert, too—though her family had left it in 1912, before the inferno. Along with her American-born siblings, Mardiros (Martin), Margaret (Margie), Mikael (Michael), and Shake (Charlotte), Siroon had enjoyed a splendidly ordinary American life.

Actually, she preferred to be called Sarah. It was like Sara, her mother's name, and easier to pronounce, but these were only the excuses. In fact, Siroon and Sarah were but two sides of the same conflicted spirit. Siroon, meaning "pretty," was a refugee without a homeland. Sarah was an American girl. Siroon labored in vineyards and canneries. Sarah idolized Clark Gable. Siroon was the daughter of a disciplinarian; she called her father *hairig*. Sarah called him "Daddy." Siroon should have seen it coming, but the last thing Sarah expected at age seventeen was to be married.

It did not matter; the decision was made. Der Sarkis and Kaspar put on their suits, climbed aboard the Model T, and drove along the Visalia highway to the Nalbandian farm—a popular farm in those days of Prohibition because of Sarkis Nalbandian's famous home-brewed "white lightning," the *rakhi* he stocked in a trench in the backyard.

Sarkis towered over Kaspar and Der Sarkis. He was tall, severe, and handsome, and dressed elegantly, but Kaspar saw straight into his parochial country heart. The fact was that Kaspar was a man of Kharpert, a nephew of Der Sarkis, and a member of the ARF, and Sarkis simply did not have the imagination to foresee a better husband for Siroon. So as his wife stood powerlessly by and his children played innocently in other rooms, Sarkis Nalbandian met with Kaspar and Der Sarkis to negotiate the end of Sarah's childhood.

When the callers left, the girl emerged from her room. "Who was that man?" she asked. "Why did he come here?"

Sarah's protests and tears did not change her father's heart; his decision was absolute. In July 1927 the seventeen-year-old Sarah became Siroon for good.

SIROON HOVANNISIAN PERFORMED WITH QUIET obeisance all the duties of a young Armenian wife, but she did not know the man she served. She did not understand what Kaspar found in that newspaper *Hairenik*, daily delivered from Boston. She did not understand why he rushed off to Fresno for a funeral one morning, who the dead general Antranig really was. But she did not need to understand Kaspar. She lived in his house on K Street, and she had the seed of a new generation of Hovannisians inside her.

Kaspar took pride in his home and wife, but he lived with anticipation of greater things. It had not been the quill or sword but rather that third symbol of the ARF flag—the spade—that Kaspar longed to control. He wanted his own farm, and he would have to earn it. Every morning he put on a suit and tie and walked down K Street to the red-brick building with a neon sign: "Tulare Hotel—Air Conditioned." At the first-floor barbershop of that hotel, Kaspar spent the day practicing the horticulture of the head and the pleasantries of country conversation.

Siroon's classmates were now in their senior year of high school, and here she was doing chores, knitting, and reading the "page devoted to things feminine" of the *Tulare Advance-Register*. Sometimes, when she saved the money, she went to the pictures. (In 1928 *The Green Hat*, starring Greta Garbo, was all the rage; it was written by the British Armenian writer Michael Arlen.) Kaspar would not return until the late evening, and that suited his wife just fine. She was married to Kaspar, but Siroon had no love for the strange foreign shadow that slipped into the bedroom at midnight and cast itself upon the sheets.

Siroon surrendered to Kaspar, but she did not surrender to his ways. When her first son was born in the spring of 1928 and Kaspar named him Hovhannes, she quickly changed his name to its English equivalent, John. She would name all her children, in fact. Kaspar would not protest, not with John and not with Ralph (Siroon's improvement on Raffi), who arrived in 1930; he allowed his wife the small victories. And on November 9, 1932, the day the Tulare newspaper declared a "Roosevelt landslide," Siroon named their third child. She had been praying for a girl, someone who would grow to understand her.

The birth certificate read: Richard Gable Hovannisian.

The embarrassment of naming an Armenian child after a Hollywood actor was not lost on Kaspar, but again he did not protest. This time he had a secret reason: the name Gable actually reminded Kaspar of the infant boy he last had seen on the banks of the Euphrates, his brother Gabriel. The middle initial *G*—and it would be only an initial from then on—was much more complicated than Siroon had intended.

The stock market crash of 1929 was not supposed to disturb small-town Tulare, but by 1933, it was clear that a great depression had settled all across the United States. Yet, unbeknown to his friends and family, a roll of cash was thickening in Kaspar's trouser pocket. From seven in the morning to eleven at night, Kaspar kept up his exhausting cut-and-chat routine at the Tulare barbershop. Customers were fond of his sociable style, their children of the candy he gave out. Kaspar would collect twenty-five cents a head—which translated, incredibly, to a hundred dollars a week.

Kaspar allowed himself only one pleasure, and that was the pleasure he felt in the company of other Armenians. On the weekends at the community hall or the Der Sarkis farm, Kaspar would be beaming. He was the youngest of the men, and he enjoyed the respect of the elders, as they enjoyed his vitality. He talked loud and laughed heavy, and often Kaspar would force the men out of their seats around the card table and onto an open patch of grass, where he would hold competitions: who could jump the farthest, run the fastest, lift the most. These brutish physical activities confused the children and embarrassed the young wives, who could not understand why mature men insisted on behaving like teenagers, as if they never had a childhood.

THE HOPE FOR A FREE, independent, united Armenia was dead. Kharpert, Garin, and the Armenian provinces of Western Armenia were now the junkyards of Kemal's Turkish Republic. The campaign of race extermination had been successful; Armenians would never live on those lands again. Eastern Armenia was still living, but only at the mercy of Joseph Stalin, who commanded from Moscow the Armenian economy, church, and culture. By the mid-1920s, he had reneged on earlier promises and transferred Mountainous Karabagh and Nakhichevan to Soviet Azerbaijan. Those who protested, or those who were suspected of being sympathetic to the ARF, vanished from the streets of Yerevan.

The Western Armenians of the diaspora were, for the most part, indifferent to the news from Soviet Armenia—which, the ARF argued, was not a homeland at all, but rather the colony of elite Russian Communists. There was one problem with that argument, and it was not a minor one. The Holy See of Etchmiadzin—the conscience of the Armenian people, the headquarters of the Armenian Apostolic Church, the site where Jesus himself was said to have descended—stood twenty kilometers from Yerevan, at the center of Soviet Armenia. It was the church, in fact, that was about to give the diaspora its first major scandal.

The spiritual leader of the Armenian Apostolic Church was the Catholicos in Etchmiadzin, and his representative in the United States was Archbishop Ghevont Tourian. On July 1, 1933, Nationalities Day at the Century of Progress Exposition in Chicago, the archbishop was set to begin a speech when he noticed the red, blue, and orange flag—the tricolor of the Armenian republic of 1918—upon the stage. Tourian asked that the rag be taken down. He was a servant of Etchmiadzin in Soviet Armenia, after all, and he could not acknowledge the treasonous symbol of a defunct ARF government.

On December 24, 1933, before the eyes of an Armenian congregation at the Holy Cross Armenian Church on 187th Street in New York, Archbishop Tourian was stabbed to death.

"Death to all murderers! Death to all Dashnaks!" Chanting these slogans, a mob of anti-ARF Armenians gathered outside the New York courthouse and demanded the conviction of the seven identified conspirators. And in every American city, town, and tenement where Armenians lived, the ARF faithful were unrepentant. Old friendships broke; the center could not hold.

The murder of the archbishop shocked the Tulare Armenians out of their peace. On adjoining farms, the Kazarian brothers, one ARF and the other Ramgavar, severed their family ties. Sarkis Nalbandian was arrested based on an anonymous report that he was carrying a knife. At the small community center, the Armenian men of Tulare stood face-to-face. On one side: Arakelian, Margosian, Kazarian, Nalbandian, Der Sarkisian, Hovannisian. On the other: Aronian, Assadourian, Ametjian, Choboian, Sarkisian, and another Kazarian.

"Traitors!" one side yelled.

"Priest killers!" answered the other.

And there, in the middle of it, stood Kaspar Hovannisian with roguish grin and furrowed brow, listening as words grew callous and demented. A folding chair crashed on the head of Der Sarkis, and the men brawled. On that winter's night in 1934, the Armenians emerged bruised and cynical from the hall where they had once danced and prayed together. One side kept the keys, the other kept the property deeds, and in broken mutters, as they made their way back to their homes, the Armenians of Tulare vowed never to forgive each other.

THE DAILY ROUTINE EXHAUSTED KASPAR, but financial security had liberated his curiosities. On his morning walks to the barbershop, he began to notice a new generation of boarded-up homes and dilapidated buildings, and he imagined what those places could become in five or ten years. He spoke with his customers about the slumping real estate market, and when he heard that a piece of farmland on the Visalia highway had been put up for sale, he moved to buy. The farmhouse had burned down—only a dusty cellar, filled with gopher snakes and bootleg wine barrels, remained—but the property itself was perfect, twenty acres located within a quarter mile of the Nalbandian farm and a mile of the relevant ARF Armenians.

Kaspar acquired a foreclosed house—a creaking, wooden wonder going for $2,000—and commissioned a professional mover to saw it off from its foundations and haul it, by truck, to the property. He painted the house white and built a shed and a barn. And beyond a small backyard, Kaspar began to plant the seeds of his dream: a vineyard. It was there, in that well-traveled house and the twenty acres on which it sat, that Kaspar built his kingdom, the playground of his children, and the new headquarters—now that Der Sarkis was feeling his age—of the ARF Armenians of Tulare.

Almost every weekend the Nalbandians, Der Sarkisians, Kazarians, Gavroians, Margosians, and Arakelians gathered to feast in Kaspar's dining room. By two or three in the afternoon, the women would have set the table and Der Sarkis would have said the blessing. The men sat at one end, the women at the other—the pecking order was unshakeable—and they turned to devouring the paper-thin *lavash* bread, cheese, black olives, salads, and the Mediterranean delicacy called *kheyma*—seasoned raw beef. A main course of lamb kebab and buttered rice pilaf would follow, served alongside *sarma* and *dolma*, grape or cabbage leaves wrapped around rice and beef. *Choreg*, Siroon's specialty dessert, would signal the sweet finale.

"*Vay, vay, vay!*" Kaspar would exclaim. "Look at all this food!"

From a record player in the living room floated ancient melodies—whether they were Turkish, Kurdish, or Armenian, nobody actually knew—and one by one the men rose to offer toasts to happiness or friends, but every so often a toast from deeper quarters. A glass of *rakhi* would be tilted toward the kitchen, where the children sat, and a modest hope expressed: that the children never see what their parents had seen.

There was no threat of that. John, Ralph, and Richard, along with the Kazarian kids, Hagop Gavroian's son, Cache, and Siroon's youngest sister, Charlotte, were living the real American life. They knew about their parents' past, but they were not bothered by it. In the kitchen they spoke of football and farms, and if they ever spoke of an Armenian, it was probably Ali Baba the Terrible Turk, a villain on the San Joaquin Valley wrestling circuit and a childhood hero of the boys.

Not Richard's hero, though. Maybe he was young or maybe he was different, but there was no doubt that Richard lacked the thunder and machismo of his brothers. "Sissy," they called him.

The fact was that the boys took mischievous pleasure in oppressing Richard. John, by right of seniority, might punish Richard for telling on him a whole month or year earlier. And once the boys placed a tin can on Richard's head and took turns shooting at it with a BB gun. So naturally Richard preferred, during these weekend gatherings, to stay away from the boys, to help his mother with the dishes, to play—much to his father's sharp disappointment—the daughter Siroon never had.

After lunch, the men and women would leave the heat of the wooden house for the shade of the green backyard. The California sun would have mellowed through the afternoon, and with luck a breeze would cool the conversation and the card games. The boys would head for the vines, and Richard, chubby and green-eyed, would totter out behind them. Often he would venture too deep into their territory, and he would return to the backyard with a sour face and wet eyes. Siroon would comfort him, then send him off again.

Richard wandered barefoot about the farm. Early on he had developed a passion for solitude. He made up songs and characters, and invented realms where he would be the ruler, not the victim. One of these, Tottyville, which Richard borrowed from his favorite radio show, *Let's Pretend*, was populated by kings and queens, witches and wizards.

Richard was fond of animals. When his father sent him to the barn to fetch a chicken for dinner, his heart would swell with pity; he released the chickens as soon as he caught them. And Bud the goat was among his closest friends. So one day, when he encountered a newborn pup by his mother's favorite sycamore tree, Richard was overjoyed. He lay down in the grass to play with him. It could be that he was consumed in a fantasy world, but by all accounts of this world Richard took the tip of the pup's tail into his mouth and bit it off. The pup cried in pain. Realizing what he had done, Richard hugged the pup and cried with him.

Richard lived as long as he could in make-believe worlds, but the reality of Tulare had a way of taking over. There was, in fact, much reality to observe, for the Tulare farm was a wondrous realm in its own right. The tracks of the Santa Fe Railroad lay only a half mile to the north, and in those days the trains were delivering to the San Joaquin Valley thousands of migrant hobos and refugee Okies who had escaped the historic Dust Bowl of Oklahoma and Texas. They were poor, tattered indigents, and on any given day two or three of these characters might be sleeping in Kaspar's shed, near the wood yard. Siroon would serve them warm leftovers, perhaps the previous night's string bean dinner, or stale goodies from a local bakery—surplus cakes and pies sold in twenty-five-pound bags.

The American experience of the 1930s, with its trademark events and personalities, surrounded the Hovannisians. It did not define their lives. For those six or seven hours at Kaspar's house, in fact, America did not exist. The Armenians were living in Bazmashen.

The men played two-deck double-handed pinochle; the women played a card game called *iscambil* or else made quiet conversation nearby. Richard preferred the company of the women, especially the older women—the generation of his grandmother Sara. They were different, these women. They had none of the coarse, rambunctious manners of the men, or the boys who imitated those manners without understanding their cause. There in the backyard, huddled around cups of Armenian coffee, they would whisper stories from their past, crying and laughing at the same time.

Throughout the day, Richard would inhabit his various roles—the victim in the vines, the wanderer with an imagination, companion to the women, inspector of the men. Richard was baffled by his father; he seemed so different here, in the company of other Armenians. He seemed to be a happy man, a *good* man, even. But Richard knew the other side of Kaspar—the violent resentment of his youngest son's inadequacy. Richard knew that after the sun set and the Armenians left for their farms, Kaspar's smile could swiftly vanish, a belt appear in his hands, and manic shouts of "Richard! Richard! Richard!" echo in the house.

Sometimes, when his father and grandfather Sarkis played on opposing teams in pinochle, Richard would fix the score against his father. He was rigging his revenge, casting his anonymous ballot in the dispute between the Hovannisian and Nalbandian families.

"HEY, OLD MAN!" YELLED THE son-in-law.

Marriage had destroyed the pretensions, and Kaspar, no longer enfeebled by poverty, was making up for lost insults. He did not hide his disdain for the provincial Sarkis and Sara, nor for their son Martin, who had lost some of his sense in a childhood accident.

By the late 1930s Kaspar could afford to express his animosities. He was still barbering, but he now owned several properties, including the barbershop on K Street and the nearby building that he leased out to a madam for use as the town brothel. He was always buying, too, and buying so much that Siroon, who was outgrowing her own feebleness, found the courage to intervene. *"Al herik e!"* she would yell. "Enough is enough!"

Naturally, Kaspar never allowed himself to be distracted by the pestering of a woman. He sought the rare bargain and the big opportunity, and he found both in the ashes of the Happy Go Lucky, a popular dance bar that had recently burned to the ground. A bigger, better building could be constructed there, Kaspar thought. So he purchased the Happy Go Lucky, though he knew very well that it lay adjacent to the Nalbandian farm and that Sarkis had wanted to buy it.

John, Ralph, and Richard were sheltered from the tribulations of the Armenian community. They grew up as ordinary American boys under the protective nurture of their mother, who taught them proper dress, proper manners, and proper Tulare country English. They learned Armenian, too, but this from their father and in smaller doses, because Kaspar was always busy at the barbershop. It was only in rare moments that he opened up to his children, casually whispering some foreign phrase or memory into American ears.

Childhood sheltered the boys from the trouble in their parents' marriage, too. They did not know that Kaspar and Siroon were bound together less by love than by responsibility. They did not know that sometimes, late into the night, Siroon would wonder if her husband really was at work or if he was visiting the J Street gambling houses and saloons, which had surfaced from the underground on the very night in 1933 that the Eighteenth Amendment was repealed. But they did know that Kaspar was a complicated man. He was supremely generous and strived to be a good father; most every Saturday he treated his wife and children to foot-long hot dogs and a movie at the Tulare theater. But Kaspar was also an angry man, a man consumed by a ferocious, unpredictable temper.

It was in the vines that Richard came to understand his father. That is where Kaspar led his boys in hard, physical work. He taught them how to identify and uproot johnsongrass, the terrible weeds that suffocated the vines and ruined the grapes. He taught them how to sulfur the vines before dawn. And in the fall, when the backbreaking year was finished, he taught his boys how to arrange the seedless Thompson grapes on paper trays. If the September rains held off long enough and the boys respected the slow, meticulous process of flipping and rolling, the green grapes would eventually shrivel and brown into raisins, and the whole farm would be captured in that pungent aroma of transformation. All that would remain was to pack the raisins into two-hundred-pound-capacity sweat boxes, and in such a way that the wet and deformed raisins would not be found by inspectors.

John and Ralph inherited their father's passion. Ralph, especially, proved to command powers over the earth; he could make levees, repair broken tools, and delight Kaspar with his ingenious farming. But Richard was a different case. He loathed the endless labor—the sweat boxes with their black widow spiders, the johnsongrass and the bermudagrass that would sprout again as soon as they were chopped, and the sticker plants that grew in the depths of the vineyard and punctured his bare feet.

Very often, instead of making his rounds through the vines, Richard would lie on his back and look into the sky. It was a clean sky with big, white, beautiful clouds—clouds with shapes to them, and secret stories.

"That son of a gun," Kaspar would say. "He'll never amount to anything!"

Richard, eight years old, longed to escape the dysfunction of home. He was most happy during family trips to the Boghosian farm in Selma, where he would play twelve continuous hours of rummy with his second cousin Lucylle, and the Armenian picnics by the King's River in Kingsburg. When the picnic ended, Richard hoped that his father would make a left on Highway 99. A left turn meant that Kaspar had decided to accept an invitation to visit the Hampardzoomians or Kazarians—which meant also that in the trunk of his Ford there was probably a box filled with red licorice and Mr. Goodbar chocolates. A left meant that the family was headed to Selma, Fowler, Sanger, or Fresno—where about this time two young men were composing a hit song: "Come on-a my house, my house, I'm gonna give you candy." The writers were William Saroyan and his cousin Ross Bagdasarian (David Seville), the pianist-producer who would create the animated music troupe *Alvin and the Chipmunks*.

But Richard did not depend on his father's moods; he planned his own escapes. By the age of ten, he was hitching rides with a neighbor to the First Baptist Church at the corner of King Avenue and M Street. That church had no theological connection to the Armenian Apostolic Church of his parents, but the fact was that no such church existed in Tulare and only twice a year would the family make the pilgrimage to Holy Trinity in Fresno. It wasn't that Richard was deeply religious, just that he needed an excuse to leave the vines. He spent every possible Sunday in the company of white American Protestants who spoke to him of a God who was frightening, punishing, and not very different, it turned out, from his father.

> Now I lay me down to sleep,
> I pray the Lord my soul to keep.
> If I should die before I wake,
> I pray the Lord my soul to take.

Every night, in bed, Richard recited his prayer and descended into dreams. Finally, his mind was free. For those few hours, at least, all the wars and quibbles were muted. The town replenished itself—the johnsongrass, too—and only the distant whistle of a passing train and the infinite rustles of the San Joaquin Valley and the deep splintered breaths of a displaced wooden house let on that time was still ticking in Tulare.

But then, suddenly, a few sharp screams tore through the dark. They were coming from Kaspar's room, from Kaspar himself—the fearless, defiant man whom night and memory had returned to his childhood, to the banks of the bloody Euphrates. He was shivering, his hands clasped to the headboard, and it was his young wife—her heart pounding with contagious fear—who would have to awake Kaspar, to hold him, to remind him that he was in America.

"*Vay, mairig, vay!*" Kaspar would cry. "Oh, Mother, oh!"

ON DECEMBER 7, 1941, PEARL Harbor burned and the United States entered another world war. In Tulare the glass of streetlamps was painted black and boys were collected for war. Mike Nalbandian, Siroon's brother, was one of them. Kaspar, meanwhile, did what good Americans were supposed to do. He bought war bonds—so many bonds, in fact, that he won prizes for his patriotism, usually cows and other animals. He later sold these at the auction yard.

The war had an altogether different significance for Richard, coloring as it did the context of his late childhood—his years at Wilson Grammar School and then Cherry Avenue Junior High School. It was during these years that Richard's deep desire to escape matured into a more purposeful interest in the humanity around him. Richard read the historical novels of Kenneth Roberts and his mother's magazines, *Life* and *Look*. He read the national newspapers that were filled with reports on the mass murder of Jews and other undesirables in Germany. "Go, kill without mercy," Adolf Hitler had instructed his generals. "Who today remembers the annihilation of the Armenians?"

Just about the time Rouben Mamoulian became the first director to stage the musical *Oklahoma!* on Broadway, Richard began to look beyond the fantasy of America. He was not a prodigy by any stretch, or even a truly avid reader, but his imagination was growing wings and taking him to actual realms: Greece, Rome, Russia. But rarely to Armenia. Armenia did not exist. Armenia was only the encyclopedia's blank, mocking space between Armageddon and Armistice Day, the burning whiteness in a classroom atlas that had neither room nor political will to identify the tiniest of the Soviet socialist republics.

Those blank spaces haunted Richard.

Kaspar was pleased with Richard's curiosities and the academic achievements that justified them; Siroon was overjoyed. She eagerly followed Richard through doors that had been locked for her. At school, she enrolled in the parent-teacher organization. At home, she protected Richard from the men and cherished him even more after giving birth in May 1946 to Vernon (Vartkes), whom nine months of prayer had not turned into a girl. On Mondays, Kaspar allowed Richard to leave the vines and help his mother with the wash. His favorite chore was to feed the newly washed clothes, piece by piece, through an electric wringer before they were taken out and hung to dry fully.

By the fall of 1946, when he enrolled as a freshman at Tulare Union High School, the school from which his mother never graduated, Richard had declared an interest in teaching and history. Of course, the boy had no understanding of Armenian history. The field did not exist. An interest in teaching was, for a Tulare farm boy, ambitious enough—and, for Kaspar's son, offensive enough to the ways of true men. It was ironic that Kaspar, the great Armenian patriot, so doubted the son who showed the most interest in Armenia.

The Armenian identity, as Kaspar knew it, was safe. It had survived his naturalization in 1932 and Siroon's in 1940, and it continued to flourish. They were Americans now, but Kaspar and Siroon never did renounce their titles in the Armenian diaspora—he as a firebrand of the ARF and she as the sweetheart of its sister organization, the Armenian Relief Society. Their children, too, were given an education in national pride. In March 1947 Kaspar hosted the inaugural meeting of Tulare's chapter of the Armenian Youth Federation, the youth wing of the ARF. The Hovannisian, Kazarian, Mamishian, and Garabedian children filled its ranks. Richard was elected treasurer.

But at school, most students did not know what an Armenian was, and Richard had neither the popularity nor the confidence to explain. A childhood spent on Kaspar's farm had plundered his self-esteem and scarred his psychology. His English was, beyond anyone's doubt, sown and reaped on a farm. And his hereditary chubbiness disguised his more striking inheritance: a pair of pure green eyes. So Richard compensated with his sense of humor, which had been trained by Jack Benny and Laurel and Hardy. He joked constantly. He laughed heartily. Soon he became "Hovie," the delightful oddball nobody could hate.

He did not play sports, as his brothers did, but Richard compensated for that, too; he became a fan. He turned up religiously at the Tulare Redskins football games and cheered rowdily for his team. He liked to win, so Richard developed simultaneous loyalties to the

Golden Bears of the University of California, Berkeley. Under coach Lynn "Pappy" Waldorf, the Bears had not lost a regular-season football game for years. This pleased Richard so much that he dreamed, as very few Tulare boys dared to dream, that one day he would attend "Cal."

In the meantime Richard acted—in school plays such as *I Remember Mama* and in games of political simulation organized by the Junior Statesmen of America. As John attended barbering college and Ralph studied agriculture, Richard spent weekends in Bakersfield and Fresno, passing resolutions supporting free trade and condemning Communist infiltration. At one session, Richard sponsored a resolution to overturn daylight saving time. Calling himself a Roosevelt Democrat, he reasoned that the time shift forced farmers to begin the day's work in the dark. Secretly he wished to shave off an hour from his after-school shift in the vineyard.

Richard was named valedictorian of the Tulare Union High School class of 1950. Over the previous three years, his mind had broken out of its shackles, and his English, owing to several demanding teachers, had acquired sound grammar—and even found a style. But Richard's childhood sensitivities did not wear out. "I, Richard Hovannisian, leave Ruth (Blythe) Fields my beautiful physique and evenly distributed weight," he wrote in a graduation day publication. And he remained, for everyone who last saw him at that podium, the plump, comic figure of Tulare Union High School—in words scribbled in the final yearbook, "a boy who keeps a smile on his face and everyone in class."

It was all smiles that night at the Happy Go Lucky dance hall, erstwhile battleground of the Hovannisians and Nalbandians, where Richard was the toast of the night. On any other night, the building would have been soaked in beer and vibrating with Western music. But it was all Armenians now, more than a hundred of them, and they had come to honor Kaspar's son. *Rakhi* was the drink of the night, and the dialect of old Kharpert filled the hall. Siroon was glowing in redemptive delight, and even Kaspar was fully, deeply proud.

Yet Richard, having finally scored a smile on his father's face, was anxious to escape. Somewhere in the thick Tulare night, his Junior Statesmen friends were waiting for him, and he wanted to celebrate with them. So when he found the right moment, Richard slipped out of the Happy Go Lucky. He left behind his parents and brothers, Sarkis and Sara, Der Sarkis, and so many Armenians who would not even notice he was gone. As the Armenians of Tulare celebrated that magnificent night of 1950, Richard left behind the farm, the *rakhi*, the Happy Go Lucky—he left behind everything and dashed through the dark, toward his freedom, across the Visalia highway and onto the other side of a dreadful century.

Richard had heard that old joke about his father's dance hall: "Happy to go, lucky to leave."

———∞∞∞———

Chapter Four

ONWARD, IMMORTALS!

I t was a boy's Hail Mary pass from a vineyard on the Visalia highway, and everybody knew that the football would never make
it to the golden hills of San Francisco. It whirled hopelessly against
the burning winds of the San Joaquin Valley and fell, forty-five miles
later, onto a small house on Floradora Avenue in Fresno, California.
This was the house of an Armenian widow who in the fall of 1950
let rooms to Ralph and Richard Hovannisian. The older brother was
completing a technical degree in agriculture, the younger brother
taking up history at Fresno State. The older brother had left his heart
on his father's farm in Tulare; he was ready to return. The younger
brother was not far enough from the farm; he was only beginning to
leave.

The way Richard saw it, Fresno was a latticework of vineyards and
cotton fields, railroad tracks and packing houses. It was a city still in its
youth, an adolescent that did not quite understand its role in the vast
valley, yet it was a city already hardened in its ways. Managed by elite
whites and sustained by Mexican labor, Fresno was an economic machine. It had no place for that strange breed of immigrants called the
"Fresno Indians." These were the Armenians, and it would seem from
that strange epithet that they had been stereotyped by their big noses.

There were thousands of big noses in Fresno, some very famous ones. The Armenian general Antranig had lived and died there in the 1920s. And the writer William Saroyan, winner of a Pulitzer Prize and an Academy Award, could still be seen riding a bicycle about his native town. Saroyan's, however, was a special case; Armenians were not common contenders for awards or even jobs. They were tormented by their neighbors and snubbed by the city powers. The malice was so demoralizing that some families left Fresno for good, while others changed their names. The Hodge, Lyon, and Paul families were Armenian.

Yet most Armenians, having inherited that ancient talent of survival, lived quietly and patriotically on. They kept to themselves in their own churches and cottage houses and the offices of their political parties, waiting for the day that the terms of public opinion would be renegotiated in their favor. Until then they endured in isolation. Only the courageous and the fortunate endeavored to blend into the mainstream of white society. Richard was among the fortunate; he was well equipped with green eyes, a fair complexion, and an American country tongue—and quite a modest nose.

Richard kept up with his American curiosities. He excelled in Senior Statesmen of America, the Young Democrats, and the College Y at Fresno State. He also joined the Cosmopolitan Club, the weekly hangout of sophisticated international students and those who wanted to know them. Richard was apprehensive about his identity, but he was drawn by the identities of others. One time, in an early act of daring, Richard claimed the dance floor and swerved his large, sweating body to the light-footed Russian melody of the *korobushka*.

A young woman chuckled at the sight of him. She was an Armenian, too, but the spins and claps of the *korobushka* had a special significance for her. They conjured up not the imaginary world of tsars and ancient history, as they did for Richard, but an actual world she had left behind. Not long before, she had been among the *Pioner*, the prized students of Lenin and Stalin, in Soviet Ukraine. Vartiter Kotch-olosian was now nineteen, attractive with dark hair and dark eyes, and she knew Richard from a high school convention of the California Scholarship Federation. To Richard, Vartiter was the fierce, philosoph-ical Armenian he was ashamed to be. To Vartiter, Richard was a drift-ing spirit who needed a direction.

Richard found the beginnings of his Armenian identity at the in-tersection of Ventura and M streets in downtown Fresno. At the Holy Trinity Armenian Apostolic Church, he sang in the choir. Across the street at the Asbarez Club, the Fresno headquarters of the ARF and its newspaper *Asbarez*, he attended meetings of the Armenian Youth Federation. But Richard's newfound pride was not easy to express beyond the closed doors of the Asbarez Club. Outside, the Armenians were still second-class citizens.

Richard encountered the prejudice for the first time during a road trip organized by the College Y. It had been a pleasant drive through the mountains, but at the sight of a speeding car up ahead, the girl sitting next to Richard was infuriated.

"Must be an Armenian!" she exclaimed.

Richard was shocked by the outburst, and he knew he had to re-spond. But how did one respond to such bigotry, more habit than conviction? Was he supposed to make a grand statement about intol-erance and to leave the girl floundering in guilt? In the heat and panic of the moment, there was no time for a breath of thought. Terror commanded the senses, and from somewhere deep inside Richard a frail and sensitive Armenian soul transmitted its first shout of protest to the outer world—a few muffled words that, as he spoke them, left the bitter taste of cowardice upon his lips.

"Must be a Mexican," Richard mumbled.

The pleasant journey and the pleasant conversation continued, an ordinary retreat on an ordinary Fresno afternoon. The moment had already passed for everyone in the car—the reckless driver and

the reckless comment already filed and forgotten as just another epi-
sode of harmless human conflict on the highway—and nobody could
guess that it had deeply contaminated Richard with the complexes of
a diasporan identity.

DURING HIS FIRST YEAR AT Fresno State, Richard tested his various
interests—in history, in diplomacy, in the Armenian Question. The
windows of his mind were flung open to the world, and he welcomed
everything that was new, strange, mysterious. He sharpened his literary tools in English Composition; in a profile titled "The Pink Lady,"
Richard wrote about a vagabond Armenian woman who talked to
parking meters. Through the lectures of Professor Herbert Phil-
lips, he learned that history was dead only if it was forgotten—that
it could be resurrected on command and made real again. And, of
course, Richard still dreamed of Berkeley—that empire of mind and
football that lay beyond the Golden Gate.

On September 8, 1951, Richard joined three thousand spectators
at the San Francisco opera house to witness the signing of the treaty
that formalized the end of World War II in the Pacific. He was enchanted by the practitioners of living history surrounding him on
the main floor: President Harry S. Truman, Secretary of State Dean
Acheson, and the delegates from all over the world. And then Richard noticed the Turkish delegate—the first Turk he had ever seen. His
heart pounded. He felt it again: the need to respond, to identify himself. Except this time courage overpowered fear, and Richard headed
directly for the Turk. He peered into his eyes and said: "Are you still
killing Armenians?" The Turk merely smiled.

His coursework was geared toward a transfer to Berkeley, but Richard was beginning to identify with the Armenians of Fresno. His close
friends were no longer the sophisticates of the political clubs but the
first- and second-generation Armenians of the Armenian Youth Feder-

ation (AYF), who spoke about the fantasy of a "free, independent, and united Armenia," the problematic reality of Soviet Armenia, the first great genocide of the twentieth century. By this time Raphael Lemkin, a Polish lawyer of Jewish descent, had coined the word *genocide*. Influenced in part by the 1921 trial of Soghomon Tehlirian, Lemkin himself had applied it to the events that unfolded in the Armenian provinces of the Ottoman Empire.

In the circles of the AYF, an unlikely friendship blossomed between Richard and Vartiter. Actually, it was not really a friendship, nor did it quite blossom the way a valley flower was supposed to. It would be more accurate to say that a series of awkward encounters took place between two dissonant souls. One belonged to an American farm boy for whom Armenianism was a chosen escape, something he had to practice. The other belonged to a refugee who had spent her early childhood in the industrial suburbs of Kharkov, Soviet Ukraine, and the ethnic camps of fascist Germany. Neither hammer nor swastika had shaken her nationalism. They had only emboldened her, and America had emboldened her, to become a staunch, unrepentant Armenian.

No romantic motives spoiled their conversations. Richard was too sloppy and sensitive to command Vartiter's notice; she was too eccentric and intimidating to attract his. Her heart was heavy, her mind's eye focused always on the *baikar*, the struggle. But that, the intensity of her convictions, was exactly what made Vartiter so fascinating to Richard.

IN THE SUMMER OF 1952, Richard traveled to New York to attend his first national AYF convention. With the enchanted eyes of a new convert, he examined the chic, intellectual Armenians of the East Coast. They spoke with unembarrassed enthusiasm about a historic homeland and, when they sang the AYF anthem, their faces glowed with that powerful, almost frightening passion:

Harach nahadag tseghi anmahner,
Vets taru anmah vrezhi zrahner.
Gadarn haireni, lerants herakuyn,
Ertank gotoghel troshag yerakuyn.

Onward, immortals of our martyred race,
The armor of six centuries of enduring revenge.
To the summit of our distant mountains,
Let us go and plant our tricolor flag.

There was excitement in the air at the convention of June 1952 because several AYF members had been caught in an act of insubordination to the central executive—an act of treason, some said. They had organized a basketball game with the boys of the Armenian Church Youth Organization, a group from "the other side." This had offended many ARF hard-liners who could not understand why true Armenian patriots should want to play ball with Communist sympathizers—common enemies of a free United States and an independent Armenia.

Richard was troubled by the drama of excessive passions, but the fact that such lofty issues as loyalty and patriotism were even being discussed electrified his own passions. The truth was that Richard was captivated by the young men and women around him—American teenagers who lived ordinary American lives but who were actually on a special mission in a foreign land. During the coming meetings and conventions of the AYF, Richard would become Dick and eventually Dikran, namesake of the ancient Armenian king who achieved, in the first century B.C., a *dzovits dzov Hayastan*, an Armenian empire that stretched from the Mediterranean to the Caspian Sea.

KASPAR AND SIROON HAD BRAGGED for months that their son was going to Stanford, but it was at Berkeley, of course, that Richard began his studies in September 1952. At the magnificent Beaux Arts halls of an intellectual citadel, Richard could finally follow his cravings into the depths of history. The problem was that Armenian history had not been invented; a Southeast Europe course was the closest he could hope to come. So Richard would have to learn of his past independently—and this was a dangerous thing, because in the 1950s Armenian history was being written not by academics but by the ideologues of rival political parties.

It was fortunate, then, that Richard met at Berkeley many young Armenian intellectuals whose views were different from his own. Richard Sarafian became his closest friend, challenging Richard in private ten-hour marathon debates. These were not the mock dialogues of yesteryear—the negotiations of imaginary policies at Senior Statesmen meetings—but real-life discussions about the death of Joseph Stalin, the execution of Julius and Ethel Rosenberg, the coronation of Queen Elizabeth II, and Ernest Hemingway's new fisherman novella. They were civil but difficult dialogues about the political division between the ARF and non-ARF, the destiny of the Armenians.

But these were political times, and even independent thinkers often failed to transcend the black and white of party pamphlets. In fact, Richard's letters from this era reveal a true party man in the making. In 1953 he was elected the president of the AYF West Coast Council. Through his very own column published in the *Hairenik Weekly*, Richard demonstrated that California was not a mere protectorate of the East Coast ARF but a parallel federation of an emerging West.

Yet, as he coached a young generation of Armenian Americans in the doctrines of Armenian nationalism, Richard began to reconsider his future in the AYF and the party he was expected to join. At the June 1954 convention in Albany, New York, as yet another chapter was suspended for crimes of insufficient nationalism, Richard finally felt disenchanted with the AYF leadership. Hunched over a notepad, he spent the weekend hours silently scribbling, drawing out over and over again the thirty-nine letters of the Armenian alphabet.

KASPAR HOVANNISIAN FOLLOWED RICHARD'S JOURNEY into the vistas of the Armenian diaspora, but that journey caused him no vicarious pride. He still did not understand how that apple had fallen so far from the family tree. But he had two others—and potentially one more, if only the young Vernon would ripen as planned—and those two, John and Ralph, were filled with the proper virtues. John was already a barber at his father's shop, and Ralph had taken over the vineyard on the Visalia highway. They were both married—John to Varsenig and Ralph to Marian. By April 1955, Varsenig had given Kaspar the good news of two boys, and Marian to Siroon the gift, finally, of a girl.

That Kaspar should have overlooked the non-ARF stock of Varsenig and Marian was a reflection of a mellowing Armenian community in Tulare; time had healed wounds and returned to his weekend feasts some of the wrinkling faces of old friends. But the fact was that Kaspar himself was mellowing in middle age—his love of Armenians outgrowing his love of party. When business found him in a new town, Kaspar would search the phone book for last names ending in "-ian" and call up strangers for conversation. So when visiting Armenians found themselves in Tulare, they did not need a phone book. They showed up at Kaspar's front door, knowing that a round, jolly face would appear to lead them to a dinner table.

Simon Vratzian, the last prime minister of the Armenian republic in 1920, was among Kaspar's guests. So was Ahron Kerkorian, a Fresno man better known as "Villa" (a nickname he owed, along with his formidable mustache, to Pancho Villa), who sought Kaspar out to plead for a small loan. Like Kaspar, he had a story about a prodigal son. His youngest, an amateur welterweight boxing champion, had recently put his entire life savings into the Los Angeles Air Service, a charter airline that shuttled the wealthy and the famous from Los Angeles to the budding casinos of Las Vegas, Nevada. Villa was certain that Kirk Kerkorian's was a hopeless case.

Kaspar gave Villa the loan; he could afford it. With John and Ralph tending to the family business and farm, Kaspar had been devoting more time to his ventures in real estate. He still owned and collected rent from several properties in Tulare, but he had recently taken up another business—the delicate art of raising houses from their under-pinnings, having them lifted onto a truck, then moving them onto other properties. It was the art, though the symbolism was lost on Kaspar, of moving homes.

RICHARD GRADUATED FROM BERKELEY IN the summer of 1954 and stayed on to acquire secondary-school teaching credentials. His final year at Berkeley overlapped with Vartiter's first at the medical school on the same campus. They both lived in the International House, and the proximity allowed the friends to rediscover each other. The conversations that had once flourished on a diet of faith and fatherland were renewed, but turned increasingly to more personal subjects.

From time to time he spoke in embarrassed whispers about an unhappy childhood on a Tulare farm. She spoke about an even darker childhood—memories of a Ukrainian evening when her father was taken away by Soviet secret police and of a German afternoon when the Allied bombs fell over the labor camp near Stuttgart and, for a moment, she thought that her sister Nazik was dead. She spoke mostly about her father, who had fought, as Richard's father had, to recapture Western Armenia after 1915. Richard listened patiently to Vartiter's stories. He was beginning to understand how her severe patriotism had evolved.

One story in particular amused Richard. It was set at Sanger High

School the year after Vartiter's family arrived in the United States. Every morning the students of Vartiter's class would place hands over hearts and recite the pledge of allegiance to the American flag. Vartiter refused—she was faithful to another flag—and she sought by post the advice of Prime Minister Simon Vratzian, the unofficial warden of the Armenian diaspora. A response was soon delivered from Beirut. When you walk into your neighbor's house, Vratzian wrote, you take off your shoes. This was a matter of respect, not principle.

It was a difficult thing, to take off one's shoes yet walk with poise, but that is exactly what Richard and Vartiter were set on doing. They were walking politely through the American system—she was one of only two women in her class at the UC San Francisco School of Medicine—but they were walking as amateur ambassadors of a dispossessed Armenian people. The problem was that Richard did not speak Armenian. Once again it was Simon Vratzian who would offer the solution.

With his abundant white hair, white mustache, and thick glasses, Vratzian arrived in San Francisco in early 1952, on a tour of the Armenian American communities. He had been appointed the director of the Hamazgayin Nishan Palanjian Jemaran, the great academy of Beirut, and he was here to preach the cause of Armenian education. Richard attended the lecture and, afterward, approached the prime minister for a few words. Instead he received the offer of a lifetime. Richard should spend a year at the Jemaran, Vratzian said. He could audit any number of classes and begin, finally, to learn the Armenian language.

"Dghan khentatser e!" Kaspar yelled. "The boy's gone mad!" For several weeks in the spring of 1955 a telephone wire connecting Berkeley to Tulare was hot with the quarrel of a rebellious son and a stone-set father. The outbursts were getting the son nowhere, nor were the commands of an offended father making the expected impact.

It was Siroon who brokered the peace, who persuaded the son to apologize and ultimately told Kaspar that they had to let their son go. She would see to it that the dreams of her washday companion would not be overruled as her own dreams had been so many Tulare afternoons before. "We lost a son"—that is what Kaspar would say when asked about Richard. And maybe so. Maybe Kaspar had lost a son, but Vartiter knew that something more important was about to be gained. In the post the day he left, Richard received a letter from Vartiter, a prophecy enclosed:

> *The fateful hour approaches—to the one who will leave a physical soil that is his by birth, and who will enter the most significant of all, the ideological soil, that is his own by heritage and choice. He will leave a land endowed with the best blessings given to him in this particle-earth, and he will step into the land that is the monument to the Ignored.*

WITH HIS CALLING IN HIS pocket and his life stuffed into a suitcase, Richard G. Hovannisian began his journey eastward. He spent two weeks in Boston and New York, then boarded on August 5, 1955, the SS *United States*, the country's largest ocean liner. Richard knew there was something reversing about all of this. He waved goodbye to the Statue of Liberty, and he knew how absurd that was. And soon he was off, sailing against the waves of the blue Atlantic, with a jumbo case of red licorice, edible memories of Tulare.

In the early morning of August 10, Richard stood on the deck as the ship pulled closer to Le Havre, the port city of northwestern France. He was awestruck by the majesty of its cliffs and cathedrals. He did not know that exactly thirty-five years earlier, some young and unknowable version of his father had been searching for a ship at that very port, longing to reach the New World.

The *United States* docked first at Le Havre and then at Southampton, England. That is where Richard disembarked. In Stratford-upon-Avon, he saw *Twelfth Night* with Laurence Olivier and Vivian Leigh. Then, with speed and economy, he plowed through the continent: France, Belgium, Holland, Germany, Switzerland, Austria, Yugoslavia, and Italy—his stock of licorice diminishing but new enlightenments reached at every stop, the sensation that everything he had read in his textbooks had actually happened. On Venice's St. Lazarus Island, Richard visited the Armenian Catholic monastery where Lord Byron had studied Armenian in 1816.

In Istanbul, Richard was stunned by the destruction. A few days earlier Turkish mobs led by soldiers and policemen had stampeded through minority neighborhoods. Greeks had been the most desirable victims—ninety churches and forty-five hundred homes destroyed—but ethnic hatred had proven to be contagious. "Today I used the word 'bastard' over a hundred times," Richard wrote in his journal on September 19, for there was really no euphemism that could contain such pure, innocent hatred. At the Seraglio Museum, he spat on a portrait of Sultan Abdul Hamid II, the engineer of the first set of Armenian massacres in 1895.

But standing amid the ruins in Istanbul, Richard consoled himself with the conviction that the evil empires of all history had not achieved their ends. Greek and Armenian shops and restaurants along the Bosphorus were boarded up but back in business. The surviving victims were once again on the streets, speaking their conspicuous languages. In Istanbul, the capital of their tormentors, the Greeks and Armenians were determined to survive.

"Always eat in smashed shops," Richard wrote.

ON THE EVENING OF SEPTEMBER 20, 1955, Richard arrived in Beirut. He was met at the airport by Antoine Keheyan, an English teacher called "Sir" around the Jemaran, and Hrayr Kabakian, a medical student from the American University of Beirut. They were sent by Simon Vratzian, but at first sight of that clumsy American they wondered what the prime minister had seen in him. They welcomed Richard and escorted him into their city upon the Mediterranean, through the narrow streets of a hillside neighborhood, and to the iron gates of the Armenian academy. Beyond a courtyard of palm trees and statues stood the Jemaran itself, a former French admiralty building, accompanied by its dormitories.

Richard began to work on the first night. He had won a family war and traveled the globe not for pleasure but for the tough business of learning the motions of his native tongue. He would first unlearn the little Armenian he knew—a dialect infested with Turkish words and inflections of vanished Kharpert—and only then begin to learn the actual language. But then there were two Armenians: the Western version, that of the diaspora, and the Eastern version, that of the existing Soviet state. In Western Armenian the word *rojig* was applied to a sweet dessert made of walnuts and grapes. In Eastern Armenian the same word, *rochik* in conversion, meant "salary" or "payment." Hrayr, Sir, and Armand Keosian, Richard's roommate, spoke Western Armenian. Simon Vratzian spoke Eastern Armenian. So did Vartan Gregorian, a young Armenian from Iran, who took up the task of teaching Richard the difference.

Mostly, though, Richard learned from the original masters. All alone in the library of the American University of Beirut, he opened the books of the nineteenth-century romantic novelist Raffi and began to read—trudging carefully through the new terrain, patiently climbing up and down the steep sentences, pausing at the unknown words, transferring them onto flash cards. He also audited the classes of Jemaran professors, most notably Garo Sassouni, a leader of the Republic of Armenia, while teaching an English class of his own. Richard kept himself so serious that the young female teachers at the

academy began to search for its source. Richard wrote of their specu-
lations to Vartiter:

> *It seems as though I am madly in love with a girl in*
> *California, but my parents object to her and don't want me to*
> *marry her. After a lot of talk, it seemed as though my father*
> *(who likes Armenian things) made an agreement with me*
> *that if I go to Beirut and learn Armenian in a year, he would*
> *give permission for me to marry my loved one. And for this*
> *reason, I'm very serious so that no bad reports get back home*
> *or to the girl. . . . Beirut is a famous place for its beautiful*
> *fairy tale stories. They can tell you what you've done before*
> *you've thought of doing it. So please take care of my beloved*
> *one and when you have time, please let me know who she is.*

In reality a true romantic drama was unfolding overseas. Back
in the United States two women, a beauty and a journalist, both had
seen—and liked what they had seen—in the large frame and disheve-
eled dress of Richard Hovannisian. They were writing letters to
Richard, competing for his affection. Of course on this matter, as on
all important others, Vartiter had her opinion, though this was not
always easy to decipher. "Be cool, reserved, detached, and very pre-
cise in your intentions," she wrote in a letter in the fall of 1955, "unless your reason and that other thing have told you to act differently.
Therefore, remain true to yourself, your own self, and not to certain
virtues which have been made into a part of yourself." In the United
States, Ray Charles had just sung "I Got a Woman" to the top of the
Billboard singles chart.

It was no longer obvious which self was real: the comic or the
emerging curmudgeon, the introspective scholar or the public activist, the American who still dreamed of Cal football games—and
sometimes, in the embrace of intoxicated Beirut evenings, sang the

university's fight songs—or the Armenian with his burning nationalism. These were the tensions of a man in the making, but also of
a unique man, a one-of-a-kind phenomenon that had never before
existed among the Armenians of the diaspora.

Simon Vratzian was not yet convinced of this. The director of the
Jemaran was suspicious of the Armenian Americans. He had lived
in the United States before the Genocide—from 1911 to 1914 he had
edited the newspaper *Hairenik*—and he had found its Armenians on
the brink of assimilation. "Going to America is like dying," he had
told his student Vartan Gregorian, who was about to begin a famous
journey into the American dream. As for what Richard had done,
leaving America for the Armenian academy, that was a revolutionary
feat indeed. It was this journey that gained for Richard the graces of
Simon Vratzian.

Retreating into blindness behind thick glasses, Vratzian looked
the part of an oracle. He clasped his hands together and he spoke
slowly and deliberately, and with great affection for his words. There
seemed to be no artifice to the man. He did not blunt his sharper
opinions, nor was he embarrassed to speak his admiration. When a
doctor inquired about his vision, Vratzian responded: "Those people
whom I love I can see from a hundred meters, and those I don't like I
cannot see even when they are under my nose."

In a way, Simon Vratzian was also the classic father figure,
though he had fallen out of practice. His daughter was living abroad
and his wife apart, and his son had long ago been murdered by
Russian Bolsheviks. That is why, perhaps, he was so sensitive with
Richard, and why Richard regarded him with such awe. They grew
close in conversation: about American academia, about the conflict within the Armenian communities, about Vartiter, whom the
prime minister remembered from her letter about the flag. Once
Vratzian made an astonishing confession to Richard. The judgment
of history frightened him, he said. He was, after all, the *last* prime

minister, the one who had dismantled the republic and "sold Armenia to the Soviets."

Richard comforted Vratzian, as much as the young are able to comfort the old. And it was possible that the prime minister was consoled, because he had developed the secret conviction that Richard himself would one day write the true history of the Republic of Armenia—that this unlikely Tulare boy would actually be his final judge. *"Dikrane bid dzaraye mer badmutiane,"* Vratzian confided to Sir. "Richard shall serve our history."

In Richard, however, the historian's dispassion was still competing with the patriot's enthusiasm. On one hand, Richard had decided against joining the ARF; he jealously cherished his intellectual independence. On the other hand, Richard's neutrality allowed him to express his nationalism more honestly. Richard was bold enough, for example, to attend the Hunchakian Party's annual celebration of Armenia's sovietization, and then bold enough to refuse to clap. Another time he walked out of a dance organized by young ARF activists. The famous verse of The Four Lads' swing-style song "Istanbul (Not Constantinople)" had thrilled the crowd and revolted Richard: "Why did Constantinople get the works? / That's nobody's business but the Turks!"

FOR CENTURIES THE ARMENIAN FAITH had been administered from various high churches across the Armenian homeland. The Holy See of Etchmiadzin, near Yerevan, always had enjoyed the widest jurisdiction: all Armenians living in Eastern Armenia, as well as the key patriarchates in Istanbul and in the Armenian Quarter of Jerusalem. The Holy See of Cilicia, in Sis, had presided over much of Western Armenia. But after Western Armenia was destroyed in 1915, the Holy See of Cilicia relocated to Antelias, a few kilometers from Beirut. Since then the Catholicos at Antelias had been on cordial terms with the Catholicos at Etchmiadzin, a man under the supervision of the Communist Party in Moscow.

But in February 1956, three years after the death of Catholicos Karekin I of the Holy See of Cilicia, it was believed that the pro-ARF clergymen and lay representatives in Beirut would elect not a Soviet sympathizer but, for the first time, an anti-Communist—Bishop Zareh of Aleppo. Richard was delighted by the commotion around him. Posing as a reporter, he gained access to the church complex in Antelias, where bearded clerics in capes whispered to each other. Most of all he enjoyed talking to Father Karekin, a highly educated priest called a *vartabed*, whose views on the election impressed Richard so much that he predicted, in his his notebook, that the *vartabed* would one day become Catholicos.

The election results of February 20, 1956, surprised no one at Antelias—thirty-two out of thirty-six votes were cast for the anti-Communist Zareh—but the abrupt shakeup in clerical power disoriented the Armenian communities. Ramgavar- and Hunchakian-dominated churches severed ties with Antelias, while anti-Soviet churches hailed the new order. Scores of these churches in the Middle East, Greece, and especially the United States—Holy Trinity in Fresno, for example—established ties with Catholicos Zareh I. The Holy See of Cilicia had effectively dissolved its allegiance to Etchmiadzin and transformed into a sovereign diasporan power, the refuge of the orphan ARF-loyal churches.

In hot political times the Armenians returned to the prejudices of their own parties. Richard did not. In the evenings, alone in his dormitory, he tuned into Radio Yerevan, a Soviet propaganda station that was the only link between Armenia and its diaspora. He took mischievous delight in the proud announcements of how many bushels of apples the Soviet Armenians had produced that year, but also true pleasure in the sound of Armenian opera and poetry. His emotions were not ruled by politics, and the victory of the Antelias churches did not seduce him into the party of his father. As he slept one night, Richard dreamed of an AYF convention. He saw long rows of seats and hundreds of faces. He did not recognize any of them.

BY THE TIME HE LEFT Beirut in May 1956, Richard spoke and wrote Armenian fluently, and in their final meeting he told Simon Vratzian that he had finished reading the *Republic of Armenia*. This was Vratzian's thick and complex work of history, written in Eastern Armenian, and Richard claimed, quite implausibly, to have understood all of it. There was only one confusing detail, Richard said. Why were the ministers of the Armenian republic paid not in traditional paper currency but in *rojig*, the sweet walnut-and-grape dessert? Vratzian laughed. He knew that Richard had read the book.

Then the prime minister turned serious. When Richard returned to California, Vratzian said, he would marry Vartiter.

Richard would have many late nights to ponder Vratzian's astounding prophecy, but for now he was on an eastward adventure through Iraq, Iran, Pakistan, India, Burma, Thailand, Singapore, Indonesia, Vietnam, the Philippines, Taiwan, Japan, and Hawaii. He stayed in cheap hotels and ate rarely. Knowledge was his obsession, economy his pride. By the time he arrived in San Francisco six weeks later, he had lost thirty pounds. It was curious to consider, but Richard Hovannisian had been strong and handsome all along. Except now everybody could recognize his good looks. His green eyes were no longer lost to the world.

The moment he arrived in San Francisco, Richard made the phone call to Fresno. Vartiter picked up. She was thrilled to hear Richard's voice, but she could not understand what her dear friend was saying, why he was insisting that she immediately board a bus and meet him in San Francisco.

Chapter Five

⸺⸙⸺

MONUMENT TO THE IGNORED

Vartiter hung up the phone in the living room of 3312 Lowe Avenue, and with great anxiety approached the stern, balding man who ruled her universe. Hovagim Kotcholosian had been a compassionate father; he had denied Vartiter nothing. But to see her go off on summer break—and to meet a man—was an affront to propriety and a potential source of gossip for an interweaving Armenian community. Still, in this modest home on this shady street of southeastern Fresno, trust had always overcome convention, and so it did now. Within a few hours, Vartiter was on a Greyhound bus headed for San Francisco, where her old friend and an unexpected twist of fate were waiting for her.

Richard was different. The evidence of a chubby childhood had melted from his body. His face had found a sharp, handsome shape. He was tanned to a movie star's bronze. But there was something else that allowed new, once-unimaginable currents to pass between two friends. Richard had learned Armenian—the language of Vartiter's inner circle, the language of a vanished republic, the only language with enough sound and melody to express true Armenian patriotism. In Beirut, Richard's Armenian identity had been activated.

It was a match made in history—conceived first in the mind of the visionary Simon Vratzian—yet the brief courtship of Richard and Vartiter did not immediately achieve the blessings of Kaspar and Siroon Hovannisian. And this was odd, because the Kotcholosians were, by all accounts, a model Armenian family. Hovagim was a staunch patriot; in Western Armenia, after the Genocide, he had fought for the legendary partisan commander Keri. His wife, Khengeni (or Khenguhi), was the consummate mother, overflowing with empathy and love. Vartiter and Nazik, their daughters, were models of the new Armenian woman, combining as they did a keen respect for the lost world of their parents with the confidence necessary to navigate the new one.

Yet the Kotcholosians were marked with a pair of conspicuous scarlet letters: DP. They were part of a community of displaced persons who had not only suffered genocide during World War I but also lived through the terror of World War II. With great scars these Armenians had arrived in the United States in 1949–50. They were not, nor could they pretend to be, real Americans, as were the wives of John and Ralph and the children of all Armenians who had taken refuge here soon after the massacres of 1915. Vartiter might have been a daughter of the Armenian Revolutionary Federation, but this would not excuse her insufficient fluency in American society—the world of Elks Club brothers and Emblem Club sisters where Kaspar and Siroon had found a place, side by side with their Armenian associations.

It did not matter. Richard would not allow his own history to be written by other men. He began, with a set of untested romantic tools, to build a new relationship with Vartiter. This was not easy. Vartiter was taken aback by the sudden boldness of her old friend. She had been given no opportunity to adjust her own feelings, yet there they were, stealing awkward glances at each other in Richard's turquoise Chevrolet, the panorama of San Francisco unfolding before them. Richard was acting strangely decisive, and Vartiter, too, was breaking out of character. She presented Richard with a cross on a chain, even though she was ambivalent about that symbol.

He taught history and geography at Oakland High School and commuted to Berkeley to complete coursework toward a master's degree in history. She was already in her third year of medical school, which included intensive training at the County Hospital in San Francisco. There was, in other words, not much time for merrymaking. A few sparse evenings at the San Francisco Opera in the fall of 1956 were the only outward signs of contemporary courtship. But then Richard and Vartiter might not even sit together: they were working as volunteer ushers.

They found love in difficult, collaborative work. Richard had decided to focus his master's thesis on the Sovietization of the Republic of Armenia in 1920, and his research came to depend on Vartiter, who would translate for him the era's Russian political writing. During one of these sessions, as Vartiter was reading aloud the recollections of the Georgian diplomat Zurab Avalishvili, something remarkable happened. Overwhelmed by unprecedented emotions, Richard unclenched his right hand and delivered a powerful wallop to Vartiter's ear. He did not understand what he had just done, but he apologized profusely, the way he had once apologized to a crying pup on his father's farm.

On March 2, 1957, after a traditional wedding ceremony at the Holy Trinity Armenian Apostolic Church in Fresno, hundreds of Armenians filled the Veterans Memorial Building in Tulare. Pilaf and kebabs were served to the tragic-nostalgic music of Western Armenia—produced by the clarinet, violin, oud, and *dumbeg* of an Armenian band. Siroon, her gray hair done up in a perm, smiled her happiness. Khenguhi cried hers. Kaspar and Hovagim, men among men, were possessed by the shameless liberty of youth. Clasping arms, they twirled around like children. They did not recognize each other, did they? They had been only boys then, but Kaspar Hovannisian and Hovagim Kotcholosian had stood among the same cheering crowd in March 1918, when General Antranig arrived in Garin.

The Armenians of the San Joaquin Valley assembled for the circle dance. Linking their fingers, they moved in rhythm: *right step, right step, right step, left kick, right kick. Right step, right step, right step, left kick, right kick.* And by that logic, ongoing and unchanged, they danced to exhilaration. At the center of the circle were Richard and Vartiter, dressed in white, more handsome and lovely than ever they had been. Vartiter moved her arms above her with such unexpected grace that it seemed she could feel contours in the air. Richard's movements were more reserved. His arms extended, the groom stepped unsurely around his new bride, a young matador around a bull, the way men had done for centuries in distant lands.

It was not their style, but Richard and Vartiter did take a day's honeymoon in Carmel, a quaint town upon the Pacific not far from the birthplace and stomping grounds of John Steinbeck. The following afternoon, Richard was back at Oakland High School and Vartiter at the County Hospital. She linked her wedding ring to a chain and wore it around her neck.

In August, under the terms of the Reserve Forces Act, Richard entered Fort Ord for mandatory basic training. Six months later, he emerged from the Presidio of San Francisco with a good grasp of the Russian language and the outline of his thesis. He wrote feverishly through the spring of 1958 and made it, in June, to the grand ceremonies at Memorial Stadium in Berkeley. He received his master's degree, Vartiter her medical degree, and together the historian and the doctor journeyed back through the Golden Gate of their dreams. A small vacant lot had turned up on Alta Avenue in Fresno, and Kaspar had found a house and hauled it there. It was a cozy spot in a neighborhood of Armenian immigrants—only two blocks from the Kotcholosian home on Lowe Avenue and across the street from Longfellow Junior High School.

Richard taught geography, history, and English classes at Long-fellow. His students were by turns terrified and inspired, but ulti-mately left clueless about their teacher's true persona. Sometimes when the students were taking a test and the classroom was quiet, Richard would open his desk drawer and take out a world atlas. He always flipped to the same page, the map of the Soviet Union, and gazed endlessly at the same unnamed republic lingering between the Black and Caspian seas. He was indebted to it—that magnificent myth of death and survival, which had pulled him out of a pathless education and given him a history to yearn for.

TWO THOUSAND CONTRABAND DOLLARS HIDDEN in his socks in the summer of 1959, Richard entered the Soviet Union. At the train station between the Finnish border and Leningrad, a grim colonel stepped on board. He read through some twenty passenger names.

"Hovannisian," the colonel said.

"Yes," Richard answered.

"Are you Armenian?"

Richard said that he was. Then he noticed that the colonel did not look Russian. Those were not Russian eyes.

"Tun hai es?" Richard muttered. "Are you Armenian?"

The colonel did not answer. He continued to read off the passen-ger names, but as he did he smiled so gently that only a person who wanted to see a smile there could see it. Richard smiled, too. No one around them knew what was happening.

A guide from Intourist, the official tourism organization of the Soviet Union, was assigned to Richard. In the afternoons he followed her through an approved tour of Leningrad and then Moscow. Inside the mausoleum at the Red Square, Richard shuddered at the sight of Lenin and Stalin, their evil and compelling greatness embalmed for all eternity. But nationalist cravings he would have to satisfy in stealth, scurrying off at night to visit Armenian churches and to purchase exquisite Armenian brandy, which had so warmed the heart of Winston Churchill at the end of World War II that Joseph Stalin sent up to four hundred bottles to him every year.

Then on July 12 Richard boarded a DC-3 airplane and took flight. He peered out of his window, fresh eyes awaiting rapture. And soon he had it. The plane descended through clouds, and Richard cast his glance upon an ancient landscape: the mountain chains, golden fields, and fast-flowing rivers of the Armenian homeland.

On the sixth floor of the Armenia Hotel in Yerevan, Richard found his room—a suite reserved for Western guests, and wired to monitor them—but he did not immediately take notice of its luxuries. He stepped onto the balcony and gazed, as Armenians have always done, upon the snow-crowned peaks of majestic Mount Ararat. Once upon a time those blue mountains had been the meeting point, the geological celebration of the union of Eastern and Western Armenia. Now they served as the boundary between Soviet Armenia and the Turkish Republic—the colossal coverup of the historic crime scene on the other side.

A camera hanging from his neck, Richard spent the week navigating the Yerevan avenues and alleys that somehow always returned him to Lenin Square. He watched the Armenian men in their newsboy caps as they played backgammon in parks and the strolling women in ornate dresses, because a walk through the capital was an event for them. His ears slowly became attuned to Eastern Armenian, which had absorbed so much Russian into its vernacular. On an electric tram stuffed with sweating factory workers, Richard was inspired out of his private nature and into chance conversations with strangers. He could not believe it, the sight of Armenians everywhere. And they could not believe it, the blissful smile of an American.

Richard was enchanted by Soviet Armenia, but he was not blinded by his patriotism. He was revolted by the clamor of Armenians inside the Holy See of Etchmiadzin, the ill will fermenting between local Armenians and the one hundred thousand Western Armenians who had arrived in the 1940s as part of a Soviet experiment in repatriation, the statue of Stalin that stood on a hill overlooking the city, like Jesus upon Rio de Janeiro. *Not much longer*, Richard thought. That very week, the television of the Armenia Hotel lobby was lighting up with the images of a kitchen set, where Soviet leader Nikita Khrushchev and American vice president Richard Nixon were actually talking about ideas.

The day before he left, in the garden of a first-floor flat in central Yerevan, Richard found Khenguhi's long-lost mother, Hranush, and brother, Hovhannes. They had not seen Khenguhi since Stuttgart 1945, when the family had been torn in two. Khenguhi, along with her husband and two daughters, had sought a new fate in the free world. Her mother and brother had decided to return to the familiar world in Soviet Ukraine. That night Hranush and Richard exchanged photographs and stories of a broken family—but in whispers, always in whispers, because there was something so wonderful in this reunion that it could not be tolerated by the Soviet authorities, visible and invisible.

SHORTLY BEFORE MIDNIGHT ON FRIDAY, November 20, 1959, Raffi arrived at the Community Hospital of Fresno, California. He had brown eyes, black hair, and a relentless smile, and he spent the first few weeks of his life in the arms of his mother, happily receiving the blessings of countless Armenians. "Raffi is growing," Richard reported to Simon Vratzian. "He is laughing. He does not know what the future has in store for him. He does not yet know that he has been born into a race in which all children, if they are good, must suffer."

On June 28, 1962, a second sufferer was born. He was named Armen.

Turkish gendarmes commence in 1915 the deportation of Armenians from Kharpert, called by the United States consul Leslie Davis the "slaughterhouse province" of the Ottoman Empire.

(Project SAVE Armenian Photograph Archives, Watertown, Massachusetts, courtesy of an anonymous photo donor)

A family of deportees passing through the Syrian desert. The photograph was taken by Armin T. Wegner, a German soldier stationed in the Ottoman Empire in April 1915.

(© Armenian National Institute, Inc., courtesy of Sybil Stevens [daughter of Armin T. Wegner]. Wegner Collection, Deutches Literaturarchiv, Marbach & United States Holocaust Memorial Museum)

As Americans in the United States organized relief efforts for the "starving Armenians," General Antranig, pictured with his men in 1917, rushed to defend the remnants of his Western Armenian homeland. An army of orphans was waiting for him in Garin.

(Top photo: United States National Archives)

Soon after his arrival in the United States in 1920, Kaspar Hovannisian posed for his first studio photograph in Boston, then hastened across the country to the San Joaquin Valley of California, where the simpler village life of his native Bazmashen, Kharpert, was being reinvented. In Tulare he married Siroon Nalbandian and emerged at the center of a new brotherhood of Armenians. Der Sarkis is seated to Kaspar's right. Sarkis Nalbandian, with tie, stands to his left.

John, Ralph, and Richard were raised to respect their father's vines, but one of them secretly dreamed of leaving. Photo from the early 1940s.

Kaspar at the barbershop in downtown Tulare, early 1940s.

Richard Hovannisian (rightmost) and Vartiter Kotcholosian (at center, in black) attend a Model United Nations convention in 1952. It was Simon Vratzian, the last prime minister of the Republic of Armenia, who envisioned—and inspired—the greater collaboration. Richard and Vartiter were married in 1957 and attended joint graduation ceremonies at Berkeley's Memorial Stadium in 1958.

The family of Kaspar and Siroon Hovannisian, 1965. Richard stands behind Raffi on the far right.

The family of Hovagim and Khenguhi Kotcholosian, 1970.

Raffi, Richard, and the family station wagon—"We are Armenians"—in 1976.

Mr. and Mrs. Raffi K. Hovannisian
Րաֆֆի Կ. եւ Արմենուհի Յովհաննէսեան

A family crest first appeared on the wedding invitations of Raffi and Armenouhi Hovannisian. The ceremony was held in June 1985 at the Holy Trinity Armenian Apostolic Church in Fresno, California.

On December 7, 1988, the towns and villages of northwestern Armenia collapsed. Raffi rushed to the homeland to help relieve—and document—the suffering.

(Photo by Robert Arsenyan)

The pals and the professor convened in Fresno for Armen's wedding in May 1989. Raffi, Armen, and Garo are at center.

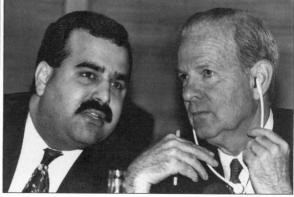

Raffi was appointed the new Republic of Armenia's first minister of foreign affairs. In December 1991 he joined Levon Ter-Petrosyan, Rouben Adalian, and Alexander Arzoumanian in a White House meeting with President George H. W. Bush. In March 1992 he raised the Armenian flag at the New York headquarters of the United Nations. In May he conferred with Secretary of State James Baker.

(Top photo by Joyce Naltchayan, the White House. Middle photo by Harry L. Koundakjian)

After his resignation, Raffi traveled in January 1993 to Martuni in Mountainous Karabagh, where he visited Monte Melkonian (right), his old friend from Berkeley.

Siroon and her sons, John, Richard, Ralph, and Vernon, 1995.

The family of Richard and Vartiter Hovannisian, January 2001. Ani is the bride.

In November 2005, tens of thousands of Armenian citizens followed Raffi in the republic's first movement of civil disobedience.

(Top photo by Onnik Krikorian. Bottom photo by Herbert Baghdasaryan)

In the summer of 2006, Richard and Vartiter journeyed to Western Armenia. Richard found the cabbages of his mother's village of Keserig, Kharpert. Vartiter found the family home in her father's village of Tsitogh, Garin.

As Richard continued his endless lecture tour, Raffi launched from Yerevan the underdog campaign of his life. In the spring of 2007 the Heritage Party entered the National Assembly with seven members of parliament: Raffi K. Hovannisian, Anahit Bakhshyan, Larisa Alaverdyan, Zaruhi Postanjyan, Armen Martirosyan, Stiopa Safaryan, and Vardan Khachatryan.

(Top right photo by Avetis Ghazanchyan. Bottom photo by Mamikon Sargsian)

Raffi and Armenouhi with their children, 2008. Clockwise: Van, Armen Richard, Shushi, Garin, Daron.
(Photo by Hakob Petrosyan)

Yerevan stretches toward Ararat.
(© Mikhail Pogosov, 2010; used under license from Shutterstock)

Richard took deep delight in his sons. They and very few other things in life could cause him to smile so deeply, so without shame— and smiling was almost always shameful, because it meant that one was weak or, worse, enjoying life. His relationship with Raffi and Armen was a joy that he could confess, for a change. That was important for a man who too often wore the educator's frown. Together with his sister-in-law Nazik, a teacher in the Fresno school district, he had organized an Armenian weekend school in Tulare. More recently, in Fresno, he had begun to teach courses in Armenian language and culture for an extension program of the University of California, Los Angeles.

Gustave von Grunebaum, the director of the UCLA Center for Near East Studies, was impressed by Richard's performance—so impressed that he invited the young lecturer to join his center in Los Angeles. It was an offer that Richard could not believe—or refuse. In the summer of 1962, he helped his parents move from Tulare to Fresno. Then, loyal to the rebel logic of his life, he left Fresno for Los Angeles. At UCLA, a green island of scholarship disconnected from a senseless, sprawling city, Richard would join one of the nation's strongest history programs—as a lecturer and soon, also, as a Ph.D. student.

In 1963 Vartiter and her boys joined Richard in Los Angeles. They came to live, after a spell of apartment hopping, in a three-bedroom house at the end of a cul-de-sac called Terryhill Place. As Vartiter worked in the internal medicine department of Kaiser Permanente Hospital, Richard hastened toward his doctoral degree. By the fiftieth anniversary of the Armenian Genocide on April 24, 1965, when hundreds of thousands of Soviet citizens staged an unprecedented demonstration of daring in Yerevan, Richard had begun to write his dissertation. The following spring, he defended "Armenia on the Road to Independence," an inquiry into the background of the Armenian republic. He had earned his Ph.D. in three years.

Simon Vratzian smiled. Blind, sick, and dying in Beirut, the prime minister took the sole pride available to him in his late age: the prospering of his students. "I am proud and happy that your superhuman work has been crowned by success," he wrote to Richard. "I am happy also that Vartiter served as your working partner, and that she will support you through future volumes. I hope that soon Raffi, too, will become your collaborator." Indeed, a full generation of collaborators was coming to life: Ani was born in 1964.

The Armenians of the United States were swept up in the whirlwind events of the 1960s: the political assassinations, the riots, the war protests, the student movements raging on university campuses. The new American-born generation especially was inspired by the civil rights movement to pursue its own national ambitions. By the late 1960s, private Armenian schools were flourishing in major cities of the United States. Educational societies, most notably the National Association for Armenian Studies and Research, were establishing endowed chairs in Armenian studies at major universities. The first chair had been created at Harvard University in 1955; Boston had been the Armenian sanctuary then.

But it was to Los Angeles that the diaspora slowly began to look. In the warm, fertile soil of California, many believed, an emerging community of Armenian patriots could plant the seeds of even greater victories.

RAFFI K. HOVANNISIAN, FIVE YEARS old and a third-generation American, was horrified to find on his first day of school that he could not understand the language of his classmates. He spent the day an outcast in his own country, his eyes wet and wandering on the playground of Brentwood Elementary School. Yet Raffi had already come into a kind of adult severity, a furling of the brow, a passion for endurance. Much to his father's satisfaction, he was speaking English in no time and delivering perfect report cards to Terryhill Place.

Richard was lecturing at UCLA, but now also keeping a full-time job as an associate professor of history at nearby Mount St. Mary's College. Unbeknown to his colleagues, he was also beginning a much greater journey. Having published *Armenia on the Road to Independence* in 1967, Richard was following that road to its natural end. He would devote the next three decades of his life to the Republic of Armenia, exhausting the archives of the United States, France, Great Britain, Germany, and the Armenian delegation to the Paris Peace Conference. It would be an enormous undertaking, and he would have to make sacrifices. He would cook and play and read Armenian with his children as often as he could, but mostly he would have to guide Raffi, Armen, and Ani by example.

Vartiter, meanwhile, was a daily teacher and constant guide. Almost every Friday, with or without Richard, she would load the children into the family station wagon and drive north through the mountains, oil rigs, grapevines, and orchards of the San Joaquin Valley. It would take about four hours to reach that familiar wooden home with its front porch and overhang, 3312 Lowe Avenue, and each time Hovagim would cry at the sight of his grandchildren. Hrair, Arpi, Vahe, and Aram—the children of Nazik and her husband, Vartkes—would meet them there, and together the cousins would spend the day feasting on oranges and apricots, singing the nationalist songs of their *babi* Hovagim, listening to the gentle aphorisms of their *mami* Khenguhi.

After breakfast the following morning, the Hovannisian children would leave Lowe Avenue for the the basement hall of Holy Trinity. They would have to endure three hours of Armenian language lessons before the weekend could resume—now at a sprawling ranch-style house in the Sunnyside neighborhood of Fresno. That was Hovannisian headquarters, a dusky home with green shag carpets and a spacious backyard, from which Kaspar had ruled over his family since 1962. He would be there, a deeply engraved smile on his face, running after his grandchildren, threatening them with tickles or a bite on the nose.

The years had humbled Kaspar. Having achieved power, he no longer sought to wield it. His fancy suits and showy shoes were left unworn in his closet, and he had adapted a new slogan: "Walk softly and carry a big stick." He had begun to hand over the reins of his real estate empire to John and, slowly, to the young Vernon. He was proud, as always, of the down-to-earth craft and spirit of Ralph. And he was coming to see Richard for who he was: a man, quite simply, born out of context. This is not to say that Kaspar had shed his manly habits—breakfast was still a shot of whisky—just that he had arrived at new sensitivities. He had allowed Martin, Siroon's stuttering, philosophizing brother, to live in his house.

"Can't live with him, can't live without him," Siroon would say of her husband, and she was responsible for Kaspar's mellowing. She had encouraged his involvement in non-Armenian groups in Fresno, and on a few occasions persuaded him into a tuxedo and onto the dance floor of American socials, where he, son of Bazmashen, did not belong. But as she tugged her husband into American life, Siroon seemed to be overcoming her own anxieties over being a true American. She volunteered at the Armenian Relief Society, the sister organization of Kaspar's party, and at Holy Trinity.

In the summer of 1967 Kaspar, Siroon, Vartiter, and Khenguhi followed Richard on a journey to the eastern homeland. A card-carrying member of the ARF and an evangelist for national independence, Kaspar was uneasy with Soviet Armenia: the streets named after dictators and the statues of Bolshevik thugs. But Yerevan the city was not the ideology-painted dungeon of Kaspar's imagination. That statue of Stalin, for example—it was no longer at the top of the hill. It had just been replaced by the statue of Mayr Hayastan, Mother Armenia, an armored woman extending a welcome but also bearing a sword.

He had been living without a homeland for half a century, but Kaspar was slowly realizing that Armenia, or some version of Armenia, had been his all along. By the end of the trip, he was racing from one water fountain to another, slurping the water that had remained cold and delicious through Soviet rule. He was dancing at each sight of Ararat.

But good feelings were soon to vanish, because the next stop was Istanbul, and that prejudice Kaspar could not overcome. On the streets of an ancient metropolis, he was rubbing up against Turks, and every Turk was the one who had murdered his mother. Dizzy and sweating, Kaspar stumbled through the streets. There was no way he could spend another moment in Istanbul. An early exit was his only salvation.

IN THE SPRING OF 1968 the Armenians of the United States achieved a milestone—an eight-column monument unveiled at Bicknell Park in Montebello, near Los Angeles. It had taken almost five years of city hall meetings, town hall debates, and community fund-raising to consecrate, in a public park, a monument dedicated to "the 1,500,000 Armenian victims of the genocide perpetrated by the Turkish government 1915–1921, and to men of all nations who have fallen victim to crimes against humanity." Unknown to city inspectors, the skull of an Armenian Genocide victim was buried under the monument. Karekin, now a bishop at Antelias, had arranged for Richard to transport it clandestinely to the United States.

The idea was conceived in the mind of Michael Minasian, a leader of Montebello's large displaced persons community, but the monument at Montebello was the work and testament of countless Armenians, from all sides of community politics. ARF, Ramgavar, Hunchakian, Apostolic, Catholic, Protestant, and every other category of Armenian converged at Bicknell Park for the opening ceremony of April 21, 1968. California senators sat solemnly onstage. A Marine Corps band played. But no one, not even the most optimistic organizers, had expected that so many Armenians—more than ten thousand—would flock to Montebello. Ronald Reagan, the governor of California, would be sure to show up for the following year's commemoration. His proclamation that day was read by a state senator named George Deukmejian.

The chairman of the board of the Armenian Monument Council and one of its founding members, Professor Richard G. Hovannisian stood as the master of ceremonies. He commanded the scholarship and the passion, a careful Armenian and a supple English, the faith of the ARF and the faith that transcends all parties. This was the day that Richard welded worlds—the day the Armenian diaspora was united in him. This was the day he made Kaspar proud—the day that a professor and his father could begin, so late and without words, to overcome their history of hard feelings.

Yet as he presided over that epic event of diaspora history, Richard was thinking only about Simon Vratzian—the prime minister, the prophet, and the great teacher—who had sown so much promise in him but who could not be here to see the harvest. It hurt Richard to know that, somewhere in the hills of Lebanon, a legend was on his deathbed. He would die in 1969, not knowing that men could walk on the moon, that his unlikely student had been given tenure as an associate professor of history at UCLA.

HIS HAIR WAS WHITE AND withdrawing, his stomach plump from endless festivities, but at the age of sixty-nine Kaspar betrayed no sign of surrender. He had not stopped working, and he could still beat his grandchildren in backyard sprints. He was overjoyed by the continuation of his life in all of them—the free, brave American spirit of John's and Ralph's children, the heavy Armenian spirit of Richard's children: Raffi, Armen, Ani, and the newborn Garo. Kaspar loved all of them, but he was especially fascinated by Raffi, ten years old but already singing nationalist songs and sending letters to the newspaper *Hairenik*. Kaspar was moved by one of these to write a letter of his own, in Armenian, to his grandson:

Dear Raffi,

These few lines have more value than an entire book. I wanted to read aloud these words, so that Grandma, too, could find joy in them. I was deeply stirred. Tears formed in my eyes. I could not read without stopping. It was not in vain that you were given the name Raffi. We keep the hope that one day you will raise the Armenian tricolor on Ararat. Raffi was a great novelist. With his writing, he inspired the Armenians to revolution, to fight against the Turks, so that we could have our historic lands. Today we have a small Armenia, but this is not the end. Through the work of your generation, we will once again achieve the Great Armenia, where all Armenians will gather. Raffi, you know that your father is doing important work for the Armenian people. These things you will understand better in a few years, and so will your brothers and your sister Ani. A few days ago I told Babi Hovagim and Mami Khenguhi about your writing. They were very happy, too. We are proud of you, Raffi. Please keep us updated about your works. Kisses to Armen, Ani, and Garo. And a big kiss on your forehead.

Babi Kaspar

Kaspar traveled once more to Armenia in the summer of 1970. When he returned, he changed his will. He would not leave his money to the ARF, as party faithful were supposed to do, but to Armenian schools in the diaspora. And then he allowed Richard to record the stories of his childhood. In the living room of his Sunnyside retreat, Kaspar spoke to his son's forty-pound reel-to-reel recorder. He spoke about his mother, Heghnar, about his brother, Gabriel. He spoke generously, emotionally, plainly. He remembered everything in fresh detail: the stroke of the sun and the scent of the mountain flower. It was as if a part of him had stayed behind in 1915, stayed with his mother and brother, stayed to die with his people.

IN THE LATE AFTERNOON OF October 21, 1970, the phone rang at the end house of Terryhill Place. In his corner office, Richard picked up. It was Vernon. He was crying. Richard listened for a moment. Then he dropped the receiver. His heart shook and his eyes began to burn. He walked to the bathroom. He had been growing a beard for some months. He shaved it. Then he told Vartiter to put the children in the station wagon. They were going to Fresno. The children were not told what was wrong.

No hope or bliss of ignorance could survive the ghastly sight of Grandma Siroon sitting in her gray armchair. She was swaying side to side, screaming her uncontainable anguish. Her grandchildren were shocked by her suffering. To them, Grandma had been an indomitable woman. Now, for the first time, she was striking those complicated, sorrowful chords.

John and Ralph explained to Richard how their father had died. Kaspar had been on the job that afternoon, checking up on a house near Fresno City College that was soon to be lifted and moved. He had collapsed in the middle of the street. The coroner said that he had died of a heart attack; there was no doubt about that. Only one detail had startled him. The deceased, Kaspar Hovannisian, was dressed in old work clothes: his shirt soiled, his shoes worn. So the coroner could not quite believe what he found in Kaspar's trouser pocket: a thick roll of cash.

Armenians filled the Holy Trinity Armenian Apostolic Church on October 24, 1970. The priest performed the service, and Richard poured Armenian earth over his father's chest. Vernon placed a bottle of Armenian cognac in his vest pocket.

"Bye, Dad," he said, and the casket was closed.

In the company of his family and countless friends—an attendance suitable for the Armenian king of the San Joaquin Valley—Kaspar arrived at the Masis section of the Ararat Cemetery of Fresno. He would be among his people, the fossils of Western Armenia. A few yards away, under the statue of an eagle slaying a snake, lay the hero Soghomon Tehlirian, who had slain the mastermind of the Armenian Genocide.

As Kaspar descended into the soil of Fresno, Siroon wailed and someone began to sing:

> *Verkerov li jan fedayi em,*
> *Taparagan dun chunem.*
> *Yaris pokhan zenks em krgel,*
> *Mi degh hankisd kun chunem. . . .*
> *Aha hankisd hogh ge mdnem,*
> *Huyses tuk ek engerner.*
> *Sharunagek mer surp kordze,*
> *Dashnaktsutian veh kacher.*

> I am a fighter covered with wounds,
> A rover, I have no home.
> In place of my love, I embrace my rifle,
> Nowhere is there sleep in peace. . . .
> And now, at peace, I enter the soil,
> You are my hope, my dear comrades.

You must continue our sacred work,
Noble Dashnaktsakan braves.

Nothing was lost, only transferred quietly to those who understood, to those who agreed to understand. In silence, the grandchildren of Kaspar Gavroian Hovannisian stood at the Ararat Cemetery,
looking at each other. Who would it be? How would they share that
great responsibility, engraved on the tombstone of Babi Kaspar? Richard had chosen the epitaph, *Ayskan charik te moranan mer vortik . . .* , a
line from the poet Avetis Aharonian: "If such great wrongs our sons
forget . . ." But not everyone, not even most people who might visit
Kaspar over the coming decades, knew the words that fell on the other
side of the ellipsis: *Togh voghch ashkharh hayin garta nakhadink.*

Raffi knew the poem: "If such great wrongs our sons forget / Let
the world's curses the Armenians beget."

Chapter Six

ALMOST HEAVEN

L ate in the afternoon of Christmas Day 1970 the doorbell rang at family headquarters in Fresno. In the backyard the grand-children of Siroon and Kaspar Hovannisian stopped in their tracks. Bats and balls fell onto the wet earth. The cousins stampeded inside. No purer combination of fear and joy existed for them than this once-a-year miracle: the creaking open of a winter's door and the first sight of the rotund bearded man in a red suit. The children, lined up on the green shag carpet, began to sing a Christmas song. "Ho! Ho! Ho! Merry Christmas!" Santa Claus chortled, charging like a bull through the crowd.

"Santa's tired," the man in the suit said, always in the third person. It was the same excuse every year. Santa was tired because he had just finished delivering gifts to the children of Armenia. But Santa never forgot about the Hovannisian children, because they were his favorite children in the entire San Joaquin Valley.

Grandma Siroon sat on the golden sofa next to the Christmas tree. Her eyes swelled with tears. She remembered Kaspar, and she knew that theirs had not been a marriage from the fairytales. It had been often cold and broken, and the years of their lives had been spent on the mending of it. But Siroon had grown to depend on Kaspar, even to love him. For the past few months she had felt so unbearably light, as if gravity itself had been extinguished.

All alone now, Siroon presided over this extraordinary family—a family brokered between a genocide and a dream, but a family that seemed, slowly, to be losing its character. They played together all through this winter's evening, but the fact was that Siroon's grandchildren were nothing like each other. They were brunette and blond and Nalbandian red, farm boys and city people. Their very names told of the troubles of Armenian life in the United States, a sad allegory of dispersion and memory: John, Cheryl, David, Florence, Ralph, Gary, Raffi, Siroon, Armen, Ani, Garo.

"WHEN I HEARD THE NEWS that the El Toro Marine color guard and band was ordered not to play on Armenian Martyrs Day on April 24, I was shocked," Raffi wrote to President Richard Nixon in May 1971. "This is my country of justice and freedom. I want it to stay that way." He was only eleven years old, but Raffi's instincts were already jumping at the Armenian cause. He shared the wrath of all Armenians who had carried out their annual commemoration at Montebello absent the pomp and pandering of previous years, when governors and senators had turned up to lay flowers at the monument. Phone calls made by Turkish consuls to Sacramento and Washington had been sufficiently confusing. There had been no genocide in 1915, the voices said, but rather a world war tragedy during which both Armenians and Turks had perished.

The submission of the United States government was truly outrageous, falling as it did out of synchrony with its own record of "the greatest crime of the war." That formulation of President Theodore Roosevelt was supported not by the briefings of Armenian or Turkish lobbyists in Washington but by American accounts filed in the National Archives of the United States: the testimony of Leslie Davis, the consul in Kharpert, who recorded in real time "the most thoroughly organized and effective massacre this country has ever seen," and of Henry Morgenthau, the United States ambassador to Turkey, who wrote to the Department of State about a "campaign of race extermination"—the dictionary definition of *genocide*, though Morgenthau wrote it long before the word itself was coined.

But already the Genocide was fading from the American memory. There were new calamities upon the world, and one strong wave of Turkish denial might wash away its last vestiges from Washington. The Armenian National Committee of America (ANCA), the activist group affiliated with the Armenian Revolutionary Federation, had been the first to safeguard Armenian interests in the capital. But because the ranks of the ANCA were drawn almost exclusively from the ARF itself, the organization did not represent the views of the Ramgavar, Hunchakian, and other political communities that did not buy into the staunch anti-Communism of the ARF. Many of these Armenians, aligned by a general sympathy for Soviet Armenia, had so far consolidated their patriotism in their own associations, most notably the Armenian General Benevolent Union (AGBU).

Cooperation between the ARF and its political rivals had been achieved on rare occasions, but finally, with a common enemy in sight, a comprehensive partnership seemed possible. That epiphany first visited two Armenian professors on the campus of George Washington University in Washington. John Hanessian was a member of the AGBU, Haigaz Gregorian a leader of the ARF, yet the two men discovered in conversation that they agreed on more issues than either of them cared to confess.

The founding whispers of a new assembly were heard first on the East Coast, but it was not long before they reached community leaders in California. One of these, in the early 1970s, was Richard Hovannisian. Earlier that year the University of California Press had published volume one of *The Republic of Armenia*, an exhaustive study of Armenian independence and the most serious and original work of scholarship completed by any Armenian historian in the English language. The book had electrified the Armenians—never before had the fragments of a broken democracy been collected into a complete history of hope, illuminating not the destruction of a homeland but the rebuilding that followed.

In 1972 Richard was promoted to professor of Armenian and Near Eastern history. "He has demonstrated that he possesses, to a superb degree, all the qualities of an outstanding historian: vast erudition, rich linguistic skills, critical judgment, and boundless energy and determination," the committee at UCLA reported. "Combined with the presence of Avedis K. Sanjian, Chairman of the Department of Near Eastern Languages and Literatures, who is a specialist on medieval Armenian language and literature, Professor Hovannisian's presence at UCLA gives us by far the strongest and most well-balanced program of Armenian studies in the United States." These sentiments were signed by three scholars, including the chairman of the committee: Professor Stanford J. Shaw, professor of Turkish and Near Eastern history.

He was building a reputation as a historian and intellectual, but beyond the gates of academia Richard remained the inexhaustible civic activist. Long before the philosophy of Armenian unity had been institutionalized in Washington, Richard had been taking weekend trips across the United States to make his own pitch for peace. And he was continuing his tour, addressing ARF crowds and non-ARF crowds, earning with his just scholarship and nonpartisan patriotism the respect of both. He did not plead with the Armenians, nor did he appeal to their sense of dignity. He merely proved to them that Soviet Armenia would never have existed without its predecessor, the Armenian republic of 1918.

Richard's weekend travels had enriched his understanding of the dispersed Armenian people. Very often, the survivors of a specific town or village in Western Armenia had reconvened, now more than a half century later, in a single American city. The Armenians of Kghi and Evereg were now living in Detroit, Michigan. Hajn had been transferred to Binghamton, New York; Sepastia to Springfield, Massachusetts; Tadem to Waukegan, Illinois; Malatia to Philadelphia; Palu to Providence; Bazmashen to Whitinsville and Tulare. As in their historic towns, the Armenians were often working as a collective: in Worcester, Massachusetts, for wire factories; in Watertown, Massachusetts, for Hood Rubber; in Racine, Wisconsin, for Case Tractor Parts.

The professor's expeditious climb up the ivory tower and his rapport with competing Armenian communities did not go unnoticed by the advocates of Armenian unity. He was invited to join the board of directors and to attend the first meeting, in May 1972, of the Armenian Assembly of America.

At the Airlie Center of George Washington University, a mansion set on twenty-five hundred acres of meadow and wetland in Warrenton, Virginia, Richard discovered that old antagonisms were finally losing their license with the Armenian diaspora. Here were Robert Aram Kaloosdian and Dennis Papazian and Haig Der Manuelian, ostensible rivals, together confronting the diaspora's defining questions: Should the Armenian Apostolic Church, now divided between Etchmiadzin in Soviet Armenia and Antelias in Lebanon, be united once and for all? What should be done about an emerging Turkish campaign to deny their common genocide?

As an Armenian political elite haggled over answers, an aging architect, engineer, and Genocide survivor named Gourgen Yanikian decided to take history into his own hands. On January 27, 1973, in his room at the Biltmore Hotel in Santa Barbara, California, he retrieved a Luger pistol from a hollowed book and shot two Turkish consular officials in the face. He was hoping to draw public attention to the forgotten first genocide of the twentieth century. That same year the Turkish government opposed the use of the word *genocide* in a report of a United Nations subcomission on human rights. The word was deleted.

Survivors of the Armenian Genocide had long been hiring lawyers and trying in vain to win back lost properties in Western Armenia. But it was time now to draft a pan-Armenian plan of action. At the meetings of the Assembly, the questions sharpened: Should the Armenians wage a war of public opinion or advocate for recognition in the chambers of American politics? Should the Armenians also demand restitution and lands? For years the members of the Assembly squabbled over such questions, and often it seemed that they took greater delight in the answering than in the answers.

Richard's patience expired. At one of the early conventions, Richard famously strode to the podium, furrowed his brow, and drew himself toward the microphone.

"Words into action," he said deliberately.

And then he returned to his seat. With such words did Richard Hovannisian break the record for the shortest speech ever delivered by an Armenian leader.

Yerevan, Armenia Hotel . . . Started diet because of hospitality . . . Opera then room, drunkards around . . . Yelling. Threw water at them from the hotel room, and then we snoozed into a unique world! July 8 . . . Ararat is clearly seen. We saw a rabbit being killed and skinned. Poor thing . . . This country is rising against communism for last night at the play they said about bribes. . . . I ate on a full stomach, as I am a Bazmashentsi. . . . I told you about my diet. . . . It starts and it ends every minute. . . . Paps told us to speak

Armenian, and gets nervous before plane trips, not answering any questions.

These were the pieces of father and fatherland being collected in the summer of 1972 by twelve-year-old Raffi. The entire Hovannisian family—the matriarch, Siroon; her sons, John, Ralph, Richard, and the newlywed Vernon; and their wives, sons, and daughters—had embarked on a pilgrimage dedicated to the memory of Kaspar Hovannisian. They had marched through England, France, Egypt, Lebanon, and Russia, and now this strange, loud, celebratory gang from the United States was parading through the streets of Yerevan, doing what Babi Kaspar had done the summer before he died: slurping water from public fountains; soaking in the celebration of *vartevar*, the transfiguration of Jesus Christ, when water fights broke out across the country; discovering that Lenin, when his statue was viewed from a secret angle, appeared to be exposing an embarrassing bit of anatomy. For the Hovannisian cousins, it was as if each woman dragging a broom, each group of men huddled around a chessboard, each stray flea-infested dog, and each ramshackle building was a carefully placed ornament in some Soviet Disneyland.

One afternoon, as Raffi and his cousins prowled about the Armenia Hotel, Ralph and his wife, Marian, led a small family delegation through a tangle of narrow streets, which was the Vartashen district of Yerevan, and to a house with a beige Volga parked outside. That was the house of Gaspar and Takouhi Khatchikian, who shared with Ralph's wife, Marian, a lineage to the same village in Western Armenia, Chomakhlu. To roaming Armenian hearts, this was as vital a connection as any. As Gaspar and the elegant Marian spoke about lands they had never seen, Takouhi set the table. She was helped by her three daughters, Alvard, Karine, and Armenouhi, the dutiful children of a traditional family, who expected that they never would see the Hovannisians again.

July 14: We then drank the last water, took in the last air, and looked at the last of our Hairenik. . . . Georgia . . . Paris . . . We saw California, then Los Angeles's city, the wondrous democracy.

"STAND TALL! FEEL TALL! THINK tall! You *are* tall!"

The daily command of Mr. Kahn, physical education instructor at Paul Revere Junior High School, had not been lost on Raffi. He had entered Revere in the seventh grade a chubby, self-conscious tenderfoot, the perpetual loser in the Friday six-hundred-yard races—the boy with the dark skin and the fuzzy, never-shaven mustache. He had not been able to climb even one foot on the schoolyard ropes. But then he had asked his parents for a set of weights and spent his adolescence on a masochistic morning routine of sit-ups, push-ups, and lifting. Nature and nurture had cooperated for Raffi—the first lifting him to a tall, lean physique, the second padding him with muscle and confidence. By the time he was in the ninth grade, Raffi was climbing to the top of the schoolyard ropes in five seconds, with no support from his feet.

It was remarkable what a little confidence could do to a teenager's philosophy—and his wardrobe. Suddenly Raffi was looking through fashion catalogs, obsessing over his appearance. Very often at seven-thirty in the morning he could be seen walking up Barrington Avenue to the Sunset Boulevard bus stop in blue jeans and a bright button-down shirt, kept open at the chest. He wanted to be noticed. He was reading William Saroyan's *The Human Comedy*, Mark Twain's *Huckleberry Finn*, and Henrik Ibsen's *Enemy of the People*, admiring the different versions of the same protagonist, "an independent person, needing no help." Asked in one assignment to identify his favorite folk heroes, Raffi answered: Davy Crockett, Daniel Boone, Wild Bill Hickok, and David of Sasun—the mythic protector of Western Armenia.

The list might be a true reflection of Raffi's taste in heroism, but it is more important as a relic of the strategy that he, at the age of fifteen, already had designed. First he would prove his Americanism—a reference to Davy Crockett, for example—and then, just as he had earned the native's grace, he would sabotage himself. In the last possible moment, almost by accident, Raffi would slip in a "David of Sasun" or a "Mount Ararat" or anything, for that matter, that would identify him as an Armenian. "Academic acrobat of Armenian ancestry," reads a yearbook inscription from 1974. There would never be an assignment, speech, poem, or public offering that would not, in some stealthy last-second phrase, honor his heritage—and, in that way, help offset the unbearable national debt he had inherited from his father.

On a cool September morning in 1974, Raffi walked up Barrington to the bus stop at Sunset. On his right he noticed, as he always did, the corner store that sold red licorice and nearby the bins of free girlie magazines. He was about to leave one temptation for the other. This time Raffi was journeying farther from home, leaving Brentwood for the quiet hills of the Pacific Palisades. When Sunset reached Temescal Canyon Road, just before the Pacific Ocean, Raffi disembarked and set foot on the campus of Palisades High School—a school where George Lucas held auditions for *Star Wars* and where on sunny days PE classes headed to the beach for surfing lessons, but also a school that had a big parking lot for buses arriving daily from Compton and Crenshaw and Watts.

Especially in the languages and humanities, Raffi proved to be an aggressive learner. He made the student council and the junior varsity football team. He acceded to the various honor rolls. He was welcome in every campus clique. It helped, of course, that Raffi's face and figure had hardened into adult contours early in life. It helped that he could bench-press three hundred pounds. It helped that he could talk like a white boy, but talk about an ethnic heritage as no white boy could. It helped that his complexion was just fair enough yet just dark enough, as if it had been made for camouflage. It helped that, by grace of nature and power of will, Raffi could get away with exchanging loud, flirtatious greetings with the black belles of Pali High.

The cause and motives of Raffi's extroversion had many interpretations but only one effect on those who witnessed him at that school on the Pacific: "Oh my God, there goes Raffi Hovannisian!" The messages of classmates in his yearbooks simply leave no room for a more modest explanation: "sweet, good-looking, intelligent"; "masculine"; "macho"; "golden boy"; "very sexy"; "Armenian tough guy"; "overintelligent"; "a rare man with class and charisma"; "kind, thoughtful gentleman"; "so beautiful a person"; "intriguing"; "sweet and foxy"; "brilliant"; "humble character and hardworking soul"; "genius"; "hunk of man."

Raffi's self-diagnosis was different. "Puritan-deist-romanticist-transcendentalist," he wrote in a notebook. He wanted to be a troubadour. But then, every weekday afternoon, the eastbound bus returned Raffi to the Sunset bus stop. He walked down Barrington Avenue and to the end of Terryhill Place, just where the roots of a ficus tree cracked open the pavement. A Chrysler station wagon was parked there. HAI ENK, the license plate read: WE ARE ARMENIANS. His home stood just beyond, and this was no place for a transcendentalist or a troubadour. This was a colony of some past or future Republic of Armenia, and Raffi, Armen, Ani, and Garo were raised to play the part of its good citizens.

This is not to say that the Hovannisian children were deprived of an American childhood. They followed, as American teenagers did, the television shows *Mission: Impossible*, *The Brady Bunch*, *Hawaii Five-O*, and *The Addams Family*. They joined the Scouts and took piano lessons, kept a dog, and acquired an American appetite for college sports. It was a good time for this, too. Basketball coach John Wooden had led the UCLA Bruins to nine national championship titles in the previous eleven seasons. He was assisted by an all-star cast including Bill Walton and Lew Alcindor, Richard's student who later changed his name to Kareem Abdul-Jabbar.

American diversions were, however, carefully monitored by Vartiter. They were rare treats that had to be earned by a steady, healthy Armenian diet. Raffi complained to his journal in September 1974: "Maybe they expect too much of me. I'm getting great grades, I come from a proud people, but they're putting over-responsibility on my shoulders—soon the backbone will break. Explosion!" A few months later, Raffi charted up his "Declaration of Freedom." His inalienable rights: "Love, Pleasance of Life, and the Complete Pursuit of Freedom." His charge against the state: "a history of repeated injuries and usurpations, all having the indirect object of an absolute tyranny over my soul."

It was a classic revolt—hurtful, upsetting, and necessary—by which a son comes to delineate his turf apart from his father. For Raffi this meant shaving his head, wearing black turtlenecks in summer's heat, and declaring weeklong hunger strikes. But the curious fact was that in all his protest against family, Raffi never lost faith in the family philosophy. Once upon a time it had consisted of a few inherited catchphrases, a mouthful of tunes, and a picture of a mountain, but now the memories of lost Armenia seemed, inexplicably, to be his own.

ON A SUNNY SEPTEMBER AFTERNOON in 1974, Raffi was dropped off at Holy Martyrs Ferrahian School, an Armenian private school in the San Fernando Valley and the weekly meeting site of the Simon Vratzian chapter of the Armenian Youth Federation. They did not know each other yet, but the twenty boys and girls who found themselves at that first meeting had been assigned to a great mission: to develop

a diasporan identity that brought into balance the competing philoso-
phies of the Armenian and American dreams.

Raffi was a natural leader, which is to say that he achieved power
quite without trying. The depth of his voice, the mysterious sense of
national purpose—the very qualities that helped him navigate the social labyrinth of Pali High also distinguished him in the AYF. Raffi was
elected vice president and then president of the Simon Vratzian chapter,
and he proceeded, as was his nature, to outdo himself. In November 1975
the members of his club served dinner and staged an original play titled
The Trial of Soghomon Tehlirian. Anahid Tehlirian, the widow of the real-
life hero who had assassinated Talaat Pasha, joined hundreds of Armenians in watching memory in action. Raffi played Soghomon Tehlirian.

Soon Raffi was part of an AYF brotherhood known as "the pals"—
Armen, Hrair, Raffi, Greg, Moushig, Khajag, Armen, Ara, Steve, Garo,
and Kevo. After the week's meeting, they would sit around greasy tables at diners and fast-food joints and talk of Armenia together. "The
important thing is this: To be able at any moment to sacrifice what we
are for what we could become." These words, printed in an AYF pam-
phlet, referred to the idea of *veratarts*, the return of a new generation
of diasporan Armenians to a free, independent, and united homeland.
Raffi was already preparing for that return, and in a big way. When
asked about his career plans, he was quick to respond: "president of
Armenia." Raffi could have said "president of the United States"—at
least there was such a title. But Armenia was not a republic. It had no
president. It was not free, not independent, not united: not real.

It could be too easy to forget, caught up in the conversations of
a national destiny, that the pals were American teenagers who were
not unmoved by the tides of youth. Very often, after midnight, the
boys would crawl out of beds, jump out of windows, climb into cars,
and race to the beaches of the Pacific Ocean. A few AYF girls would
join them there. The crackle of a campfire, the clank of bottles, and
soon the boys and girls would be singing under the stars.

When possible, Raffi would convert the music hits of the day into alternative Armenian national anthems. Lynyrd Skynyrd's "Sweet Home Alabama" became, by moonlight, "Sweet Home Armenia." The lyrics of Bread's love ballad "I would give everything I own just to have you back again" Raffi sang not to a woman but to the memory of a free homeland. And John Denver's hit song "Country Roads" evolved into a masterpiece of Armenian nationalism:

> Almost heaven, West Armenia—
> Ararat mountain, Arax River.
> Life is old there, older than the trees,
> Younger than the mountains,
> Blowin' like a breeze.
> Country roads, take me home
> To the place I belong—
> West Armenia, mountain mama,
> Take me home, country roads.

They stripped down to their underwear and broke into the surf. The waves were cold and powerful, and the boys dived into the darkness. They swam deeper and deeper, testing their fears that they might conquer them. When they returned to land, they played a drinking game called Thumper and then a game of physical endurance called *esheg*, or donkey, which had traveled generations from homeland to oceanfront. As the girls looked on, one of the boys was blindfolded. His friends hovered around him, and he waited for the moment when someone would thrash him on the head. He would absorb the pain, take off the blindfold, and try to identify the assailant. Only if he did this successfully could he rejoin the boisterous crowd.

The beach was friendship. The beach was love. The beach was a training camp for national commitment. At the beach, the boys were invincible. They felt that together they could kick anyone's ass, that they could avenge the murder of their ancestors. They were keeping each other strong, keeping each other Armenian. Raffi was keeping his generation faithful to the possibility of a miracle—a chance opening in history. He said to them and they said to him again and again: "If Armenia becomes free and independent, I will move there."

In summer the boys attended AYF camp in the Angeles National Forest. It turned out that they were not the only boys taking oaths to an imaginary fatherland. There was a whole army of dreamers here. They were living in the same cabins, singing the same songs, praying the same prayers. Here the Armenian *engers*, or comrades, were refusing to integrate with the American reality. They were actually doing the opposite, changing their American names, at least for those two weeks, back to their ethnic equivalents: Steven to Stepan, Greg to Krikor.

Among the many characters that populated AYF camp, the most magnificent was Ruben Keoseyan, an Armenian from Mexico City who once declared a one-man protest against the camp director. "I would cordially like to inform you that we are on strike," he yelled through a bullhorn. He wanted an end to morning calisthenics and afternoon kitchen duty. Ruben's grandfather was Kerop Arakelian, survivor of the Genocide and devotee of the ARF, and one day he summoned Raffi to his home in Beverly Hills. "My grandson admires you," Arakelian said, and then he asked Raffi to promise him that Ruben would marry an Armenian woman. Raffi agreed. He would save Kerop Arakelian's grandson.

In 1975 Lebanon cracked—Maronite, Druze, Shiite, Sunni, Palestinian, and other militias shuffled into baffling alliances and clashed—and the Armenians were caught up in the bloodshed. It did not take much time for tens of thousands of refugees, a new wave of immigrants, to replenish the Armenian organizations of other diasporas. In California, their children joined the AYF. They were Sako, Vahe, Vicken, and a whole set of young men who had been transplanted from the inferno of Beirut to the cool beaches of the American West. Soon they descended upon summer camp wearing camouflage pants, and they did not like what they found: barbeques, dances, and educational seminars. The Armenians had to prepare for serious struggle, they explained to their American *engers*, or they would lose the mountain for good.

Walking around the camp in shorts and a muscle shirt, Raffi could have been the leader of that movement. Until then, he had represented the AYF's hardline. But under the recent influence of militant politics imported from Lebanon, Raffi believed, the line might be hardening too much. He did not fear unpopularity; in one of his first AYF camps, when a mock National Assembly of the Republic of Armenia was called, he had chosen to lead not the majority ARF faction but the minority Ramgavar Party in opposition. And now, sitting around a bonfire, tensions heating, he was about to make a statement of another kind. The boys were singing the old revolutionary song about a band of Armenian soldiers:

> *Menk chenk uzum azad gamki prnutiun,*
> *Ukhdel enk grvel, ayt sirov mernel,*
> *Hamozvadz enk vor miayn zenkov ga*
> *Hayots prgutiun.*

> We defy the suppression of free will,
> We have sworn to fight and die with that love,
> We are convinced that only with guns
> Can the Armenians be saved.

Raffi changed the words. *"Miayn miutiamp,"* he sang, in discord— only through unity can the Armenians be saved.

RAFFI MADE THE TRIP TO the San Joaquin Valley less often now that AYF activities competed for weekend time, but when he made it, once or twice a month, he realized it was a pilgrimage. He was older now. His grandparents were older now. He knew that Babi Hovagim and Mami Khenguhi and Grandma Siroon and their generation would not live much longer. They were soon to graduate into memory, and to take with them all evidence of that great catastrophe of 1915. Really, the Turks only had to wait.

Hovagim sat on the porch at 3312 Lowe Avenue, and now Raffi sat next to him. He peeled his grandfather's oranges and listened to his stories: Turkish killing fields, Soviet prisons, German labor camps, an Armenian republic. Hovagim re-created a world so far removed from this hot, lazy Fresno street that it might as well have been a forgery of the imagination. But one thing, Raffi was certain, could not be forged. Many nights at Lowe Avenue, he would awaken in a panic and hear the terrifying screams of a man and a woman coming from the bedroom. And Raffi knew exactly what was happening. His grandfather was fighting his grandmother in sleep, thinking she was a Turk.

ON THE AFTERNOON OF JUNE 17, 1977, Raffi approached the podium set upon the football field of Palisades High School. It would have been impossible not to recognize him. On that very grass he had played football for the Dolphins. He had acted in school plays. He had founded the Armenian Cultural Society, with its membership roll of two-and-a-half Armenians. He had packed the school auditorium that April 24 for a spectacular commemoration of the Armenian Genocide. He had served his principles with passion; it was due to his great determination, for example, that doors had finally been mounted on the stalls of the men's bathroom.

"Once we followed, now we lead," Raffi began. The way he dragged his words and paused and rhymed for effect, he sounded almost deliberately like Martin Luther King Jr. Indeed, his deep cries for racial justice were obvious echoes of the civil rights movement, which had helped awaken his own sense of national struggle. "White has become part black, black part white, and both part Armenian," Raffi said. "At long last superior statues have begun to fall."

In September 1977, as Americans mourned the mysterious death of Elvis Presley, Raffi arrived at the University of California, Berkeley. He lived at the International House and enrolled in history and political theory courses. These, the science of the past and the art of possibility, were now officially in competition. In the next few years Raffi would have to bring his passions to order. Of course his axiomatic passion would not change. Already the chairman of the AYF West Coast Central Executive, Raffi joined a small group of Berkeley students in reactivating the university's dormant Armenian club.

Some fifty Armenian students had settled in the Tan Oak Room of Berkeley's Academic Union and the first meeting had just begun when a young bearded man in rubber sandals entered the room. Raffi, who was running the meeting, watched as the man distributed packets of photocopied material. He made out the title: "How to Make a Bomb."

Aggravated by attacks on the memory of the Genocide in the 1970s and inspired by Gourgen Yanikian's assassination of Turkish diplomats, some Armenians in the diaspora had come to adopt violence as a tool of political struggle. A new group called the Justice Commandos Against Armenian Genocide, in sympathy with the ARF, sought the recognition of the Genocide and the unification and independence of an Armenian homeland. The Armenian Secret Army for the Liberation of Armenia (ASALA) had similar fantasies, only wrapped in a greater Marxist-Leninist vision. The revolutionary groups shared a strategy: the assassination of Turkish diplomats across the world.

Monte Melkonian, the radical pamphleteer at Berkeley, was a follower of the Marxist-Leninist ASALA, and Raffi was compelled, on the day of their first meeting, to distance himself from him. But he soon discovered another side to Monte. He was from the San Joaquin Valley, apparently, and through the coming months he proved to be a true intellectual and a tireless activist. In fact, it was with Monte's help that Raffi organized, in the spring of 1978, a grand exhibit of Armenian culture and history at Berkeley's Doe Library—an exhibit that was swiftly shut down, however, because the Turkish consul general of San Francisco had phoned to protest the display of a counterfeit genocide.

Immediately the Armenian presses, ARF and anti-ARF, growled together. At Berkeley the Armenian club came to life. Richard drove up from Los Angeles to join journalism professor Ben Bagdikian in a town hall event, which was teeming with hundreds of student activists possessed by the rebel spirit of an earlier decade at Berkeley. Except now the administration would not ignore them. Shortly before the scheduled end of the exhibit, photographs of the Armenian Genocide were restored to Doe Library. The librarian resigned. The Turkish consul was eventually transferred to Libya.

And now Raffi had a new thought. Maybe the victory at Doe was not a fluke. Maybe the Armenians, who had been content during much of their history merely to endure, could now afford to invest in greater ambitions.

RICHARD FOLLOWED THE TRAJECTORY OF Raffi's rise through the Armenian community but took caution never to convey his pride. Nothing, Richard believed, spoiled a man more than flattery. It was with a few self-deprecating remarks and a trademark frown that Richard had accepted the many heavyweight titles of his own intellectual life: Guggenheim fellow, associate director of the G. E. von Grunebaum Center for Near Eastern Studies at UCLA, and a place on the board of directors of too many organizations.

Due in great part to his own work over the past twenty years, but also to the work of a pioneer generation of scholars—Sirarpie Der-Nersessian, Ronald Grigor Suny, Vahakn Dadrian, Robert Thomson, Dickran Kouymjian, and Nina Garsoian, among others—Armenia was now back on the map. The field of Armenian studies, a small, undeveloped plot of scholarship when Richard entered it in the late 1950s, was now part of the recognized landscape of European and Near Eastern studies in the United States. Founded by Richard's initiative in 1974, the Society for Armenian Studies had become its official forum.

Unfortunately, the Armenian communities were facing problems no scholarship could settle. A Turkish diplomat would be assassinated in Paris or Rome or Beirut, and soon the *New York Times* would phone the Armenian Assembly of America for a comment. Would the Assembly care to "deplore" the killing, or merely to express its generic "regret"? Ten hours could easily be squandered on parsing the distinction before the whole matter was thrown out and the preeminent Armenian organization of the United States informed the American press that, actually, it would not comment on a major political event directly related to it.

Yet that same problematical passion, to gain international recognition for the Armenian Genocide, was also inspiring the Armenians to more civil actions. In 1975, House Joint Resolution 148, a project of the Armenian Assembly of America, cleared the United States Congress. Designating April 24, 1975, as National Day of Remembrance of Man's Inhumanity to Man, the resolution called on President Gerald Ford to honor "victims of genocide, especially those of Armenian ancestry who succumbed to the genocide perpetrated in 1915." In a subsequent success in 1976, a team of scholars led by Richard Hovannisian testified to the House Subcommittee on Future Foreign Policy, offering the lessons of the Armenian Genocide to the engineers of international relations.

The Genocide was neither his specialty nor his obsession, but

Richard could not escape it. Since the early 1960s, before denial had become standard protocol in Turkish circles, Richard had been sending his students to record the stories of a dwindling community of Genocide survivors. The subjects had not known each other, but their stories—eight hundred recorded so far—were nearly identical. They confirmed, through one cohesive oral history, that in 1915 the Young Turk authorities had endeavored to erase the Armenian people.

Richard collected the living proof of the Genocide in his office on the sixth floor of Ralph Bunche Hall, a waffle-iron building overlooking UCLA's sculpture garden. On the fifth floor of that same building, a professor of Turkish history was working out the theory that something altogether different had happened in 1915. In the second volume of *History of the Ottoman Empire and Modern Turkey*, published in 1977, Stanford Shaw argued that the Armenians of the Ottoman Empire had been preparing, under cover of world war, to revolt. "It would be impossible," Shaw explained, "to determine which of the Armenians would remain loyal and which would follow the appeals of their leaders." And so the Turkish authorities ordered the relocation of the Armenians, but with instructions that they "were to be protected and cared for until they returned to their homes after the war."

Richard took it upon himself to write the definitive refutation of Shaw's theories. In his review for the *International Journal for Middle Eastern Studies*, he exposed his colleague's selective methodology, the fabrications, and the deliberate choices of language that could convert "deport" to "transport" and the unbearable "Syrian desert" into a place called "central Syria." The review, along with the many public lectures Richard delivered in the coming months, closed the case against Stanford Shaw.

But then, at 3:50 a.m. on October 3, 1977, a makeshift pipe bomb blasted through the front door of Shaw's Brentwood home. The case was open again. The professor was shaken but unharmed, and the

FBI launched an investigation. Agents in suits trailed Armenian and Greek political leaders, clerics, and students—including Monte Melkonian. An investigator for the FBI even showed up at the Terryhill Place home of the Hovannisians. Shaw had implied that the Armenian professor might know something about the incident. The professor did not. Neither the Justice Commandos nor ASALA claimed responsibility for the bombing, and many Armenians came to believe that the Turks themselves had orchestrated an explosion of sympathy.

THE DEATH OF HOVAGIM KOTCHOLOSIAN on May 3, 1978, was the first great loss of Raffi's life. It had been different with Babi Kaspar. Raffi had been ten years old; he had not really known his grandfather. But Raffi knew Babi Hovagim. He knew his nightmares. He knew that the stern bald man who worked as a night guard and lived quietly in a modest Fresno home was indeed a great man—no more, perhaps, but certainly no less than that whole generation of men who had been boys in 1915, who had witnessed the death of their families and joined the armies of Western Armenia and then dispersed throughout the world and become night guards.

At Berkeley, Raffi spent the year earning perfect grades, but losing, in the dormitory cafeteria, the lean figure that had been the pride of his adolescence. He was outgrowing his flashy clothes, his vanity, and even his rebellion. The death of Babi Hovagim had suggested to him that the time for play had passed, that Raffi should be a man now and go home, go to UCLA, where a professor was waiting—or expecting; that was the word Richard would have used—the return of his son.

When he arrived at UCLA in January 1979, Raffi immediately joined the Armenian club on campus, but he did not forget the true and secret reason of his homecoming: to try on his father's shoes. Quite on his own, he began to conduct interviews with Genocide survivors, then submitted the recordings to the UCLA oral history collection. He also enrolled in his father's class. Sitting anonymously among forty students, Raffi admired his father really for the first time. With his natural English and accumulated Western wisdom, the professor was giving more elegance to Armenian history than the history probably deserved. He was explaining how empires had appeared and disappeared but how the Armenian people had survived—through kingdom, serfdom, genocide, republic, and Soviet rule.

The yearlong survey of Armenian history was among the most difficult courses offered at UCLA, but it proved especially difficult for Raffi. He would study endlessly for exams, only to be rewarded by the professor's ruthless markings: "unnecessary"; "much time wasted"; "specifics?"; "nothing from readings?"; "overcrowded"; "not focused"; "adequate"; and only sometimes "good," which was the most a family member ever got from Richard. The grade at the end of the first term was a B+, Raffi's lowest.

As he learned the history of modern Armenia, Raffi did permit himself to pursue alternative curiosities. In the spring of 1979 he worked part-time in the law offices of Ronald Sohigian, and that summer he headed to Capitol Hill in Washington, D.C., where he interned for Congressman Nicholas Mavroules, a newly elected Democrat from Massachusetts. Raffi's fellow intern, Adam Schiff from Stanford University, was just beginning his own journey toward the chambers of American politics. He would one day have an office of his own on the Hill.

Raffi remained a leader of the California AYF, but he was no longer a true believer. In the past few years the radical politics of Armenian Lebanese party leaders had been winning converts in the United States. In the AYF, Halloween parties and athletic competitions were replaced with military training exercises on campgrounds that had, until then, seen nothing more than water balloons. The Jewish radical Irv Rubin turned up at one AYF meeting to motivate the young Armenians; criminal records would be expunged at the age of eighteen, he said. And in 1979, as the Ayatollah Khomeini realized an Islamic revolution in Iran, it was decided that the AYF would be renamed the Armenian Revolutionary Federation Youth Organization (ARFYO) and effectively subsumed into the party itself.

"Good Afternoon Comrade! I feel it necessary to schedule a meeting immediately with the underground to discuss recent developments. I will await word from you." Such notes, written and delivered with dramatic stealth to bunk beds across the AYF campgrounds, announced a meeting of the pals and several sympathizers. They would gather in the forests to listen to Raffi's latest protest against the new AYF authorities. "Let us agitate," he would say, "even at the expense of risking our standing as good Armenians and Americans. In the end, we shall be the ones who effected, who accomplished, who were mocked, yet who advanced the cause of self-determination, of democracy, of humanity."

Party loyalists were concerned with Raffi's extracurricular activities, but none more than the event he organized on February 26, 1980, at UCLA—a question-and-answer event with Kemal Arikan, the Turkish consul general of Los Angeles. The courteous man from Ankara was a known denier of the Armenian Genocide, but just a few weeks earlier, when Raffi visited him at his office in Century City, he had made an extraordinary confession. Leaning close to Raffi, he had declared himself off the record and with no qualifications acknowledged that the Turkish government indeed had committed a genocide in 1915.

A bomb threat was phoned in to UCLA, and the event was canceled in progress. Raffi was disappointed; he knew the callers were probably Armenian, people he knew. They were probably the same people who would summon him the following day to answer to the Central Executive of the AYF and, ultimately, force him into decisive action. In the following months Raffi collected the signatures of hundreds of AYF members and announced, on May 17, that five chapters—Los Angeles, Montebello, San Francisco, Fresno, and Mexico City—would be rejecting the ARFYO name. They refused to become instruments of the ARF.

The next day Raffi sent his letter of resignation to the Central Executive and thereby severed his last formal ties with the organization of his parents and grandparents, the party of the Armenian republic. He did not disown his friends or burn the bridges of his return, but he did believe that at this delicate moment of diaspora history, the way to honor the true revolutionary movement of Babi Kaspar and Babi Hovagim was to leave it.

The secessionist AYF chapters did not last. Raffi had neither the time nor the passion for vengeance to make them last. In June 1980 he graduated from UCLA summa cum laude. He won the award for outstanding honors thesis for his paper on the February 1921 rebellion in Soviet Armenia, when Simon Vratzian, Garo Sassouni, and the leaders of a just-sovietized people staged their first act of revolt against the new occupants. And he earned a full scholarship to begin another school year at UCLA, this time as a graduate student in history.

But now, finally, Raffi knew that he did not belong in history. He would take off his father's shoes. He was a man not of the past but of possibility, of change, of the future.

Chapter Seven

THE PARTY'S OVER

L ooking more like a poet than a politician, with a thick beard and pondering brown eyes, Raffi stepped onto the grounds of Tufts University and crunched over dead autumn leaves to the Fletcher School of Law and Diplomacy. Set upon the hills of a colonial Medford, Massachusetts, campus, the red-brick building was a sanctuary of the privileged and the ambitious, the crème de la crème of aspiring diplomats. They did not yet know it, but these one hundred graduate students had arrived during a most critical season in the history of international politics—just when the cold war between the United States and the Soviet Union had frozen to absolute zero. Whether the ice would thaw or crack—that was the great question of November 1980, when Ronald Reagan defeated Jimmy Carter in the U.S. presidential elections.

He had enrolled in a two-year master's program in law and diplomacy, but Raffi proved himself during the weekend wine-and-cheese receptions. There was something so charming in his idealisms, how he could catalog the woes of civilization and then conclude, with a sudden burst of fresh logic, that "we shall overcome." Among his classmates and within himself, he endeavored always to reconcile enemy ideas: pragmatism and idealism, naturalism and positivism, the efficacy of force and the elegance of good diplomacy. And he did this with none of the generic language expected of a political man. He opened a research paper on the philosophers of the Enlightenment, for example, with these words: "Man is born to wander, and yet everywhere he is plagued with sore feet."

The diplomatic milieu of Fletcher—the receptions, the networking, the points and counterpoints of the *Fletcher Forum*, which he edited—could not, of course, overthrow Raffi's primary passions. By instinct or habit or duty (it was too late, by now, to delineate the difference) Raffi returned to the Armenian cause. He revamped the Tufts Armenian Club and counseled its members through its many commemorations and celebrations, as in April 1981 when President Ronald Reagan publicly recognized the "genocide of the Armenians." He spent Sundays in the parking lots of the local Armenian churches. Windshield to windshield, he spread the news of a coming confederation, an alliance of Armenian students from all over Boston.

On the university intramural field—the turf of Richard's cousin John Baronian, the Tufts lineman turned trustee-philanthropist—Raffi relived the heyday of his powers. The contours of a firmer football player had faded into a thinking man's body, but Raffi still thrived on a physical challenge. Several times during his stay in Medford, he tested himself through two weeks of starvation, shedding thirty pounds each time. Then, almost by duty, Raffi turned to the more enjoyable task of undoing the fortnight's accomplishments. With his friend Greg Koobatian and occasionally with his cousin Nancy Gavoor, the Tufts women's track coach, he would embark on midnight eating sprees at the pizza joints and ice cream shops of the college town. Without food there could not be a complete communion of friends.

Raffi knew he had made the right decision coming to Fletcher. The archives of history would have suffocated his faith in Armenia; the world of diplomacy was allowing it to breathe. Still, in his second year at Tufts, Raffi registered to teach a course in Armenian history at the university's Experimental College. He also decided to title his dissertation "American Foreign Policy and the Republic of Armenia, 1918–1920." He was testing himself again, but he was also showing his father that he, too, believed in the history of his people, just that he had found a road of his own—a road worth traveling for at least a lifetime.

Early in 1982 Raffi read of the assassination of Kemal Arikan, the Turkish consul general whom he had invited to UCLA two years earlier. He had thought often about that well-mannered diplomat, the startling confession he had made. It was only a matter of time, Raffi had thought, of time and good diplomacy, before men like Arikan would find the courage to confront their own government. Yet there he was, a corpse in a car in Los Angeles, courtesy of the Justice Commandos.

The murder in January of Kemal Arikan and the natural death in April of Martin Nalbandian, Grandma Siroon's brother, haunted Raffi on his last stretch at Fletcher. It was with soured sentiments that he received his master's degree in international law and diplomacy. But there was much to be excited about. Raffi had landed a major summer internship at the Department of State in Washington, where he would take charge of the Norway, Denmark, and Iceland desk. "Sources described applicant as an articulate, brilliant, and capable individual with good analytical skills and popular with most individuals," his background report disclosed. "Two sources stated that the applicant was at times arrogant and tended to be too brash as well."

But it was something else entirely that supported Raffi's spirits. Upon the conclusion of his internship at the State Department, Raffi and his brother Armen would be traveling to the Republic of Turkey—to Istanbul then Ankara and then to the eastern frontiers, to the wastelands and dreamlands of Western Armenia.

IN THE SUMMER OF 1982, as Raffi's policy briefings and memoranda were gaining the notice of his superiors in Washington, Richard was lugging a case of blue hardcover books through the streets of Los Angeles, Fresno, San Francisco, Detroit, Boston, and New York. The second volume of his *Republic of Armenia*, which towed the storyline from the Versailles Treaty of 1919 to February 1920, had been a decade in the making. It was a work of scholarship; it had not been conceived as a crowd-pleaser. Yet, due in part to the accessibility of Richard's scholarship and in part to the intellectual hunger of the Armenians, the saga of a failed republic was drawing large crowds to the libraries and church halls of the diaspora.

The Armenian republic was Richard's subject, but his community had bestowed other responsibilities upon him. In June 1982 the professor was preparing to take part in a watershed event at Tel Aviv University. The Israeli government and the Institute on the Holocaust and Genocide, founded by Israel Charny, Shamai Davidson, and Elie Wiesel, were hosting the International Conference on the Holocaust and Genocide. Professor Charny, a Jewish American scholar who had repatriated to Israel, believed that genocides should be examined side by side—especially the genocides of the twentieth century, which shared so much character and methodology that it seemed that each one depended on the precedent of the one before it, and the first one, the Armenian Genocide of 1915, on an original pattern made in hell.

The conference had not yet been convened when Israeli phones began to ring. Earlier that year, the Turkish government had established in the United States the Institute of Turkish Studies; it had formally entered the war over history. And now, having discovered the term "Armenian Genocide" in a preconference news story, Turkish officials informed their Israeli allies that such a term was unacceptable— indeed, that its continued circulation would threaten the safety of thousands of Jews who were using Turkey as an escape route from Iran to the West. The state of Israel pulled out as a sponsor of the conference. Elie Wiesel withdrew as keynote speaker.

A cyclone of scandal passed through Tel Aviv, but a small battalion of scholars remained standing. Under the leadership of Israel Charny and Shamai Davidson, the conference was opened in late June, and half of the scheduled speakers arrived to investigate the greatest crime ever invented. The conference was a smash success for the Armenians: the facts of the Genocide and the tactics of its deniers surfaced to the top pages of the international press. The Armenian papers presented at the conference, meanwhile, were collected by Richard into a book. *The Armenian Genocide in Perspective* would go through five printings.

After the events in Tel Aviv, Richard returned to his class in Los Angeles, to a flourishing oral history project, to another unwritten volume of *The Republic of Armenia*, yet the life of the scholar was slowly ceding ground to his other life as an activist. He was invited almost every weekend to a conference or a town hall meeting, where he was confronted by the frustrated questions of his people. The professor was not as cheerful as he was expected to be. He did not hide his fear, the cardinal fear that Armenian leaders were supposed to banish from their communities: that in another fifty or hundred years, an Armenian diaspora—lacking the gravitational center of a true homeland—would fade into oblivion. "I work like an optimist and believe like a pessimist," Richard would say.

The room would grow quiet, and then somebody would ask the one question Richard most hated to answer: "What can we do?" And here Richard, the troubled guardian angel of Armenian studies in the United States, would fall into a somber mood. He would pause for a moment, allowing his thoughts to settle into a new order, and then he would say: "I don't know. I am not the great theorist. I am not the mastermind. I do hope that the masterminds will come. I do hope they can develop for our people a strategy for survival."

ON JULY 27, 1982, AT 2:05 p.m., a group of twelve tourists—an elderly couple, a doctor and his son, two middle-aged men, a professor, and five university students, including Raffi Hovannisian, age twenty-two, and Armen Hovannisian, twenty—boarded a Pan American airplane at John F. Kennedy International Airport in New York. Half a day later, they landed in Istanbul.

Raffi wrote in his journal.

7/ 28/ 82—ISTANBUL

Unadjectivable feeling when put Armenian foot, U.S. shoe on Turkish ground.

Passport control—looked at no one's picture but mine.

Different uniforms. Same guns.

7/ 29/ 82—ISTANBUL

When I marry, my wife will have to represent all that's good in all Armenian girls, past-present-future, their humility, their eyes, their beauty, their transcendent look and touch of mystical, yet see-through love, as if evolved over the harsh mountainous centuries.

7/ 30/ 82—ISTANBUL

My mood is romantic and detached. Its drawbacks are clear. Its advantages are overlooked and mustn't be forgotten.

I love them all, and there is a void in me that I cannot fill. Just a chance to transfer these boys and girls and all like them to a free east. Just a chance to know them through a common land, to be brother and father and son to them just once, to embrace them and nourish their souls. . . . Go ahead and laugh at this dream, but it will come true, and whether or not you know it, it rests in the essence of all our beings.

8/ 1/ 82—ANKARA

Turkish multitudes, inquisitive eyes, boys in groups, and smiling kids, whose grandparents did and didn't do this or that, and with whose kids and grandkids we will one day have to fight or coexist.

8/4/82—MALATIA

On the road to HARM (Historic Armenia).

And of a sudden, dry, brown, almost white hills and mountains without greenery.

Their bodies and souls burnt here.

Groves and groves of apricots on the brown, curving hills.

I feel like spending weeks in each place, becoming encompassed in its historic whole. As it turns out, I feel, as my people, like a vagabond, a refugee. I am unsettled and incomplete.

Armenians everywhere. Nationalism—narrow, but all we have. Internationalism—bigger, more noble, more attractive, but will dilute former. A healthy equilibrium possible, or both are mutually rejecting magnets? Hope there's a balance, but that failing, and for now at least, will pursue internationalism within the framework of nationalism rather than the reverse.

If I become lazy when I return home, and if I forget about this place and don't return here again to help up Historic Armenia, let it be known that I condemn myself prospectively and unconditionally.

8/5/82—THE EUPHRATES

Crossed very narrow (one-lane) bridge across Euphrates. Went, swam the blue, once red, very cold waters. Held up bus. Scratched knee, and gave my blood to it, and it—its waters to me. As if by fate (destiny).

8/5/82—BAZMASHEN, KHARPERT

Brown dirt, cats, dogs, apricot pelts on the ground. One of these—the house, or at least the plot where our grandfather was born, lived and watched his family be chopped up, shattered, totally detached from him. . . . I can't believe I was there—and touched the earth and breathed the air of Babi Kaspar. What trees, what homes, what streets, what earth, what waters he must have seen, breathed, walked, tilled, and drunk. Where had he walked exactly, if we only knew. Someplace there we and our grandfathers crossed paths and planes, just at a different time. . . . That was truly a dream, a reverie with which I have been unable to cope thus far—an experience that can never be given over in its full meaning. To touch your grandfather, your people, transcending time.

God, I want these lands as my honeymoon destination, and hopefully someday as my home. All these lands, all our lands, which we will share equitably with our neighbors.

8/ 8/ 82—Bitlis

As entered bus—8:00 p.m.—learned thru Deron (from Ozcan) that apparently 2 Armenians killed 13 and wounded 75 in Ankara (we to stop there between Erzerum and Istanbul) airport yesterday—gunfire, bomb, I don't know. . . . Turkish radio broadcast—picked out words America, Ermeni, Ankara airport, terrorist, and ASALA. Put 'em all together, and you get . . .

8/ 12/ 82—Ararat

In the plain of Ararat. Westside story.

Late at night on roof—Ararat and I alone, I—unable to see it—it—watching my every move.

8/ 14/ 82—Ani

Into the hills, then valley—then back again. The Armenian Plateau!

Ani—grand city—into view—Citadel/ramparts to the right—and Soviet Armenia just beyond.

What once great, brilliant capital of Armenia, now rubble.

8/ 15/ 82—GARIN

Thinking re: international law, Armenian history, etc.—really feeling waste of time—and that each day—wasting a day of (good) life, as we all approach death. Really (urge to) categorize life into compartments now.

Need a quick, expeditious decision re: cost/efficiency of my life on this path or that, to the extent that that can be forecast and estimated in advance (prospectively).

This is it.

Defense of the Fatherland, 1000s of Armenians here killed, raped, looted, deported. Churches, Patriarch, schools, villagers, Sanasarian Institute, etc. Where?

God, I was in Tsitogh today, and didn't even kiss the land—didn't "enjoy" it. . . .

I, we were there and we saw and felt and smelled and touched—with some variation over time I'm sure—what Babi Hovagim did. We saw his roots, his home.

Tsitogh, small village life in the plain of Erzerum, I love you. We were there and always will be in our hearts, minds, souls, and bodies.

Beautiful Sunset on the golden plain of Garin.

Where and when: the self-determination and brotherhood of all peoples. I cling to that hope, and await that day.

8/ 16/ 82—GARIN

Looks like need repatriation here (as first step)—or depend (if possible) on Soviets to come in here—then Armenian independence. One percent chance—less, says Armen, that we to live here again—just history. I'll put my money, heart, mind, soul, body, life on that one percent tho'.

How much this trip to determine/influence my future, career, family, etc., time will tell.

8/ 17/ 82—GARIN

Tho' all anxious to get home, a sad departure from Tsitogh, Garin, and Historic Western Armenia, all of which we leave behind—only physically and only for a time.

8/ 18/ 82—ISTANBUL

The last day.
Friendship and peace amongst peoples.

Raffi handed his blue United States passport to the official at the security desk at Yesilkoy International Airport. The Turkish man laughed. He wasn't stupid. This wasn't an American name. The man escorted the Armenians to a table in the customs area. Five security officers, two of them carrying machine guns, were waiting. They told the Armenians to open their suitcases. They spoke to each other in Turkish, and Raffi made out a couple of words: *ermeni* and *giavur*— "Armenian" and "infidel."

In Raffi's suitcase, the officers found two socks full of soil—the soil of Bazmashen, Kharpert and the soil of Tsitogh, Garin, which were to be sprinkled upon the graves of Babi Kaspar and Babi Hovagim in Fresno. The soil was confiscated, and then newspapers, receipts, sweaters, film. The officers examined the tour leader's maps; eastern Turkey was identified as Western Armenia. They spat on the maps. The elderly woman and the doctor's son broke into tears. "Shut up!" shouted the Turks.

After the plunder, the Armenians were marched into another room, where the men were threatened into silence as the women were stripped and their bodies explored for weapons.

8/ 18/ 82—ISTANBUL

The last day.

Friendship and peace amongst peoples.

And the stark reality of its impossibility at Turkish customs.

(Lower-scale 1915 all over again.)

The dream over, we have been awakened.

And never again will we fall asleep.

THE ARMENIANS OF THE UNITED States awoke in the fall of 1982, but they woke up to different worlds, under the influence of different dreams. In September Raffi arrived at Georgetown University Law Center, hoping to find a respectable style and structure through which to realize his national longings. In October, five Armenian men, Justice Commandos between the ages of nineteen and twenty-nine, were arrested in Los Angeles and Boston. They were charged for conspiring to blow up the offices of Kanat Arbay, the honorary Turkish consul general in Philadelphia. In November, George Deukmejian arrived in Sacramento as the thirty-fifth governor of California. Tens of thousands of Armenian Americans, Roosevelt Democrats by tradition, overnight rerouted their allegiances to Deukmejian's Republican Party.

Raffi began his first term at Georgetown with a sense that history was moving again. He celebrated the election of an Armenian governor, and he hurt for the five men—the "L.A. Five," they came to be called—whose pain and patriotism had swayed them to the strategy of desperation. He knew these men. Three of them he knew from the Armenian Youth Federation, one of them as a confidant and pal. He knew him from his very first AYF meeting, from the Pacific beaches of his youth.

Raffi's heartstrings were tangled with those of his community, but his patriotism no longer depended on a party, a brotherhood, or his father. Something fantastic had happened during his journey to Western Armenia. He had witnessed his past there, walked upon its ruins. He had found the scents, songs, and accents of Fresno living in the hills of Kharpert and the plains of Garin. His heart had stung; he had developed, walking on a land of bones, an unbearable empathy for the millions slain.

"Your whole style, your flow is free-spirited and spontaneous," Raffi wrote to a friend on November 20, 1982. "Mine, on the other hand, is deliberate, cautious, and conscious that each word, as it is being written, is etching its little spot in history." He wasn't really writing to his friend. He would never really be writing or speaking or singing to any one person anymore. It was his twenty-third birthday when Raffi realized that he was not a private man, that he was a character in a national epic that someone was always watching. Somewhere around the village of Bazmashen in Western Armenia, a shadow had begun to follow him.

At the Georgetown University Law Center, a triangular campus jigsawed into the Capitol Hill district of Washington, Raffi leafed through the student directory, searching for likely members of the law school's first Armenian club. Within a few weeks the Georgetown Armenian Law Students Association (GALSA) was in business, and it proved to be far more popular than Raffi had anticipated—at least for the first meeting. Scores of students had shown up for an event of the Gay and Lesbian Students Association (GALSA).

Raffi kept up correspondence with his family and friends in California, but he presided now over a new brotherhood centered in Washington: Van, Zaven, Ara, Pakrad, Raffi, Mark. Sitting around boxes of pizza and bottles of Diet Coke, the soft drink revolution of 1982, the boys would tune into *Monday Night Football*. They relished the poetic violence of that great American sport. But when the game ended and the commentator Don Meredith sang his famous victory line, "Turn out the lights, the party's over—they say that all good things must end," the party would begin afresh. Someone would be sent to pick up Philly cheesesteaks, and by the time he returned, the television would be dark. The boys would be talking about the fatherland, Armenian music sweetening the air.

"Where is your family from?" Raffi would ask. "No, I mean, where is your family really from?" He had been asking that question relentlessly since he returned from Western Armenia. *What province? What city? What village? Did your grandparents resist the Turkish gendarmes? Which death route did they take?* The answers to these were not always known to his friends, most of whom could not even speak the mother language. Raffi would not be upset; it was not their fault. But in his brotherly way Raffi would encourage them to discover these details of their ancestry. If the Armenians of the United States were ever to return to their homes, they would first need to learn where their homes had stood.

THE SUMMER OF 1983 WAS a season of crisis for the Armenian diaspora. Two events, occurring within the same week in July, all but dismantled the cause.

The first event was the withdrawal on July 12, 1983, of the Armenian Revolutionary Federation from the Armenian Assembly of America—and the end, therefore, of the great peace, or at least the great pact of nonaggression, between the principal political establishments. The tensions had been sharpening since the early 1980s, when the Justice Commandos and ASALA had begun not only to compete but also to turn against each other. Simultaneously the ARF had been divesting its resources from the Assembly. Its own lobbying group, the Armenian National Committee of America, had opened a fully staffed Washington office in 1982.

The second event was the explosion on July 15 at a Turkish Airlines check-in counter at Orly Airport in Paris, France. Eight people were killed, fifty-five injured. Of the dead, two were Turkish. Four were French. One was a Swede. One was American. None of them was a diplomat. ASALA claimed responsibility for the bombing. The Armenian communities of the United States did not. They had accepted the killing of diplomats, perhaps even delighted in the deaths of professional genocide deniers. But not this. There was no use calling it a "militant group"; ASALA was a terrorist organization whose quest for national justice had finally been corrupted by impatience.

In the aftermath of the Orly bombing, ASALA itself exploded. Many among its ranks grew disillusioned with the obsessive violence of the organization's leader, Hagop Hagopian. Soon they broke off into a new band, vowing to struggle toward the same sacred ends, but to spare the Armenians the humiliation of immoral means. The splinter group was called the Armenian Secret Army for the Liberation of Armenia: Revolutionary Movement. Its leader was Monte Melkonian, the former Berkeley activist, and he had come to proclaim the end of terrorism in the Armenian diaspora.

"I'M NOT SURE WHICH IT is—a credit or a flaw—to be structured, rigid, planning well in advance," Raffi wrote to his parents in September 1983. "Whatever the label one attaches, it is a product of my coming to grips with my own mortality and that of all around me." Yet Raffi could not have planned for the providential phone call that found him, one autumn afternoon, in his dank studio apartment at the corner of 16th and T streets.

"Hello." It was a woman's voice. "Is this Raffi Hovannisian? This is Armine Khatchikian."

Yes, a mutual friend had phoned a few days earlier to tell Raffi about a delightful Armenian girl, a student from Occidental College in Los Angeles, who would be spending a semester at American University. "Take care of her," he had said. And then Raffi had seen Armine at a church picnic on Wisconsin Avenue, the day before her phone call. He had studied her from afar—this vivacious and smiling girl with brown eyes and long, braided brown hair, curving along a delicate figure—as she skipped cheerfully through an Armenian circle dance: *Right step, right step, right step, left kick, right kick.* Armine was wearing lace socks.

"Sorry to bother you," Armine said with a gentle accent. "Is this a bad time?"

On the other end of the line, Raffi fumbled for a response. "Cute socks," he said.

That weekend Raffi and Armine headed by car to the St. James Armenian Church in Richmond, Virginia, where Raffi had been invited to make a presentation of his "Odyssey into Historic Armenia." His friend Ara and her friend Suzy took the backseat. Armine distributed pastries. Raffi, at the wheel, was the entertainment. He joked and recited poetry. He sang folk songs and whistled the theme of *Cheburashka*, a Russian cartoon Armine had watched growing up in Soviet Armenia. Armine was impressed. *"Es bujur, yars bujur,"* Raffi began to sing another folk song. "I'm tiny, my love is tiny." Armine smiled. *Inch el bujur es*, she thought. *And how tiny you are!*

At the church hall of St. James, Raffi approached the podium. "We were going to discover the secret of that soil," he said sonorously, "why thousands of years later, there are no Armenians there." Armine studied Raffi as he spoke, images of a barren landscape projected on the screen behind him. At first he was professorial, cool and sophisticated like his father. But then his voice began to strain, then crack, then sing. Raffi plunged into lament, then drew himself up in rage. Armine sat spellbound, wondering if this was the same man who had been whistling the theme from *Cheburashka*.

In the next few weeks Raffi and Armine met regularly in the pizzerias and coffee shops of America's capital town. Armine found more reasons to admire Raffi: his stubborn chivalry, the courage of his imagination. Raffi, in his turn, was captivated by Armine: her own sense of nationalism, her irrepressible vitality. Returning to American University late one night, Raffi and Armine decided to explore the spooky vacant buildings of a campus after hours. An unlocked door opened to a recreation room. Raffi found a piano. Armine found a couch. For the next few hours, Armine watched a silhouette sway and sing to the night. It was not through words but through music that Raffi first entered Armine's heart.

Actually, her American friends called her Ann. Only Armenians knew her as Armine, and only Raffi ultimately insisted on Armenouhi. That was the full, difficult, beautiful version of her name—and Raffi delighted in uttering its ancient, mellifluous syllables. *Armenouhi*: lady of Armenia. Of course when he pronounced his own name, Raffi hardened his *r* like an American; it seemed arrogant to retain the foreign consonant. But when he introduced Armenouhi to his friends—and there were many introductions in the coming days—he uttered her name in the original. That is how Raffi made his first declaration of ownership of Armenouhi Khatchikian.

She was born in 1963 in Soviet Armenia, the youngest daughter of Gaspar and Takouhi Khatchikian, who had been among thousands of Lebanese Armenians to follow Soviet promises to Yerevan in the 1940s. Along with her sisters, Alvard and Karine, Armenouhi had been shielded from the ordeals of Soviet life. But not Gaspar and Takouhi. They applied for United States visas every year after Armenouhi was born. It took a full decade to receive approval, and it would have taken a decade longer except that Gaspar shared a lineage and a last name with Ken Khachigian, speechwriter for President Richard Nixon.

The Khatchikians arrived in Queens, New York, on the weekend of July 4, 1975, but theirs would not be a typical immigrant story.

At the age of forty-two Gaspar died of a heart attack, and it was his widow, Takouhi (meaning "queen" in Armenian), who moved the family to Los Angeles and assumed responsibility for the education of her three daughters. At Hollywood High School, Armenouhi ran the Armenian Club. She joined the AYF. And she arrived on scholarship at Occidental College in 1982, one year after Barack Obama left for Columbia University.

Armenouhi and Raffi exchanged histories in Washington. She told him about Yerevan and Queens, and he told her about Fresno.

"Fresno?" exclaimed Armenouhi. "I have relatives in Fresno." Walking down 16th Street in Washington, Armenouhi spoke of an elegant woman who had visited her home in Yerevan almost exactly a decade earlier.

"Marian?" Raffi asked.

And suddenly, by the shock spread upon Armenouhi's face, it was clear: the woman of her memories was Marian Hovannisian, the wife of Raffi's uncle and godfather Ralph.

It was evening in the capital. Raffi and Armenouhi had been talking all day. They were just about to reach his apartment when Raffi took Armenouhi by the arm, drew her close, and peered into her eyes. *Is this the one?* he thought. He said nothing, only stood there, at the corner of 16th and T, awkwardly contemplating Armenouhi. Upstairs, sitting on the dilapidated sofa of a grungy studio, Raffi took Armenouhi's hand and lifted it slowly to his lips. He was wearing a white knit sweater.

The evening dragged and thickened. Raffi and Armenouhi fell silent. Raffi set a sheet of paper on the table, and then he took a pen to it. Ararat quickly came to shape, the small and big mountains standing side by side, leaning on each other. A sun was setting between them, slowly disappearing into Western Armenia. When he had finished drawing, Raffi moved his pen above Ararat. *Garin*, he wrote. Then he dropped the pen on the table. Sunlight was forming outside. Armenouhi understood. She picked up the pen. *Chomakhlu*, she wrote a short distance from Garin. Then Raffi took the pen: *Kharpert*. Armenouhi: *Daron*. Raffi: *Van*. In a circle around the mountains, Raffi and Armenouhi wrote out the cities of their vanished homeland. They did not talk. They would never discuss this drawing. They knew what it was: a covenant.

In the spring of 1984 Armenouhi finished her semester in Washington and returned to Los Angeles, where she would soon begin her first term at the UCLA School of Law. Immediately she sought out the famous Armenian history professor on campus and asked if she might enroll in his class; she would prove herself to him directly. The professor scowled. He did not understand why of all the girls obsessing over his son, it was this one, a Soviet Armenian refugee, who had captivated him. But he allowed her into the class and found no recourse, ten weeks later, but to give her a final grade of A. The professor phoned Armenouhi at her home.

"You have a good memory," he said. "But you misspelled the word *separate*."

In Washington Raffi waited for graduation. He excelled at constitutional law and earned his lowest grade, a C, in legislation—an irony that would reveal itself in time. He continued to organize GALSA events and conducted research at the International Law Institute. But his thoughts were in Los Angeles. In the fall of 1984, Raffi phoned his father at Terryhill Place. "If you want to," Raffi said, "you can call Armenouhi and pay her mother a visit."

Armenouhi received the news of Raffi's proposal by phone, and not from Raffi. It was Richard who informed her of her imminent engagement.

"I only have one question," Richard said. "What will you call me?"

"What would you like to be called?" Armenouhi replied.

"My children call me Papa, but I don't like that. I'd rather you call me *hairig*." *Hairig* meant "father" in Armenian.

"Okay, *hairig*," Armenouhi said.

The rites of Armenian love quickly unfolded. With a box of See's chocolates, Richard and Vartiter arrived at the doorstep of a one-bedroom apartment in Hollywood. The beautiful Takouhi, Armenouhi's mother, served them Armenian coffee. It was sweet, which meant that she was pleased with the visit. A few weeks later the Hovannisians paid another visit to the Khatchikians, this one with much greater fanfare. While Raffi was writing his dissertation, "Universality Jurisdiction and the Armenian Genocide," in Washington, his uncles and aunts and cousins from Fresno packed into the Khatchikian apartment for the festivities of the *khoskgab*, "the knot of words." *"Menk egadz enk tser bardezen vart kaghelu,"* they said. "We have come to pick a rose from your garden."

Raffi and Armenouhi were engaged on June 1, 1985, and a wedding was called for the end of the same month. On the invitations, a family crest made its first appearance. A full sun floats in the background. In the forefront: two cranes, their necks entwined. One looks west, the other east. Their wings are the mountains.

ON THE AFTERNOON OF JUNE 30, 1985, the family of the groom gathered at the home of Siroon Hovannisian in Fresno. In the piano parlor, Raffi stood in his mustache and white underwear. His brothers, Armen and Garo, and his cousins, Hrair, Vahe, and Aram, helped to dress him: first the white pants, then the white shirt, the white suspenders, the white shoes. Then Archbishop Mesrob Ashjian approached the groom. The archbishop was the prelate of the Armenian Apostolic Church, the leader of the Antelias churches in the eastern United States, and he had arrived from New York with the green-and-red sashes from the province of Daron in old Armenia. They symbolized the transition from boyhood to manhood, but strapped upon Raffi's chest, they looked more like bandoliers of bullets. It was as if Raffi was a guerrilla being groomed for war. The men sang together:

Zartir vortiag, uzh per, ver gats,

Baderazmi poghn hnchets.

"Zartir," gochets tsaynn haireniats,

Genats mahu zhamn hnchets.

Awake, my son, take strength and stand,

The bugle of war has sounded.

"Awake," declared the voice of the fatherland,

The hour of life and death has sounded.

Armenouhi and her friends re-created the women's rituals at the home of Edwin and Seda Sadoian, a family cousin of the Kotcholosians. The women huddled around the crying bride. *"Dasnevets daregan, nani jan / Siro jiranum,"* they sang. "I'm sixteen years old, dear mother / In the clutch of love." Then the doorbell rang. The Hovannisian men had arrived to retrieve Armenouhi. By custom the groomsmen would be greeted at the door by a representative of the bride's family. They would stand by the doorstep, negotiating the terms of the marriage, and the emissary would dart in and out of the house, presenting each offer to the bride. But in the case of Raffi and Armenouhi, the deal had been made long before the wedding day. He had promised her a home upon Ararat. She had promised him seven children.

The ceremony was held at the Holy Trinity Armenian Apostolic Church, where generations of Hovannisians had baptized their children, married their young, and parted with their dead. Armen was the best man. Ani, Raffi's sister, was the maid of honor. The wedding was a family affair. Brothers, sisters, and cousins watched as bride and groom pressed their foreheads against each other beneath the archbishop's cross. The Armenian liturgy was read and chanted. When it was finished, Raffi lifted his wife's white veil and kissed her once on each cheek. Armenouhi wore Vartiter's wedding ring, Raffi the gold band of Babi Hovagim.

The crowd of six hundred reconvened across the street at the Centre Plaza Hotel, where the Asbarez Club had once stood. When Raffi and Armenouhi, arm in arm, walked through the doors of the banquet hall, the *zurna* pierced Armenian hearts, the *dumbeg* pounded the rhythm, and the crowd broke into dance. Their shoulders draped with *lavash*, Raffi and Armenouhi stepped toward the two plates set on the dance floor. They stomped on the plates until they cracked, dispelling evil spirits. Rice rained abundantly and the crowd cheered as Raffi and Armenouhi danced toward the head table. From the podium Armen sang the old song of Kharpert:

> *Hey, zhamanage egav, harsanike esksav!*
> *Harsn u pesan egan egan!*
> *Zhoghovurte votki elan,*
> *Dzapaharel esksan.*
> *Amenun achke harsin vra,*
> *Pesayin hale hartsnogh chga!*
> *Amenun achke harsin vra,*
> *Pesayin hale hartsnogh chga!*

> Hey, the time has come, the wedding has begun!
> The bride and groom have come!
> The people jumped to their feet,
> And began to clap.
> All eyes are on the bride,
> And the groom is cast aside!
> All eyes are on the bride,
> And the groom is cast aside!

A program of customary felicitations followed—"May you grow old on one pillow" and "May you sit at the table with seven children"—but only the music and dance, the 10/8 beat of ancient feet, could create for Raffi and Armenouhi the experience they had so wanted for their wedding: a national hypnosis. The unforgettable spectacle of the evening was the candle dance of Lake Van. The lights were turned off, the hands of hundreds linked in a circle, and a candle lit where each hand met another. In the dark, it appeared as though the candles themselves were dancing, drifting in eternal, luminous circles.

It was a spectacular wedding—a celebration and summary of all Armenian traditions, as weddings had been before 1915. It had taken seventy summers for a young bride and groom to bring justice, at least in their minds, to the tens of thousands of weddings that should have occurred, but had not, on the plains of Western Armenia. "*Ev polor martik togh urakhanan ev togh polors hbard zkank vor menk tasdiaragum enk aynbisi mi serunt vor ge bahbani hai sovorutiunnere, hai lezun, ev hayutiune odar aperun mech,*" said Takouhi, the mother of the bride. "Let everyone rejoice and stand proud that we are bringing up a generation that will guard the Armenian tradition, language, and identity on foreign shores."

Raffi and Armenouhi did not immediately leave for a honeymoon. Raffi was due to take the California bar exam in August, so the newlyweds spent six weeks at the hot wooden house at 3312 Lowe Avenue where once Babi Hovagim had entrusted to his grandson the secrets of their national destiny. The house was empty. Mami Khenguhi had moved across town to live with her daughter Nazik and son-in-law Vartkes Messerlian. The childhood home of the Kotcholosian grandchildren—the Hovannisians and the Messerlians—was deserted. But the splendid orange and apricot trees survived in the backyard.

Raffi walked out of the testing room sure that he had failed. But he would not allow such anxieties to disrupt the opening voyage of his married life. Accompanied by a honeymoon entourage of brother and pals, Raffi took Armenouhi on a two-week tour through Soviet Armenia. They visited the family of Khenguhi's brother and Armenouhi's grandfather. They found the Khatchikian childhood home. They delighted in the monasteries and mountains of an ancient homeland. And there, during that strange honeymoon of a Western Armenian man and an Eastern Armenian woman, the metaphor of a united Armenia was finally consummated.

RAFFI AND ARMENOUHI MOVED INTO the family home on Terryhill Place; that was their wedding gift from Richard and Vartiter. Raffi had passed the bar, it turned out, and in September he took a job as a litigator for Hill, Farrer & Burrill. Armenouhi, meanwhile, began her first year at the UCLA School of Law. Husband and wife had the credentials to enroll in the community of young American professionals, which was blossoming on their cul-de-sac and all about the shady groves of Brentwood. Instead, they created lives that no one on their street could imagine.

It was a windswept evening in November 1985 when the pals formally convened in Raffi's home. Since the big brother had returned from Washington a few months earlier, the old AYF fraternity had been restored to the den at the end of Terryhill Place—a small corner room with a sofa, a coffee table, and a television. Armen, Ara, Steve, Greg, Garo, Moushig, Ruben, and the rest of the gang had been gathering to watch *Monday Night Football* and to muse, as they had in their youth, about the possibilities of an Armenian homeland. But the boys had arrived today to hold a more difficult conversation. The subject was Ruben Keoseyan, that dearest and closest of pals, who had found his Armenian identity through this brotherhood, and who had just moved from Mexico City to Los Angeles and announced his engagement to a Mexican woman.

When he had first met Patricia at a restaurant in Mexico City and they had stayed up until two in the morning comparing their national struggles, Ruben had forced his heart to remain sober. He had been honest. "I want you to know that I can't marry you," he had said. And he had told his pals the same thing: "No way! Never! It'll end, you'll see." But it had not ended. His heart had been beating in unpatriotic ways, and he had been called now before a jury of his peers to answer for his actions. Now, the friends of Ruben Keoseyan had assembled for an intervention. The television was turned off. The boys were serious, and even Ruben, the immutable joker, wore a face fitting the occasion.

Armenouhi was in the kitchen preparing Philly cheesesteaks. Only for deliveries did she trespass into the territory of her husband. She could hear the brutal voices: "You lied to us, Ruben! You lied!"

Ruben himself had been silent throughout the evening. He was unmoved by his friends, all except one, and that one had been silent, too. Raffi always spoke at the end of his meetings. He listened to the opinions of everyone. Only when the bickering had finished did the chief justice make the closing speech, a synopsis of all existing views followed by a final judgment that brought them all into harmony.

Now Ruben listened.

"We are gathered because we love you," Raffi said. He looked with sorrowful, angry eyes at Ruben. "We have shared so much together. The chapter in Mexico City. The coup at camp. Our upbringing." They had shared much more than that. "We have a dream," Raffi said. "You can marry her and forget all of us, your grandparents, your blood, the future of the motherland, or you can join us in our quest to defy the odds of history and foreign soil—by staying Armenian and marrying an Armenian and having kids who will someday see a land their parents never did."

Ruben said nothing; there was no response to the logic of national pride. He merely listened: "Don't let yourself become the latest victim of genocide. It is her or us. Stay with us."

Raffi offered Ruben a room in his house and a return to the Armenian cause. He talked about the oath he had taken years ago at the home of Kerop Arakelian, Ruben's grandfather, who had feared that his family was about to lose the Armenian spirit. Ruben knew about the oath. He knew that he was failing Raffi. But there was no solution to this problem that wouldn't fail somebody, some ideal. Ruben smiled. He knew what had to be done. He stood up and walked out of Raffi's life forever.

Ruben did not hate Raffi and Raffi did not hate Ruben. They loved each other. But on that November night, they had disappointed each other to the core. Ruben had found his friend to be without heart and understanding, and Raffi had found his friend to be weak and selfish, as if Ruben hadn't learned in all these years that the life he lived was not really his.

TWO MILES EAST ON SUNSET Boulevard, in a white house with big windows overlooking UCLA, Richard and Vartiter Hovannisian were carrying on as they had for the past twenty-five years. Time had changed what it could. Richard had grown heavy and his hairline was determined to retreat; he was looking more and more like his father. Vartiter's own hair had faded to gray. Their children Armen and Ani were already enrolled at UCLA—Armen at the law school and Ani in the communications department—and Garo was soon to join them.

Yet as far as the children could tell, Richard and Vartiter had not changed. They had only hardened into the pattern of their lives— which was constant, endless work. For the past twenty-five years, Richard and Vartiter had done nothing else. They had never taken a vacation, never gone out to a movie, never had dinner by candlelight. They had spent almost nothing on themselves, and they were proud of it. They had mailed in their donations to charities, schools, and political campaigns, and they would purchase for each of their children a complete education and ultimately a house, but Richard and Vartiter refused to buy anything that smelled of American luxury. Except a Cadillac. They bought a Cadillac every ten years.

He worked on campus and she worked in the hospital, and they connected in the evenings for a half hour's chat. And then it was over. He went to sleep and she began the most rewarding part of her day. At the kitchen table, a cup of steaming water always her companion, Vartiter took a sharp pencil to the professor's writing—pausing at each word, skipping nothing, believing with the full force of her being that her husband's work mattered. In a few more hours, well before dawn, Richard would rise for another day. Vartiter would have to finish editing by then.

If Richard ever had true friends, he did not have them now—a casualty of the stubborn velocity he had chosen for his life. He buried his emotions from the world, even from his family. He could often seem cynical and, when he was accused of cynicism by his children, he merely agreed. He did not explain himself to them and almost never wrote the long, emotional, reflective letters that were common in his youth. Perhaps the last of these he wrote to Hrayr Kabakian, some thirty years after they had met at the Jemaran:

> *I hate to expose the depth of my Armenianism—perhaps not*
> *understood or appreciated by all—but thoroughly imbued,*
> *sadly gnawing, continuously weeping, perpetually angered.*
> *I live in the Armenian past unendingly. I try to relate to the*
> *ugly aspects of the Armenian present without complaining.*
> *My life is bound to the re-creation of a past period in which I*
> *live and die, in which I continue to hope knowing full well the*
> *end of the story before I have begun it, hoping against hope*
> *that somehow by my sitting before the microfilm machines*
> *for eighteen hours a day, by being bound to this typewriter,*
> *by depriving myself, by ignoring my family, jeopardizing*
> *things dear, that somehow, if I cannot change the end of the*
> *story, that I may in some little way help in the beginning of a*
> *new chapter, of giving to the future a history that will never*

probably be written unless it is done now, a subject to which
I have devoted years, and about which I live in the silent fear
that I shall not be able to live long enough to tell the story
as it must be told, to commit to print the many thousands
of pages, reels of microfilm, volumes and packets of dusty
archival materials that are stored in my mind and in my
notes. I am heavily burdened by the weight of these upon me.

Richard was fifty-two, but the evidence of a midlife crisis could not be found on the driveway of his home. He was planning a more convincing rebuttal to mortality: the creation at UCLA of an endowed chair that would require the university to allocate, in perpetuity, an annual budget to the teaching of modern Armenian history and to cover the salary of a tenured professor. But two prerequisites would first need to be satisfied: a donation to UCLA of $500,000 and the approval of the University of California Board of Regents. The university already had accepted an endowed chair in Armenian languages, and it was less than eager, in a season of Armenian political violence, to consent to a second.

The Armenian community, however, was eager. Walter Karabian, a former California State Assembly leader, began to work out the political problem. His friendship with Willie Brown, the Assembly Speaker who controlled the UC budget, was the key. Richard, meanwhile, managed the financial effort, and he found an immediate ally in Dro Amirian of the Armenian Educational Foundation. Members of the AEF, an organization that Richard's great-uncle Harry Carian had helped found in 1950, immediately pledged half the necessary amount. The other half Richard would raise from an expansive network of Armenians, including his brothers, John and Ralph, and his mother, Siroon.

In the fall of 1985 the Hovannisians were preparing for a reception for the UCLA chair around the swimming pool of Richard's home.

Siroon had come down from Fresno with a blue pot of her famous buttered rice pilaf and a tray of the doughy dessert called *choreg*. She observed with pride as Vartiter and Armenouhi set the tables for their men, the way the women of past Armenian generations had done. The guests would soon arrive, and Armenouhi was rushing a dish to the poolside. Suddenly a mysterious dizziness overcame her. Struggling to repossess her bearings, she stumbled back into the house and fell on the couch. Vartiter, the doctor, appeared at Armenouhi's side, but she was arrested by the matriarchal voice.

"Oh, don't mind her," Siroon said. "She's only pregnant."

RAFFI WAS HOLDING ARMENOUHI'S HAND in the delivery room of UCLA's medical center when their first child arrived. It had been a C-section—Armenouhi had narrow hips, the doctors said, and the coming giant was likely to destroy them—and now, just as the doctor retrieved the baby, Raffi reached out to him. Armenouhi looked on as Raffi held the screaming, slippery boy in his arms. Raffi smiled immensely. *"Tsayn me hnchets Erzerumi hayots lerneren,"* he began to sing. "A sound echoed in the Armenian mountains of Garin."

I did not yet know the man who held me, but I began my apprenticeship without protest. I listened to his songs and then his stories, and soon I learned his language; *luys*, or "light," was my first word. By the age of two I commanded the full repertoire of Armenian revolutionary anthems, the proof of a proper upbringing. And every few months I saw my father off on another trip to Armenia. He would leave with a silver video camera case and he would return, ten or fifteen days later, with the most recent footage of the fatherland.

I first saw Armenia in the summer of 1987 flickering on the television in our den. My father had just returned, and he was on the editing machine. I sat on his lap and gazed at the screen. I saw villagers singing Armenian folk songs to the camera. I saw Stepanakert and

Shushi in Mountainous Karabagh, or Artsakh. *"Shushi, dghak,"* my father said from behind the camera. *"Hai chga hos. Payts mi or. Mi or haiere gkan."* A couple of frightened Azerbaijani boys were running away from the camera, but my father was following them. "This is Shushi, my boys. There are no Armenians here. But one day. One day the Armenians will come."

By the time my father and I held our next editing sessions, in May and October 1988, the Armenian people had made significant progress toward that prophecy. The images on the screen were no longer of singing villagers but of screaming citizens, hundreds of thousands of them, who gathered day and night at Liberty Square, by the opera house of Yerevan, chanting, "Unification!" Much had happened in the past year. Inspired by Mikhail Gorbachev's democratic promises, the Armenians of Mountainous Karabagh—still three-quarters of the region's population—had petitioned the Kremlin for permission to secede from Soviet Azerbaijan and to reunite with Armenia. When Azerbaijani forces had responded in February by massacring unarmed Armenians in the town of Sumgait near Baku, a spontaneous mass movement was born.

In Yerevan, Raffi was quietly chronicling a living history; in Los Angeles, he was preparing to make it. Almost every week now, he was delivering his famous speeches—that daring combination of sermon, song, and original poetry—to the diasporan political communities, which had united against the increasingly anti-Soviet disposition of the movement to reclaim Mountainous Karabagh. In a joint statement in October they counseled faith and patience to the Armenians; agitation against Moscow would serve only to endanger the homeland. That was the same argument being made in Yerevan by the Communist bosses, most notably Karen Demirchyan, who had the audacity to confront his own protesting people: "Karabagh isn't in my pocket for me to give it to you."

Raffi understood the fear, but he had recognized in those demonstrations the beginnings of a much greater movement, one that could eventually redraw the boundaries of the Armenian dream. Before thousands of Armenians gathered in the parks and auditoriums of southern California, he defended the popular movement of Yerevan and recited his poem:

> Why must we remain Armenian
> In this foreign dominion?
> And why keep our hearts churning?
> Because, my friends, we will be returning.

By now Raffi was a lawyer for Stroock & Stroock & Lavan and a member of the board of directors of the Armenian Assembly of America, which had survived the withdrawal of the ARF. Throughout the 1980s, the Assembly had conducted a study of genocide denial in American academia, revealing that almost every major denier— Stanford Shaw, Bernard Lewis, Heath Lowry, Justin McCarthy—had received grants from organizations with links to the Turkish government. Encouraged by Governor George Deukmejian, the Assembly also had succeeded in establishing the Armenian Genocide as a mandatory component of the California public school curriculum. Raffi had submitted supporting testimony to the state legislature, and Richard had designed the curriculum guidelines.

Still, the Assembly spent most of its time on achieving internal agreement. On December 5, 1988, during a weekend meeting of the board in Los Angeles, the issues were set on the table. How should the Assembly respond to Raffi's proposal that the organization be opened for public membership? How should the Assembly interact with the ANCA, the ARF lobby? Should the Assembly encourage Armenian immigration from the Soviet Union to the United States? On this last question, the board was divided. Ken Khachigian, Ronald Reagan's chief speechwriter and the man secretly responsible for the president's historic reference to "the genocide of the Armenians," voted to encourage immigration. Raffi voted against. *Let the Armenians hang on a while longer,* he thought. *Something will come.*

Raffi did not know what would come or when. He did not know what miracle would happen to the homeland. But he was ready for it, even on December 7, 1988, even among a cheery American crowd at the Shrine Auditorium, where Armenouhi was vowing to defend her adopted land. "Against all enemies," she said, "foreign and domestic." Raffi looked proudly upon his wife. A few months earlier on that very stage, *The Last Emperor* had won the Oscar for Best Picture, and Cher, the daughter of an Armenian truck driver, had been named Best Actress. And now there stood Armenouhi, the Armenian refugee turned American citizen turned attorney at law, raising her right hand and pledging her everything to the United States of America.

Chapter Eight

FAX MACHINE

What happened in Armenia? Look here, Garin. Tell me what happened in Armenia." I was on my yellow plastic tricycle, peddling along Terryhill Place, my long blond hair waving behind me. "Garin, what happened in Armenia?" I peeked over my shoulder. He was standing there, the bearded man in a white T-shirt, the video camera a part of his anatomy. "Garin!" he yelled, catching my glance. I swerved and cycled toward him.

"*Hayastane ufig e,*" I said delicately. I was now in his shadow. "Armenia is hurting."

"Good!" my father exclaimed, a smile suddenly restored to his face. "Now, what do we say when we go to the demonstrations?"

"Karabagh is ours," I responded obediently.

"And what else?"

I covered my eyes.

"What else, Garin? What do we say at the demonstrations?"

"*Mi-a-tsum!*" I said. My face was illuminated. "U-ni-fi-ca-tion!"

In a quiet office in Suite 1800 of the Century Plaza Towers in Los Angeles, a young litigator for Stroock & Stroock & Lavan peered at the stack of deposition transcripts on his desk. Just a few weeks earlier, Raffi had stood at the fault line of history. He had been in the fatherland that dreadful winter, wandering through the debris of December 7, 1988—a date infamous but immortal in the lament of Armenian French singer Charles Aznavour:

> They fell that year,
> They vanished from the earth,
> Never knowing the cause
> Or what laws they offended.

They had fallen that year, tens of thousands of Armenians into rubble and snow, yet those who survived the earthquake—the paralyzed and the homeless—had not squandered their chance in the limelight. In the ghost towns of Leninakan and Spitak, they had stared into Raffi's video camera and confronted the world not with grief but with fury over the Soviet Union's contempt for the Armenians of Mountainous Karabagh. Mikhail Gorbachev had responded by imprisoning the Armenian leaders of the Karabagh Committee, and the Armenians had responded by organizing more protests against Moscow—demanding unification, democracy, and the shutdown of Armenia's nuclear plant, a cousin of Chernobyl.

Raffi had been there, in that season of anguish and possibility, and now he was back in his office in Los Angeles. He could not work. He rustled through the newspapers—*Asbarez, Armenian Reporter, Massis, Armenian Mirror-Spectator*—and immersed himself in that secret parallel world, unknown to his bosses, where the forces of history were awakening. The senior partners were not pleased with Raffi. They had signed off on his phone bills and travel requests so far, but it was obvious that their young litigator was terminally distracted. "Raffi," one of the partners counseled, "turn off your Armenia jets."

That phrase infected Raffi's contemplations. His personal pride could have endured an accusation of idleness, but an injury to his public pride as an Armenian was intolerable. Wounded and stubborn, Raffi resigned his position at Stroock. Within a few weeks, he had signed on with Coudert Brothers, a major international law firm and the culmination of his professional ambitions. But when Raffi moved into his new office on the twentieth floor of a Los Angeles skyscraper, he did not notice the luxurious views. He asked for, and received, a leave of absence. His superiors knew where he was headed, but just what their bright new acquisition would be doing there, on the slippery slopes of a national struggle, was beyond the imagination of metropolitan lawyers.

ON THE HILL ASCENDING TO the Matenadaran, the repository and museum of ancient Armenian manuscripts, the Armenians were gathering daily. The Supreme Soviet of Armenia—the Yerevan legislature dominated by local Communists—was endeavoring to appease the public passions. A few days before, the Supreme Soviet had repealed the ban on the Armenian republic's tricolor flag and allowed for celebrations of Armenia's independence, May 28, 1918. And now, on the afternoon of May 31, 1989, Raffi watched a caravan of cars arrive from the Yerevan airport to deliver the proof of an even greater concession.

They walked out, one by one, the men of the Karabagh Committee, released from the Matroska prison in Moscow: Rafael Ghazaryan, radiophysicist; Vazgen Manukyan, mathematician; Vano Siradeghyan, novelist; Hambartsum Galstyan, linguist and philologist; Ashot Manucharyan, organizer and educator; Babken Araktsyan, mathematician; Levon Ter-Petrosyan, scholar of history and languages. Ter-Petrosyan stood first among his equals. "Le-von! Le-von! Le-von!" The chants were unceasing, but the man who owned that name seemed to be properly unmoved by the adulation.

Levon Ter-Petrosyan was not a demagogue. A tall and hunching man with disheveled brown hair, he looked upon the city as if it were a vast public classroom. He spoke a polished, professorial Armenian, and only for special effect—most often when referring to the authorities in Moscow—did he use the vulgar Russian slang that had bled into the Armenian vernacular. His speeches were written out and read in monotone, as befitted a Soviet professor, and often they dragged on so long that the orator himself would retrieve a cigarette from his pocket. Yet the Armenians were captivated. Raffi examined them: clean-shaven men, children in school uniforms, women swaying in summer dresses. These were not the rebels of history textbooks—peasants hungry for food or power—but citizens ready for ideas. They were dressed for a polite revolution.

Raffi had seen nothing like this in the United States. So many times he had attended the rallies of American politicians—as a kid in 1968, he had cheered for Robert F. Kennedy en route to his assassination—who spoke no language but melodrama, that purplest dialect of emotional argument. But Yerevan did not need melodrama. In the capital of the smallest of the Soviet republics, the democratic drama itself was enough to sustain the hope of a people.

IN THE SUMMER OF 1989, as masses of citizens overtook the squares of Yerevan, Armenia, and Stepanakert, Mountainous Karabagh, Armenia's popular leaders officially registered a political party. The Armenian National Movement would press for reunification and democracy, of course, but now also for independence from the Soviet Union. First the Armenians would test the channels of Soviet jurisprudence—Article 70 of the Soviet constitution protected the people's right to self-determination—but if Moscow proved unwilling to negotiate, they would not deny themselves less conventional strategies of struggle.

That the Armenian Supreme Soviet had agreed in the first place to register the Armenian National Movement—to accept, in effect, the candidacy of anti-Soviet leaders in all future elections—was sure evidence that Soviet power was depreciating. It was based on such evidence that the Armenian Revolutionary Federation and rival political parties in the Armenian diaspora began to recalculate their initial position against the nationalist struggle and to sneak, slowly and awkwardly, into the throngs of a historic charge for independence. It was based on such evidence, too, that Raffi decided to leave Coudert Brothers. His imagination had grown restless, and Raffi was determined to follow it—first to the Washington offices of the Armenian Assembly of America, then to its final destination.

The family elders were not happy. In Los Angeles and Fresno in the summer of 1989, Raffi had suffered their views with a smile. "Unacceptable," Richard had said with a scowl. *"Klukht guden,"* Mami Khenguhi, in all her kindness, had said of the Soviets. "They will eat your head." Armenouhi, on maternity leave from Cummins & White, had not complained. But then she did not need to complain— she just had to sit there, Garin in one arm and the newborn Daron in the other—for Raffi to understand the injustice of his decision. Raffi listened to the dissenters, nodded at them—almost, it seemed, agreed with them. Yet in the privacy of his own mind, Raffi was waiting, not listening.

Raffi arrived at 1334 G Street in Washington at an auspicious time for the Armenian lobby. Van Krikorian, his old Georgetown classmate, recently had taken over the legislative affairs department of the Armenian Assembly of America, and he had been overseeing the effort in the fall of 1989 to push an Armenian Genocide resolution through Congress. Similar attempts in 1985 and 1987 had flopped, but Van confided his optimism to Raffi. The Assembly and the ANCA, the advocacy group of the ARF, were finally cooperating, and Senate minority leader Robert J. Dole had agreed to represent their resolu-

tion. Some forty years earlier, Dole had returned home from World
War II with a destroyed shoulder and a broken aspiration for basketball stardom. An Armenian doctor, a survivor of the Genocide, had
healed his spirits.

Raffi followed the events of his world. In Washington: the predict-
able mobilization of the Turkish lobby, the retreat of the resolution's
co-sponsors, the turnaround of President George H. W. Bush. In Moscow: the decision to lift direct control over Mountainous Karabagh
and to repair the territory to Soviet Azerbaijan. In Yerevan and Stepanakert: official declarations defying the Kremlin's decision and an-
nouncing the unification of Armenia and Mountainous Karabagh. In
Ankara and Baku: the move to seal Armenian territories from incom-
ing grain and petroleum. In Berlin: the crumbling of a wall. Across
the Atlantic Ocean, the tides of history were washing over a continent, and Raffi was living with the anxiety that he was missing out
on the defining events of the twentieth century.

He would be in Armenia soon, but Raffi had one last mission in
the United States. In January 1990 he founded the Armenian Bar Association, the first national network of Armenian lawyers, which
would organize the diaspora's ideas on the legal questions of a past
genocide and a coming republic. At the Doubletree Hotel in Marina
Del Rey, California, Raffi presided over a successful opening convention; elections for the board were held and dinner served. But Raffi
was not celebrating. His thoughts were drifting to Baku, where the
official military forces of Soviet Azerbaijan had begun to maim, stab,
and burn to death hundreds of civilians, and commenced the violent
dispersion of some two hundred thousand Armenians.

IN FEBRUARY 1990 RAFFI SETTLED into a one-bedroom apartment
off Azizbekov Square in Yerevan. Every morning he took the five-
minute walk down to the black stone building once occupied by

Prime Minister Simon Vratzian. The Yerevan office of the Armenian Assembly of America was just next door, and there Raffi spent the mornings, reading every word of every Armenian and Russian newspaper he could find. It was his job, as the Assembly's Yerevan office director, to prepare a daily report of the organization's activities, geared toward the earthquake relief effort.

He had specific instructions from Washington to avoid official association with the Armenian National Movement—"we have neither the right to interfere in Armenia's internal political process, nor the capacity to affect the future," an Assembly memorandum, dated July 20, 1990, explained—but Raffi cheerfully disobeyed. He often visited the headquarters of the popular movement on Baghramyan Boulevard, where a chaos of politicians, newspapermen, students, soldiers, and spies gathered daily to influence the greater movement. This was possible. No barricades existed between leader and citizen, and a single stranger walking in could easily make a difference or a name for himself, whichever he wanted.

In the war room of independence, Raffi met with Levon Ter-Petrosyan, Hambartsum Galstyan, and the full cast of new democrats. They came to depend on Raffi's English, French, and Russian, his network of diasporan Armenians, his cache of legal knowledge. But they were most impressed by Raffi's creative sense of dedication. He would invent his own challenges: one day he was off with the commander Vazgen Sargsyan to the front lines of the Karabagh conflict, and the next day he was arranging interviews for the Armenian leaders with the international reporters stationed in Moscow. There was something almost greedy in Raffi's selflessness, as if he wished not only to contribute but also to have contributed to every front of the Armenian cause.

In April, Richard and Vartiter arrived in Yerevan to attend the capital's first-ever Armenian Genocide conference and then a meeting of the Armenian National Academy of Sciences, the exclusive intellectual guild of Soviet Armenia, which was about to make Richard the first diasporan social scientist to qualify for membership. With a camera in her hand, Vartiter followed her husband through his many lectures and accolades, but one journey she would have to make alone. At Lenin Square that week, she stood among an uproarious crowd to witness the toppling of a statue.

In Yerevan, Lenin Square overnight became Republic Square, and all through 1990 an epidemic of nationalism swept through the Soviet satellite republics. On May 20, in Soviet Armenia's parliamentary elections, the Armenian National Movement gained a majority over the established Communist Party. And on August 23, under its new president, Levon Ter-Petrosyan, the Supreme Soviet adopted a plan for independence, a guiding document called the "declaration on independence." Raffi observed the vote from the back row of parliament. That was his favorite place in any room. Raffi was free in the back, and he relished the biblical logic: *But many that are first shall be last; and the last first.*

By the fall of 1990, my mother had brought me and Daron to live with our father in Yerevan. "A vacation," she had called it, and she believed we would soon return to our American dream. She did not consider that my father actually had no intention of living in the United States ever again, that for Raffi, the act of repatriation itself—returning liberty to native lands—was the truest expression of the American dream. Armenouhi did not know that the Yerevan press was already calling her husband the "permanent representative of the diaspora."

Due in great part to Raffi's early insubordination to his bosses, the Armenian Assembly of America was by now fused with the democracy movement in Yerevan. In September 1990 it was the Assembly that organized Levon Ter-Petrosyan's all-American tour and Raffi who was appointed his personal tour guide and interpreter.

The lawyer and the popular leader grew to know each other on the trail. In Los Angeles, Raffi treated Ter-Petrosyan to Jack in the Box hamburgers and introduced him to a thunderous crowd at the Pantages Theater, where Raffi's pals were the security officers. He accompanied him to Washington, where the State Department issued a $10 million check for earthquake relief, and to New York, where he translated Ter-Petrosyan's speech at a banquet opened by Senator Bob Dole. And then Raffi stood by as a Fifth Avenue tailor measured the presidential entourage. Hirair Hovnanian, the patron of the Assembly, was treating the Armenians to a full wardrobe of custom-made suits—the uniforms of Western democracy.

On the return to Yerevan, Raffi and Ter-Petrosyan slept on twin beds in a hotel room in Moscow. It had been a fulfilling trip, and it had brought the two men—an idealist American activist and a calculating Soviet academician—ever so close. Raffi had found some warmth behind Ter-Petrosyan's cold, grave public face, and Ter-Petrosyan had been moved by Raffi's patriotism. He had long admired Professor Hovannisian, but Ter-Petrosyan now saw an even greater future for his son. He was fond of reading the future, actually. Just a few days earlier in New York, sitting in a limousine with Hirair Hovnanian, Ter-Petrosyan had looked out the window, studying Raffi through the tint.

"You see that man?" he had said. "One day that man will be the president of Armenia."

HE HAD NAMED HIS SONS Garin, Daron, and Van; it was a confession. These were cities of Western Armenia, the coordinates of Raffi's true nationalist aspirations. They served as a constant reminder that the dreamlands of Babi Kaspar and Babi Hovagim were on the other side of the mountain. Yet it was on this side, in a disintegrating Soviet state, that the Armenians were taking their stand. The struggle was different here. The Eastern Armenians were burdened not so much by the memory of the Genocide but by a history of Soviet totalitarianism and the unrequited loss of Mountainous Karabagh.

Already, Raffi's patriotism was carrying these burdens.

On May 5, 1991, defying the pleas of his wife, his bosses, and Levon Ter-Petrosyan, Raffi picked up his video camera and climbed into a Soviet military helicopter. Within an hour he had landed at the fringes of Mountainous Karabagh, which was surrounded on all sides by the battalions of Soviet Azerbaijan, reinforced by Turkish military advisors, Russian and Ukrainian mercenaries, and Afghan mujahedeen.

Raffi spent his first day in Shahumian, a northern town nestled among blue and green mountains, walking anonymously through hospital wards to videotape the dead and interview the dying. From the remote hinterlands of a crumbling empire, he phoned in his reports of war and suffering to the international press bureaus in Moscow.

And then Raffi joined history. On the battle lines at the village of Getashen, Armenian men and women had arrived to assist the natives in organizing a defense. These were not professional soldiers. They were farmers and teachers and journalists who had left their families in all corners of the world and shown up in Mountainous Karabagh with nothing but the will to fight and the willingness to die. Raffi was among them, the volunteer fighters of Armenia, but in this case only to document their defeat. Getashen fell on May 7, 1991.

The retreat of the fighters alarmed the Armenians of Shahumian. Every morning, on the fields outside the city, hundreds of civilians cast themselves at the feet of the Armenian military leaders, begging for seats on the next helicopter out of the war zone. Seized by gout in the right foot and troubled by telephone calls from Yerevan and Washington, Raffi himself had to leave. Every morning he limped onto the fields and every afternoon his determination melted before a begging mother with a baby in her arms. Day after day, he gave up his seat. And one day, after he had performed that same act of miserable selflessness and watched the last helicopter break from the ground, frustration cracked through Raffi. He dropped his video camera to the ground and yelled into the mountains.

"What am I doing in this godforsaken land?"

Raffi flinched at the echo. He did not recognize himself. He could not believe that such a cowardly thought could originate in him. The sound of it there, on that sacred piece of the Armenian patrimony, shamed him into silence.

A few days later Raffi finally found a seat on a helicopter full of corpses, wounded warriors, reporters, and military commanders. Soldiers had surrounded the helicopter to block off the begging Armenians. There was no more room. Raffi looked at the soldiers, then at his abandoned compatriots beyond. He recognized one of them: Karine, a volunteer from the front lines of Getashen, a valiant woman who had been intercepting Azerbaijani radio signals and translating enemy messages for the Armenians. She lingered in the crowd, a duffel bag of weapons in her hands.

Overhead the blades cranked into action. Raffi caught the woman's glance. "Don't worry," he yelled out. On the field yellow flowers trembled, and Karine bolted for Raffi. The helicopter was already in the air, and Karine was running through the line of soldiers, her arms outstretched. All those years of weight training at the Pali High gym and running the obstacle courses at the AYF camps in the California mountains had brought Raffi to this test. In the eyes of Karine, at least, the bearded man who pulled her up from the inferno of Mountainous Karabagh passed the test.

The Armenians had just ascended over Shahumian and begun their journey through mountain corridors when the pilot, a Russian colonel on Gorbachev's payroll, produced a sheet of paper. It was a matter of protocol, he said, to record the identity of the passengers. But Raffi knew there was no such protocol. Something strange was happening. He looked outside, and it was obvious. The helicopter was moving not westward, to Yerevan, but eastward, to Soviet Azerbaijan.

Guns were pressed against the pilot's head, and the truth emerged: two Azerbaijani helicopters were following the Armenians. The Russian pilot had been instructed by radio to collect the identities of his high-profile passengers and to proceed to Kirovabad, Azerbaijan. The Armenians panicked; they knew what fate was being planned for them. They would not risk it. At first the pilot hesitated, but the guns proved convincing. He said that there was only one way to lose the Azerbaijani helicopters. Within a few seconds, the passengers had buckled up and the helicopter was spiraling into the gorge.

"WHEN RAFFI HOVANNISIAN WALKS INTO the halls of the Armenian government, he is greeted with knowing nods from the guards and open doors into the offices of Cabinet ministers," reported the *Christian Science Monitor* in May 1991. "At the parliament, President Levon Ter-Petrosyan pulls him over for a quiet consultation. Yet Mr. Hovannisian has no official position. He is not even a citizen." The article was titled "Nationalist Vision Draws Diaspora," and it posited Raffi as the original model of the Armenian repatriate: a successful citizen of the diaspora who gives up the good life in pursuit of the meaningful one.

The possibility of an independent Armenian homeland was galvanizing thousands of diasporan Armenians. Carolyn Mugar and Louise Manoogian Simone were investing millions in a national rebirth. Mihran Agbabian, a leader of the Assembly, was spearheading efforts to launch the American University of Armenia. Gerard Libaridian, who under Richard's tutelage had received his Ph.D. from UCLA, was advising Levon Ter-Petrosyan on foreign and security policy. Monte Melkonian, the bearded rebel of Berkeley days, was planning to organize a professional Armenian army to defend Mountainous Karabagh.

Throughout 1991, the various satellite republics of the Soviet Union raced toward independence. Gorbachev survived an attempted coup in August, but it was clear, finally, that he was finished. His government had suffered successive acts of disloyalty. His economics had been paralyzed by stagnation. His reformist socialism had lost the war of ideas against the thriving Western democracies. Time was running out, and Gorbachev could do nothing but wait as his empire broke into pieces.

ON SEPTEMBER 21, 1991, SOVIET Armenia held its great national referendum on independence. On that day a delegation of observers from Washington, including Congressman Wayne Owens of Utah and the philanthropist Vahakn Hovnanian, had been assigned to Raffi—"a bear of a man," Owens wrote in his journal, "who would scare you if you ran into him in a dark alley someplace, except that he always, always has a deep smile."

They were supposed to be touring the Yerevan precincts, but it was clear from the very beginning that neither Raffi nor the Americans intended to waste the day. On the streets of the capital, festivals of freedom were erupting: women singing, children dancing, men screaming out their unbearable liberty. On the balconies of decrepit Soviet apartment buildings, grandfathers and grandmothers were emerging, as if for the first time, with wet and frightened and enraptured eyes.

Congressman Owens was thrilled, for he saw in the Armenians what had become mere habit and ritual in the United States: that revolutionary passion for freedom, the trademark of the Founding Fathers. "To hell with observing!" the congressman declared without the slightest inkling of shame. "We want part of the action!"

And soon he was standing at the center of it, arm in arm with Raffi, surrounded by rejoicing Americans and crazed Armenians and honking Soviet cars, and beyond them the pink and gold ministries and hotels of what had just been Lenin Square, which were lighting up in the night and transforming into the headquarters of the new Republic of Armenia.

On September 23, 1991, the Central Election Commission issued the results of the referendum. Almost 85 percent of eligible citizens had voted; 99 percent had voted for independence.

In the lobby of the presidential palace, Raffi and Levon Ter-Petrosyan embraced. The Armenian republic had officially clocked into history, and Raffi knew he had to act. Two requests he made of Levon Ter-Petrosyan. To begin with, Raffi wanted Armenian citizenship. "Don't worry," Ter-Petrosyan said, a grin upon his face. "You work, and we will make it happen." Then, with greater anxiety, Raffi made his second request. He told Ter-Petrosyan that he would be honored to serve as a department head or a deputy minister in the foreign ministry of the new republic.

And now Levon Ter-Petrosyan turned serious. He shook his head. "No," he said. "There will be an appointment of another kind."

IN THE WEEKS BETWEEN INDEPENDENCE Day and the republic's first presidential elections, Levon Ter-Petrosyan and his closest advisors, with the marked exception of Raffi, convened in Aghveran, a resort town in the hills north of Yerevan. In the villas of the old Communist elite, the men met to discuss the composition of the president's cabinet. If Ter-Petrosyan should be elected president, and there was no reason to doubt that, he would be expected to announce his key ministers. Among these was the minister of foreign affairs. Ter-Petrosyan proposed to his advisors the name of Raffi K. Hovannisian.

The advisors were astounded. They did not mean to question

Raffi's patriotism and dynamism—but, really, was there anything more than that? Except for the two years he had spent at Fletcher, and a summer in Washington, Raffi had no diplomatic experience. He carried an American passport! Shouldn't the foreign minister of Armenia be a citizen of Armenia? Would it not be more prudent to appoint a seasoned diplomat, even if he were seasoned by Soviet attitudes? Levon Ter-Petrosyan allowed the objections to air, but on this matter he would not be convinced. Raffi was to serve as the Republic of Armenia's first minister of foreign affairs.

In October 1991 the Armenians participated in direct presidential elections, entrusting to Levon Ter-Petrosyan 83 percent of the vote and a popular mandate to create the foundational state. The main challenger, the popular actor Sos Sargsyan, conceded defeat; he was representing the Armenian Revolutionary Federation. A republic was coming to life, yet the international media seemed more interested in that enigmatic United States citizen, the first to head the foreign ministry of another government. On the front pages of the world's newspapers, different versions of the same story—this one from the November 7, 1991, edition of the *Los Angeles Times*—began to appear:

> Raffi Hovannisian, graduate of Palisades High School, UCLA, the Fletcher School of Law and Diplomacy and his family's home-taught school of ethnic pride, is set to take office Monday as foreign minister of Armenia. The landlocked republic is not quite independent of the Soviet Union, but Hovannisian, 32, a stocky, mustachioed, former high school football lineman—and class valedictorian—is working on it.

With a supreme smile and a monthly salary of 600 rubles, or $143, Raffi walked through the doors of a simple cream-colored building on Baghramyan Boulevard and proceeded to find that no foreign ministry existed inside. Only the must of rotting wood and the smoke of cigarettes floated through its dank, haunted hallways. Armenouhi accompanied Raffi on this tour. Fifteen years earlier she and her family had fled the totalitarian experiment in Armenia, and now she had returned with a cardboard box to collect its last idols. In the minister's chambers, she studied the framed portraits of meditative men, the bust of Lenin on her husband's desk. She peeked over at Raffi, and she knew that he would not need statues. He was setting up a fax machine—the first fax machine of the foreign ministry.

Soon the transmission began: *Armenia is free. Please recognize.*

While Raffi waited for answers from the capitals of the globe, he turned to resuscitating the ministry. From Armenia and its diaspora he recruited scores of young men and women to fill its empty offices. The republic had no budget, so he carried out his own fund-raising campaigns and tapped into his personal bank account to pay salaries. He enforced a dress code and a code of ethics. He offered public example and private instruction in diplomacy. Within a month he had transformed the ministry into an arena of bright minds, where East and West, expertise and imagination, nationalism and diplomacy were cooperating at last.

Armenouhi was devoted to her husband's mission, but she was slowly discovering a role of her own. As the Yerevan director of Project Hope, an international health care organization, she oversaw the training of Armenian doctors and the installation of advanced medical equipment in the nation's hospitals. Quite independent of her husband, Armenouhi had begun a journey into the murky, miserable depths of Armenia's netherworld.

As our parents mended a broken country—that is, in any case, what we thought they were doing—we, the brothers Hovannisian, explored the verdant groves of the government *dacha*, a walled compound where the president and his top ministers were assigned houses. Daron was two and Van was not yet one, and so it befell me, five-year-old authority on domestic roguery, to mastermind our escape from the supervision of our sitters. We explored our sprawling kingdom and spied on the children of other dignitaries. One boy was shooting dogs with a BB gun. Another boy, a switchblade in hand, was chasing after his sister. These children emasculated my rather modest American sense of mischief, but they could not disabuse me of my enchantment.

We lived in a castle. That is what it seemed like, anyway, because there was a Russian pool table on the veranda and secret service agents in the basement. I marveled at all of this, yet I knew this was not my real home. I knew that beyond the gray walls of the dacha was Yerevan, which itself was not real, and beyond that was California, where all my grandparents and uncles and aunts and cousins lived. Where I was now, this was just beautiful nonsense. I was simply walking through my father's dreams.

For the winter holidays we traveled to the United States. The Aeroflot plane was packed with Armenians, the men smoking and the women oozing so much perfume I thought it must be a funeral. The Armenians cheered as we walked toward our seats in economy class, and I knew they were cheering for my father. We settled in, and then my father got up to walk the aisle. He had to shake hands with everyone, and the Armenians loved him for it. But on that day, there was considerable embarrassment in their exchanges. I did not know why. My father did not tell me that almost everyone on that plane was abandoning Armenia.

At the Moscow airport the colonels searched our suitcases. Their faces were made of stone; it would hurt them to smile. A bust of Lenin was found, and the colonels multiplied before our eyes. "Where are your documents? What is your business in Armenia? *Who are you?*" they asked the man with the mustache who had arrived from Yerevan with a United States passport, accented Russian, and the rather incredible idea that he was the republic's minister of foreign affairs. The colonels refused to believe him, and it took the intervention of several passengers to confirm my father's ridiculous identity.

As always, we spent Christmas in Fresno, and the men of my family became boys before the matriarchs, Grandma Siroon Hovannisian and Mami Khenguhi Kotcholosian. I remember their wrinkles, histories mapped upon the skin of girls. There seemed to be no common source to their sensibilities—the country teasing "You go on!" of Siroon and the wounded, abiding melancholy of Khenguhi— yet somehow I could comprehend that these were the different faces of the same catastrophe that had closed in on the Armenian people in 1915. There was no way to look into their eyes and not know that those eyes were looking back at you from another place and time.

On December 25, 1991, the Hovannisians gathered in Grandma Siroon's living room. The sun was still basking in the sky, which meant that the children were playing football in the backyard and it would be a while before someone went to retrieve the red suit from the closet at the end of the hallway. On the golden sofa next to the Christmas tree, Siroon sat beside her sons. She was proud of each of them: John for his prospering real estate empire, Ralph for his loyalty to farm and vineyard, Richard for the road he had chosen for himself, and Vernon, too, for following in his oldest brother's footsteps.

But today the pride of Grandma Siroon was not rationed among her sons but awarded completely to Raffi, because he was the foreign minister of the republic that her husband had spent his life praying for. On the television, the traditional Christmas broadcast of *It's a Wonderful Life* was being interrupted by the two most fantastic announcements: first, the resignation of Mikhail Gorbachev and the dismantling of the Soviet Union; second, the declaration of President George H. W. Bush, in his Christmas Day message, that the United States officially recognized the Republic of Armenia.

"Our enemies have become our partners," the president said. And here Raffi's uncles and cousins burst into cheers. *"Vay, vay, vay!"* Uncle Vernon shouted, his inheritance from Babi Kaspar, and the cousins echoed, *"Vay, vay, vay!"* because they could not believe that their very own Raffi, the overeducated city kid of their youth, had helped to make it all happen. Two weeks later, on Armenian Christmas, January 6, 1992, Raffi finalized the terms of Armenian-American diplomatic relations in a Washington meeting with Secretary of State James Baker.

IN THE FOREIGN MINISTRY ON Baghramyan Boulevard, the nation's fax machine was coming to life. Several governments had recognized the Republic of Armenia in November and December 1991, but the Christmas announcement by the United States had unclogged completely the phone lines of international diplomacy. The staff of the ministry huddled around the fax machine as page after blank page entered the contraption and slowly reemerged as smeared ink, a barely decipherable communiqué from Britain or Japan or Mexico: *We recognize.*

Within a few weeks, nearly a hundred countries had officially accepted Armenia as a legitimate sovereign state, and Raffi was now preparing for more strenuous negotiations with the international organizations—most urgently, the Conference on Security and Cooperation in Europe (CSCE), the United Nations, and the Council of Europe. Fortunately, by the spring of 1992 Raffi had stocked his ministry with more than a hundred capable minds—Zaven Sinanian, Van Krikorian, and Raffi Sarrafian from the Georgetown era; Vartan Oskanian from Fletcher; Matthew Der Manuelian of the Assembly; and Christian Ter-Stepanian of France—diasporan Armenians in their twenties and thirties who had chased their idealism from the developed democracies of the West to the beginnings of an original democracy. Some local Armenians in the ministry speculated that these men were spies.

Raffi did not challenge the conspiracy theories; these he knew to be the fancies of people living in closed, secretive states. Besides, he was too busy—traveling the world, a black leather bag always at his side, swiftly gaining his republic entry to every significant international forum. As far as Levon Ter-Petrosyan was concerned, however, his appointee was doing his job too efficiently. He had chosen Raffi with the hope that a man educated in Western diplomacy would best minister Armenia's reputation in the world. He had been right. But the president had not considered what the minister would do after recognition had been gained. This minister, it was now clear, was about to take on the two monumental issues of modern Armenian history: redemption for the Armenian Genocide and liberty for Mountainous Karabagh.

This was a problem because Ter-Petrosyan and Hovannisian took two very different approaches to Armenian national issues. The president openly believed in the logic of a conciliatory foreign policy, which held that Armenia should be willing to pay—through tactful silence with Turkey and territorial concessions to Azerbaijan—for its place in the community of nations. The minister of foreign affairs, along with the nationalist opposition led by the ARF, disagreed. For Raffi, the reality of the Genocide and the rights of Armenians to their homelands, both in eastern Turkey and Mountainous Karabagh, were issues of history over which neither Armenia nor an occasionally principled West should have to negotiate.

A competition of visions had always existed in the theoretical realm, but they were quickly materializing in the real world. Since New Year's Day 1992, when the Soviet Union officially closed down and Russian troops began to withdraw from Mountainous Karabagh, Armenian and Azerbaijani forces had been rushing toward total war. Atrocities were committed and answered by both sides—Azerbaijan's Alazan and BM-21 Grad rockets rained relentlessly upon the Armenian civilian population in Stepanakert, while Armenian fighters reportedly opened fire on Azerbaijani civilians—as the region was devastated and destabilized.

Armenia's diplomatic efforts, meanwhile, were encountering unexpected obstacles. On February 28 in Prague, at a meeting of senior officials of the CSCE, an envoy from the Armenian foreign ministry was under consensus pressure to sign the first international document on the Armenian-Azerbaijani peace process. Two stipulations alarmed the envoy—first, the status of Mountainous Karabagh as a territory of Azerbaijan, and second, the permanence of all national borders as currently drawn. Hearing of this, Raffi phoned his envoy in Prague. He was to remind the European diplomats, and his own, that Joseph Stalin's impulsive gift of Armenian land to Soviet Azerbaijan could not possibly be honored in a post-Communist Europe. He was to reject the document. The envoy agreed with the minister.

So it was with great shock that the following morning Raffi read the reports in the international newspapers. The Armenians, apparently, had proven to be most gracious at the CSCE—real, first-rate Europeans, they, to sign the document in Prague, to compromise on their claims to Mountainous Karabagh.

JUST WHAT HAD HAPPENED OVERNIGHT in Prague, Raffi did not yet know, but this was not the reason for his insomnia in the early hours of March 2, 1992. A pillow between his legs and the air conditioner blowing a blizzard—ideal sleeping conditions—Raffi was still utterly awake in a cheap hotel room in New York City. In the darkness, he could make out the silhouette of his father, asleep in the other bed. Raffi was thinking about his speech. He had not written most of his speeches in the past few months, but he had written this one, and he was now imagining its words. Raffi's perfectionism was already legend at the ministry, and an impotent phrase had no chance of surviving one night in the torture chamber of his mind.

"You have the floor, sir," announced the voice of a woman. This was the closest Raffi had come to dreaming all night. He stood up from his seat in the expansive, circular, intergalactic chamber. He carried a folder in his hands, and as he walked to the podium, he struggled to button his gray suit. Raffi settled before the microphone. Before turning to English speech, he uttered a few words in Armenian—the first Armenian words ever to echo in that hall.

This was not a dream.

When the morning session had concluded, the delegation from Yerevan was escorted out of chambers and into the chill of the metropolis. Outside, by the flagpoles, a few hundred Armenians had gathered to observe the ceremonies. Amid the crowd of suits Raffi noticed his father, the tireless chronicler of the original republic. An improbable wetness had overtaken the professor's eyes. It was March 2, 1992, his thirty-fifth wedding anniversary, when Richard watched his son raise the Armenian flag—the red, blue, and orange tricolor of the first Armenian republic, and now the new one—at the headquarters of the United Nations. Above him the sky was blue and the clouds were white and swirling.

OUTSIDE OF THE WEEKLY MEETINGS of the National Security Council, the foreign minister and the president rarely met to coordinate their ideas on Armenia's foreign policy. Conformity had been the Soviet version of coordination; the tradition called "an exchange of ideas" did not exist in the post-Soviet democracies. So it was through the whispers of their staffs or else from newspapers that Raffi and Ter-Petrosyan learned of each other's diplomatic adventures. Apparently the foreign minister had presented at the United Nations his routine arguments for the international recognition of the Mountainous Karabagh Republic, while the president, in a March 5 interview with Moscow's *Komsomolskaya Pravda*, had announced that Mountainous Karabagh should remain an autonomous republic within the territory of Azerbaijan.

As Raffi traveled through the diplomatic forums, it became clear to him that he would need not only to rehabilitate the views of his Azerbaijani and Turkish colleagues and influence the moods of the international community but also to embolden the foreign policy that was being run from the Armenian president's office—specifically, to toughen the soft language of statements that had already been signed, or even drafted, by the Armenians.

The great test was a meeting of the CSCE's Council of Ministers beginning March 24 in Helsinki, Finland, where the official foundations of peace talks among Armenia, Azerbaijan, and Mountainous Karabagh were to be set—and to be set upon the anti-Armenian document passed in Prague a few weeks earlier. Raffi went to work, and he was inexhaustible. In public he spoke and in private he charmed. He reasoned and roared, then repented with a smile. By the end of the day's session he had succeeded in fortifying the founding document with new language, including the stipulation that "the democratically elected government of Mountainous Karabagh" be guaranteed a seat at the peace talks.

The Azerbaijani delegates were stunned; they were not prepared for rebuttal. So it was after a considerable delay, just as the document was being adopted, that their more savvy Turkish colleagues awkwardly broke out of their neutrality and opposed Raffi's formulations. A second round of debate followed and ultimately a more modest document was passed. But two important provisions remained: first, a reference to "elected and other representatives of Mountainous Karabagh"; second, the opening of humanitarian corridors that would link by land the Republic of Armenia with Mountainous Karabagh, which until then had been under full blockade by Azerbaijan. These provisions would prove decisive in the coming decades of negotiations, which would be supervised by the CSCE and its successor, the Organization for Security and Cooperation in Europe (OSCE).

By the spring of 1992 Raffi had become the standard for principled Armenian patriotism. When in April he and Ter-Petrosyan toured the many Armenian communities of the Near East, something happened that should never happen to a president. On the streets of Aleppo, Syria, where tens of thousands of Armenians had gathered to welcome the leaders of the republic, chants of "Levon!" were supplanted by chants of "Raffi!" The Armenians were joyful to see the president, but it was his minister, son of the diaspora, whom they lifted from the ground and carried on their shoulders. The president walked—and listened: "Raf-fi! Raf-fi! Raf-fi!"

In Yerevan, too, the president's popularity had begun to wear. As Armenian fighters were overcoming outlandish odds and triumphing in Mountainous Karabagh—on May 8, 1992, they liberated the major fortress town of Shushi—Ter-Petrosyan was still promising concessions to Azerbaijan, Turkey, and the West. These promises, compounded by the president's failure to prevent the onset of a great economic crisis, had wiped away the afterglow of independence. The opposition in parliament was more enthusiastically disputing presidential policies and, in turn, the president was losing patience. In a live television broadcast on June 29, Ter-Petrosyan laid out a case of sedition against Hrair Marukhian, the diasporan leader of the Armenian Revolutionary Federation, and announced his expulsion from Armenia.

AT THE LEGISLATURE IN THE summer of 1992, a coalition including ARF supporters was planning to reclaim Armenia's foreign policy from the hands of President Ter-Petrosyan. Its members were ready to pass a resolution to recognize the independence of the Mountainous Karabagh Republic—a resolution that the president opposed less in principle than in practice, because he believed that such a sudden move would undermine Armenia's standing in Europe. The president panicked and decided to send his own nationalist, the foreign minister, to reason with the members of parliament.

Standing before the parliamentary assembly on July 7, 1992, Raffi realized that his loyalty was awkwardly divided. He would have to carry out the president's wishes, but without supporting his foreign policy. And so Raffi presented a most fragile argument—that the independence of Mountainous Karabagh was legally imperative and politically inevitable, but that the technical act of recognition, which was an executive act, should not be robbed from the presidency. By the end of the afternoon, he had brokered a compromise. The parliament would not formally recognize its sister republic, but it would also resolve never to sign an international document that Mountainous Karabagh itself would not sign.

"Paylun eluyt er!" the president exclaimed to Raffi that evening. "A brilliant speech!"

But the following morning, over the phone, the president issued a different opinion. The foreign minister's performance in parliament had served irreparable damage to Armenia's foreign policy, he said, and given new life to the nationalist opposition.

One autumn afternoon Armenouhi was at the government dacha when her husband called. He was in Jakarta, Indonesia, negotiating Armenia's admission with observer status to the Nonaligned Movement. He had established diplomatic relations with China and India, he said, and met privately with Yasser Arafat and President Ali Akbar Hashemi Rafsanjani of Iran. "Tell the president," Raffi said to Armenouhi, "that the Iranians have allowed grain to come in." This was tremendous news: the Turkish and Azerbaijani borders being closed off, Armenians had been living with no bread.

Armenouhi hung up the phone and stepped out of the house. It was a tepid evening, and she scurried across the lawn to the presidential mansion. She was buzzed in and led to the study, where she burst out the good news: "Raffi called from Jakarta! Grain is coming in!"

Levon Ter-Petrosyan looked up from his books, casting astonished eyes upon Armenouhi. "Raffi is traveling?" he said.

ALL ROADS END IN ISTANBUL, the enchanted city upon the Bosphorus where, once upon a time, the masterminds of the Young Turk government met to decide the fate of an ancient people. On April 24, 1915, the Armenian intellectuals and clergymen of that city were rounded up and summarily executed. Then the orders went out to the empire's provinces. More than a million were killed, and another million dispersed throughout the world. It was to Istanbul that the grandson of Kaspar Gavroian of Kharpert and Hovagim Kotcholosian of Garin returned on September 10, 1992, to say a few words about history.

At the conference room of the luxurious Conrad Hotel, built upon one of Istanbul's seven hills, the Turkish government was hosting a meeting of the Committee of Ministers of the Council of Europe. The foreign ministers of the member states (France, Great Britain, and twenty-five others) were in attendance, as were the foreign ministers of several nonmember states (Russia, Azerbaijan, and ten others) who were trying to talk their way into Europe. The foreign minister of Armenia was in this category. He was anxious. Turkish diplomats had been vigorously opposing Armenia's induction to the Council of Europe, and he was being called upon, in the heart of the Republic of Turkey, to respond.

From the podium Raffi began with the expected diplomatic flourishes, proclaiming that the meeting of ministers "represents a homecoming of sorts for my country" and an opportunity to reflect on Armenia's "loyalty to its European heritage." He spoke of his republic's multiparty democracy and the steady dissolution of a hege-

monic state into a free market economy. And then the narrative of
Armenian diplomacy took a twist no one had thought possible. Raffi
paused—he believed in the pause—and then, peering into the eyes
of his colleagues, he said: "Despite the tragedy of the Genocide . . ."

And from there, as confusion and horror fell upon the room of
ministers, Raffi steadily explained why Turkey was in no position to
block a neighboring republic's admission to the European club. He
spoke of Turkey's grave human rights violations against Armenians,
Greeks, Assyrians, and Kurds; its illegal blockade; and its failure
to remain neutral in the war over Mountainous Karabagh. He argued that the conflict should be viewed not as a territorial dispute
between Armenia and Azerbaijan but as the push of a people for self-
determination—the final stage, Raffi said, of the post-Soviet decolo-
nization process.

That night, as the ministers dined at the Dolmabahce Palace—one
of Istanbul's many wonders, the work of an Armenian architect—
celebrations raged in Beirut, Aleppo, Paris, Boston, and Los Angeles.
That an Armenian had dared utter the word *genocide* in Istanbul and
presented to the world the complete collection of national issues had
inspired the diasporan communities and reempowered visions of a
"free, independent, and united Armenia." But in Yerevan, in his mansion at the presidential dacha, Levon Ter-Petrosyan was not celebrating. To him, Raffi's performance in Istanbul was an act of sabotage
that had paralyzed his project of conciliation among neighbors.

In the next few weeks the president refused to see the minister,
and the minister, not being one to beg, carried on as usual. He was
continuing talks with Azerbaijani and Turkish attachés, the UN and
the CSCE, Russian president Boris Yeltsin, and American secretary of
state James Baker. Raffi had developed a strong rapport with Baker;
he would earn a mention in his memoirs as the "American citizen
from Los Angeles, and such a dapper dresser that my security detail
came to refer to him as 'Valley Dude.'"

Raffi was also sending off the first Armenian ambassadors to world capitals and receiving the first foreign ambassadors in the Armenian capital, where the flags of the United States and Iran waved side by side. He was creating the Armenian Foreign Policy Fund to sustain the ministry, drawing support from major entrepreneurs. After a meeting with Raffi, the Las Vegas billionaire Kirk Kerkorian wrote a check for a million dollars. Raffi had appealed to Kerkorian's patriotism and teased him with an old story: Raffi's grandfather Kaspar had once made a small loan to Kirk's father.

The foreign ministry building, a fossil when Raffi had found it a year earlier, was now a vibrant chamber of ideas. Post-it notes, the evidence of Western thinking, were scattered about its offices. The competing styles of diplomacy still competed, but now in the collegial style of the foreign minister. Among his staff and people, Raffi enjoyed the reputation of a principled and tireless spokesman for the national will. "The most popular man in the newly reborn Republic of Armenia," the *Los Angeles Times* called him in September 1992. "A recent poll in the Armenian newspaper *Epokha* found that he enjoyed a mind-boggling 96% approval rating, more than President Ter-Petrosyan. Even among the long faces of a Yerevan bread line, people turned thumbs up when asked about him."

In early October Raffi was in Moscow, en route to Thailand and then an official visit in Australia, when he received a call from Yerevan. Raffi urgently returned to the capital, but it turned out there was no crisis. He knew what was happening. Within a few days his mother and brother Armen arrived at the dacha. The house was quiet and miserable for weeks, and the family waited together. Finally, on October 16, the telephone rang. It was the president's line. Raffi picked up.

"*Paron nakhagahn e*," Ter-Petrosyan said from the other side. An awkward phrase: "This is Mr. President."

Some hours later, in a brief meeting in the presidential offices,

Levon Ter-Petrosyan asked for Raffi's resignation. He could stay on as an advisor, if he wished—but of course Raffi wished for no such thing. Without any extravagant words or gestures, he left the president's office for the last time, returned to the dacha, and played awhile with his boys. Then he told Armenouhi to begin packing. He wanted to leave the dacha immediately. He could not bear to spend one more moment behind those walls, in that dream within a dream within a dream.

Chapter Nine

———

STRANGERS

E very night we heard the howls.

In gangs of six or seven they moved under moonless skies, overturning trash cans, munching on dead rats. The dogs were treacherous, and soon they turned against the humans, too. We had heard the old folk saying *"Shune tiroche chi chanachum,"* but only now, wrapped in sleeping bags in the dark and freezing winter of 1992, could we appreciate the intended terror: "The dog does not recognize his master."

My father had not wanted us to sit out in Los Angeles the winter after his resignation, so we had moved into the first floor of a house on Charents Street. We were to live as ordinary Armenians, my father had said, which meant that we survived without gas and electricity, and the only way to keep warm was to bury ourselves in sleeping bags. We ate potatoes and cheese and apricot jam. Often we had no bread, because grain shipments were not coming in. Water was a luxury, and the first opulent sound of it gushing through the pipes would send the entire family to its feet. We would take our buckets and plastic bottles to the faucets, which would be dry again within the hour.

"Inch g'nenk hos?" I will never forget that question in the dark, the trembling voice of my mother. "What are we doing here?"

The dogs did not recognize their masters, not here, not in this gloom-frozen homeland—an abyss illuminated only by candles and kerosene lamps, where even children knew that dogs, when they are starving, are not man's best friends. But there was another Armenian saying, *"Enkerovi mahe harsanik e,"* which meant that death with friends is a celebration. The Armenians were suffering, but they were suffering together, waiting in breadlines together—together waiting for spring and democracy, which had been postponed on account of a cruel but necessary war. Thousands of refugees were coming in from Mountainous Karabagh, daily refreshing the news with more suffering, more poverty, more death. But the way I saw it, through the marveling eyes of a six-year-old, we were enduring together.

My father, however, was not protected from the Armenian winter. The Ter-Petrosyan government was not only blocking his applications for citizenship but also campaigning against the very memory of him. Almost overnight, from the nation's television channels, all of them controlled by the government, the republic's first minister of foreign affairs had quite simply vanished. Old friendships had cooled, and the phone lines connecting our home with the offices of the Armenian Assembly of America had gone out of service. It was an undesirable thing, in Yerevan, to be out of power.

No satisfactory explanation of the minister's shocking resignation and disappearance was offered to the public, but the Armenians amused themselves with theories, which was one of the ways they passed the winter. The most scandalous of these, which is to say the most common, was best captured as a cartoon in an opposition newspaper. Ter-Petrosyan was shown to be consulting his mirror. "Mirror, mirror on the wall," he asks, "am I the most popular of them all?"

In the diaspora, as in Yerevan, Raffi's popularity was complete. Once a renegade and never a card-carrying member of the Armenian Revolutionary Federation, the party of Kaspar and Hovagim, Raffi was now its cause célèbre. In Los Angeles and Boston and Beirut, his name was brandished by community leaders as the symbol of principled leadership. And not just by the ARF. "The most serious consequences of the president's abuse of democracy and his dismissal of Hovannisian are yet to unfold," predicted the *Armenian Reporter*, a non-ARF newspaper. "President Ter-Petrosyan has unwittingly created the first viable candidate who could challenge and defeat him in the next presidential election—Raffi Hovannisian."

This was the message delivered, during the first blizzards of 1993, to my father's ears. If the Ter-Petrosyan government insisted on following its present path to an inevitable bankruptcy of the public faith, then Raffi would have his chance. He alone commanded the reputation—and the imagination—to save the Armenian people. This is what the whispers said, anyway, exciting whispers for a thirty-three-year-old man from Los Angeles who had ended up in opposition to the state he had spent his life dreaming of.

In Mountainous Karabagh, Raffi's mind could breathe free. The sensation of the sacred, imperiled in Armenia, was still preserved in its raw altitudes. That was a majestic place, foothills rolling green and eternal in yet another severed patch of paradise. So in January 1993, leaving behind his wife and boys, Raffi traveled to Mountainous Karabagh—not by helicopter, but this time by car, through the corridor at Lachin—to seek context for both the praise and the contempt he had incited in Yerevan.

Raffi spent his days walking through the teeming hospitals of Shushi and taking cover in the underground bomb shelters of Stepanakert, which was enduring continuous aerial bombardment. He had no purpose but to wander through this bursting space, but he was wandering with a direction, wandering southeast to Martuni, because there was someone there he wanted to see.

He was by now called Avo, a lieutenant colonel of the army of Mountainous Karabagh, the leader of four thousand men, but Monte

Melkonian was very much the same bearded romanticist Raffi had first met in the Tan Oak Room at Berkeley. Raffi had been trying to run a dignified first meeting of the Armenian club. Monte had been distributing flyers titled "How to Make a Bomb."

Since that providential encounter in the fall of 1977, Raffi and Monte had graduated from different schools of struggle. Raffi had collected his diplomas from the world's finest academies, Monte from French prisons and the radical training camps of the Lebanese underground. But ultimately, their different passions had returned them to a common source. Diplomacy and combat had cooperated more than once, as in the spring of 1992, when Monte participated in the operation to secure the Lachin corridor, the first land link between Armenia and Mountainous Karabagh, which Raffi earlier had negotiated.

Raffi stood by a pile of firewood outside the barracks. He was wearing a wool sweater over a collared shirt, but this was too much for an unusually temperate winter's day in Martuni, Monte's headquarters. Raffi waited. He was told that his friend was taking a bath, and Monte did not often take baths. He declined the commander's privileges. He did not carry a pistol. He did not curse or smoke. He never drank while in uniform. He was as common as his men, and his men adored him. He took many visitors these days, but this visitor he was not expecting.

Uniformed in camouflage and smiling intensely, Monte charged toward the man with a mustache. "Raffi!" he yelled cheerfully. The men embraced. Then Monte broke open a red pomegranate. Raffi took one seed into his mouth.

"*Adi panme che*," Monte said. "'That's nothing."

Raffi put his arm on Monte's shoulder, and they walked together.

"*Aysor shad lav or egar. Desar inch keghetsig e?*" Monte said. "You came on a good day. You see how beautiful it is?"

He was speaking in a rambunctious San Joaquin Valley version of Western Armenian, and Raffi answered in the same.

"We heard about yesterday's victories," he said.

Monte chuckled. He could brag a little to Raffi. "Yesterday," he said, "and the day before and last month and before that. We have not given up one centimeter!"

Indeed, all through the spring of 1993, the Armenians not only guarded their centimeters but advanced, confidently capturing new frontiers of Mountainous Karabagh. The Azerbaijani battalions were stunned again and again, most notably at Kelbajar, where Monte led his men through four sleepless days of battle. The recurrent defeat of Azerbaijan's elite armed forces at the hands of the amateur Armenian warriors caused considerable embarrassment to the strategists in Baku, who found no recourse but to turn to their senior allies. Citing the Armenian capture of Kelbajar, Turkey officially closed its border with Armenia in 1993.

The fact was that the Armenians were in possession of an invisible resource that accounted for their victories. It was a passion inflamed long ago, cherished by the generations, developed in repression, and finally unleashed on the battlefields of Mountainous Karabagh. That is what the international observers did not understand. The Armenians were not fighting only Azerbaijanis; they were also fighting the Young Turks, Kemalists, Bolsheviks, and all those who had conspired through history to destroy their people. They were seeking redemption, which could often look like revenge, for a century without a home.

From Yerevan, Raffi followed Monte's struggle with pride, but also with a kind of envy, because he knew that his own Armenian journey could never be so pure. He admired how free Monte was, how he seemed to live above the influence of politics and man. He admired even Monte's death, so devastating yet so exquisite, on June 12, 1993, when enemy machine guns finally found him in the village of Merzuli in Azerbaijan.

•   •   •

By the autumn of 1993 our family had moved again, this time to a place of our own, a three-bedroom apartment on the tenth floor of a rectangular masterpiece of Soviet ugliness in the neighborhood of Aygestan, "the land of gardens." We had with us an extra tenant: a baby girl. She was the only daughter of Raffi and Armenouhi, yet this had not exempted the girl from assuming one of the difficult, inflexible, meaningful, proudly uninternational names my father liked to shackle to his children. Except hers was not drawn from the provinces of Western Armenia. She was Shushi, the great fortress city of Mountainous Karabagh.

We continued to live ordinary Armenian lives. We celebrated when the water came and trained our noses to stop smelling in the elevator, because it reeked of urine and vomit, and then learned never to take the elevator because, if the electricity went out, we would have ourselves a private dungeon. My brothers and sister were looked after by a sitter during the day, but I was old enough to go to school, where I learned what Soviet Armenia really had been: fear and respect, corruption and true brotherhood—a domestic cold war between a severe social order and a secret humanity in revolt. I was astonished to find that my draconian teachers could transform, in the privacy of personal encounters, into goddesses of maternal warmth and wisdom.

Most of my learning I did after school, however, in the early hours of the afternoon, when the city's children descended with soccer balls and jump ropes onto the streets surrounding their apartment buildings. We were not unsupervised. The men playing backgammon and women cracking sunflower seeds and gossiping examined us from afar. Here it did not matter whose child you were; if you were causing trouble, someone's mother was going to yell at you. And so I was free and protected in my neighborhood and, at the age of seven, I could stay out with my friends until sunset.

By the time I got home, my mother would have returned from work to run her candlelit kitchen, a constant detonation of lemon, garlic, and mint. She had just been appointed the director of Junior Achievement of Armenia, a program funded by the United States government to promote economic education in the country. With the backing of an influential board including George Deukmejian, the former governor of California, Armenouhi's mission was to train teachers in the methods of Western pedagogy and the ideas of post-Communist economics, and eventually to create a course in economics that would be taught in every public school in Armenia.

My father would arrive sometime after my mother. He had been out for dinner with an ambassador or a meeting with leaders of the opposition. Or else he was out of the country, at a conference in Tehran or Luxembourg or Beijing. He would return with his black diplomatic handbag filled with cultural trinkets and Toblerone chocolate, and spend the dark hours eagerly recounting to his children where he had been, whom he had met, what strange delicacies he had eaten. My mother would unpack my father's bags, but she would be listening, too, because she knew the stories were really for her.

In Yerevan whispers of power and glory pursued Raffi, but he had decided not to listen to them. The truth was that after spending three decades on an acute trajectory leading from Berkeley to UCLA to Fletcher to Georgetown to the elite firms of international law and to the top office of the Armenian foreign ministry, Raffi's sense of ambition, not to say the ambition itself, was exhausted. He had come too far too quickly, and oftentimes in the adrenaline of the chase he had almost forgotten where he was going and why. His passion for the Armenian homeland had brought him in view of the mountain, but if he were to climb it to the peak, he would have to do it patiently and deliberately. The mountain was made of ice and snow and illusion, and one false move would send Raffi to his end.

For the time being, Raffi settled into less glamorous ideas of service to the fatherland. As he starved off his weight and began to look sharp in suits again, he conjured up the plans for Armenia's first independent research institution. In the offices of the republic's academics and analysts, he defended the controversial notion that public policy should be governed not by ideology but by objective research and a free competition of ideas. Through ongoing research and seminars, Raffi hoped, something of a civil society might emerge in a land where so far there was a people and a government but nothing to make them accountable to each other.

As RAFFI WORKED TO BRING yet another institution to life, the forces of regional politics twisted in unexpected ways. In May 1994, drenched in the blood of the thirty thousand slain, the republics of Mountainous Karabagh, Azerbaijan, and Armenia signed a trilateral cease-fire. Except the agreement was reached not at Minsk under the auspices of the CSCE, as had been planned, but in Kyrgyzstan under Russia, which was quietly reasserting its paternal role in the region. In response to the pro-Azerbaijani gesticulations of the West, which had been fueled by the Caspian oil fields near Baku, Russia had tightened ties with Armenia and now posed as its guardian. The Kremlin had called, and Azerbaijan had sued, for peace at a time when nearly all of Mountainous Karabagh and some territories beyond it were in the hands of Armenians.

So why was President Ter-Petrosyan, within a few months of a triumphant military campaign and cease-fire, yet again pitching concessions to his people? The president answered with supreme pragmatism. A militarized border with Azerbaijan and a closed border with Turkey were simply not in the national interest, he said. Foreign policy depended not on idealism but on reality: "how many tons of wheat are in our stores, how many bullets we have, how many cisterns of diesel fuel are available to our tanks."

The Armenians were most displeased with Ter-Petrosyan's answers, and in 1994 they took their displeasure for a walk on the streets. Only three years after independence and landmark elections that gave Ter-Petrosyan an indisputable public mandate, tens of thousands of citizens marched behind the president's erstwhile colleague and defense minister Vazgen Manukyan, this time to protest the legitimacy of their own government. The Armenian Revolutionary Federation launched parallel protests, and Ter-Petrosyan responded by shutting down the party offices and banning the ARF from Armenia.

Amid much turmoil in October 1994, the Armenian Center for National and International Studies (ACNIS) opened its doors. Absolutely no one had agreed to rent to Raffi—calls from the presidential office dissuaded successive landlords—and he would have no offices at all were it not for the personal rapport he had nurtured with Hambartsum Galstyan, a former member of the Karabagh Committee and now the mayor of Yerevan, who sublet his personal offices. On the fifth floor of a building adjoined to the Armenia Hotel, the site of the parliament of the first republic, the original research center of the new republic began its operations. Its principal benefactors were two children of Kharpert: Siroon Hovannisian and Kirk Kerkorian.

Raffi had planned to launch ACNIS with a series of conferences dedicated to developments in regional and foreign policy, but it was clear to him that domestic politics—democracy, human rights, and free speech—were now the priority. In July 1995, Levon Ter-Petrosyan ordered the arrest of thirty-two ARF leaders on charges of terrorism and conspiracy to overthrow the government. Despite the prosecutor's best efforts, Raffi was not implicated.

A liberal to the world and a tyrant to his people, Levon Ter-Petrosyan had lost his balance. But on television he appeared always cool, calculating, unworried. He knew the chessboard, and he was planning a "horse's move" no one was expecting. Catholicos Vazgen I of the Holy See of Etchmiadzin had died recently, and Ter-Petrosyan was seeking his replacement from beyond the walls of Etchmiadzin. He was looking to Lebanon, to the Holy See of Cilicia, the "other church," the spiritual center of the party he was endeavoring to destroy. It was called unity. It was called treachery. Whatever it was called, Catholicos Karekin II of Antelias accepted Ter-Petrosyan's invitation.

Yet no Machiavellian plot could regain for the president the democratic advantage he had enjoyed through Armenia's independence. By September 1996, the republic's second presidential elections, Ter-Petrosyan was moved to commit that most desperate act. The OSCE, which had monitored the elections, announced a "lack of confidence in the integrity of the overall election process," citing rampant ballot stuffing, the unlawful presence of police at polling stations, irregularities with military votes, and the remarkable disappearance of twenty-two thousand ballots from the safes of Precinct Electoral Commissions. That was the very number that pushed Ter-Petrosyan over the 50 percent threshold and gained him victory after the first round of voting.

The chief opposition candidate, Vazgen Manukyan, rejected the results of the elections. Supported by a coalition of opposition forces, including the ARF, he led tens of thousands of citizens in the biggest protests since the ones Ter-Petrosyan had organized at the close of the Soviet empire. Ter-Petrosyan, once the mild-mannered academician, now ordered city police to beat and arrest hundreds of citizens, while Armenian tanks, escorted by riot squads, descended upon Yerevan. "Go home!" policemen yelled into megaphones. "Go home!"

Armenia was spiraling into chaos, but the president, composed as ever, still the master of his game, was planning his next move. He extended his hand once again to the horse. In March 1997, upon the resignation of his prime minister, he convinced the president of the Republic of Mountainous Karabagh to resign from his position in Stepanakert and to come to Yerevan to fill the post. Robert Kocharyan, an unassuming mechanical engineer turned leader of the Karabagh movement, acceded to Ter-Petrosyan's request, but really he did not like being moved around on someone else's chessboard.

DURING THE SEVERE WINTERS AND hepatitis outbreaks that regularly shut down School Number 114, I was sent to live with my grandparents in Los Angeles. They were such mysterious people to me—especially Mama Vart, who needed only a piece of toast, a cup of steaming water, and a few smiles to survive. In the evenings, returning home from the hospital, she read through the diasporan newspapers, and I knew she was searching for news of her son. I admired my grandmother's steady hand, how slowly and carefully she cut out my father's pictures, as if she were performing surgery. The problem with Mama Vart was that she had achieved pure empathy; everything we did hurt her. She found her only solace in the laundry room. In the early hours of the new day, when the house was cold and quiet, she would warm up an iron and begin her therapy. It was her favorite chore, to make wrinkles vanish from the clothes of the men she loved.

Now Hairig was just as strange as Mama Vart, but he did not share with her that deep craving for self-annihilation. He could still quietly enjoy a UCLA football game on television and delight in the taste of a Mr. Goodbar, wherein the memory of old Tulare was preserved. He could please crowds and, when necessary, during the many events that were organized to honor him, produce upon his face a perfect mimicry of gratification. He did enjoy traveling, when he was invited to speak. He no longer worked at a typewriter but on a computer. He had accepted modernity.

But the professor was still a difficult man, fluent in the ways of his world but increasingly alienated from the world itself. That is what the mission required: a regimen of constant work and creativity. And

even then it had taken the professor thirty years to exhume and me-
ticulously commit to print the founding chapters of modern Armenian history. The final two volumes of *The Republic of Armenia* were
published in 1996, just about the time when the Armenians of the
new republic could use some reflection on the mistakes of the first.

There were exactly two rewards for an academic masterwork of
this type: public admiration and private pride. But the first, Richard
found, grew tedious in repetition, while the second, once he had
achieved it, proved not to last. His life's work complete at the age of
sixty-three, Richard sought now to do the work of other lives. He
would continue to record oral histories of Genocide survivors and
to dismantle the arguments of denial at conferences sponsored by
organizations such as Facing History and Ourselves, but he was now
reconsidering his approach to the event horizon of Armenian history.
In all the time and money they had spent on defeating revisionist
theories of the Genocide, Richard realized, the Armenians had not
identified what they had truly lost.

The loss was cited usually in numbers, a million and a half, and that
death count was so awesome that it had eclipsed the unquantifiable loss
of homeland and civilization. So the professor turned now to reconstruct,
one by one, the social, political, and cultural life of each major Armenian
community in old Western Armenia. Twice a year he invited to UCLA
Armenian and non-Armenian scholars to present original research on
that community, and then collected the papers into a book. The first conference, on the province of Van, was called for May 1997.

All the while Richard supervised a full set of Ph.D. students and
continued to teach his signature survey course in modern Armenian
history, along with courses in oral history and comparative Genocide
and Holocaust studies. Not everyone was eager to take his classes; the
rumor, circulated among UCLA's few hundred Armenian students,
was that years earlier the professor had given his famous son, Raffi,
the lowest grade of his college career. Many of them even preferred

the Turkish history courses taught by Professor Stanford Shaw, who compensated for his generally unpopular denial of the Armenian Genocide by being very generous to his Armenian students.

In the early days, before Shaw's notorious book, the academic adversaries had agreed to the terms of collegial etiquette. Shaw had invited Richard to speak to his classes about the Armenian Question of 1915, and Richard had accepted the invitations, until students informed him that Shaw had spent the following three sessions controlling the damage. But since the late 1970s, when Richard had publicly taken Shaw to task for his reckless scholarship, the relationship had soured. Outside of mandatory department meetings, the professors had scarcely met. They had kept their animosities to themselves. They had not known that before they were through with each other, they would fight one last magnificent war.

It began in October 1997 at an ordinary department meeting, the type of bureaucratic affair Richard would have skipped, except a new school year had just begun at UCLA and he did not want to seem impertinent. The history conference room was only at the other end of the hallway from Richard's office on the sixth floor of Bunche, and the professors were already filing in, taking seats, and reading over the agenda. Today there was one special item: a proposed Turkish history chair at UCLA.

Richard was appalled. He peered at Stanford Shaw, then at the chairman of the department. They had spent the summer collaborating with the Near Eastern Center, apparently, planning a counterbalance to Richard's Armenian history chair. He should have figured; retirement was looming over Shaw, and he would not consider leaving UCLA without first installing a protégé. But now it was too late, the chairman said. The terms had been endorsed by the senior administration, a contract with the Turkish government already drawn up, and all that remained was for the history department to approve. The vote was scheduled for December.

Back in his office, hidden from sight, Richard realized his classic transformation from professor to activist. He phoned his friends at the Armenian Assembly of America and the Armenian National Committee of America, the rival advocacy groups reconciled only in crisis. The Armenians went to work. Meetings were scheduled with deans, demonstrations at regents' meetings. From Colgate University, Professor Peter Balakian circulated a petition protesting the "tainted chairs"—most infamously, the Ataturk chair at Princeton University—which were being funded by the Turkish government to serve entirely political ambitions: to promulgate a sanitized version of a national history, where no Armenian or Kurdish or Cypriot question existed, and no genocide had ever taken place.

On campus, members of the Armenian Students' Association invaded Bunche Hall and lined up at office doors. The *Daily Bruin* was flooded with hundreds of letters to the editor, most of them objecting to denialist studies on campus. For the moment, the possibility of a Turkish chair had overshadowed all other issues on campus. At a town hall meeting hosted by the chancellor, a student concluded her tirade about civil rights and race politics with an outburst of frustration. "This issue is just as important as the Armenian issue!" she shouted.

Meanwhile, on the sixth floor of Bunche, the academic temper was disintegrating. "Call off your attack dogs," a professor snapped at Richard, referring to the Armenian students who had been lobbying him. The movement inside and outside the university had generated sensational publicity for the Armenians of Los Angeles, but also proved to provoke something of a backlash from UCLA professors who resented the encroachment on their intellectual "independence," the word they preferred to *infallibility*.

Shortly after 1:00 p.m. on Friday, December 5, 1997, the last day of classes for the term, with the professors eager to leave for the winter vacation, Richard arched his eyebrows to a perfect scholarly disposition and began to speak. This was not a personal vendetta, he explained to his colleagues assembled in the conference room, though the plans for the chair had been drafted behind his back. As an Armenian, he was offended by a denialist campaign, but this was not an ethnic debate, either. The problem was that a foreign government—and a denialist government—was being allowed to buy influence in American academia.

Much discussion followed Richard's twenty-five-minute presentation. Several young professors publicly declared a change of mood, while many others rose to defend Shaw. At around three o'clock a secret ballot was called. The professors voted and the secretaries collected the ballots. They counted them. Then they counted them again. Hovannisian and Shaw waited nervously.

A few minutes later Richard emerged from the history conference room. Three Armenian students were waiting for him outside. "What happened, Professor?" they asked impatiently. Richard looked beat up. *"Dghak, offices egek,"* he said. "Boys, come to my office." He did not like that they had been lingering there. So the boys followed Richard to the end of the hall and into his office. The door closed behind them, and they stood before the professor. In that room, isolated from the world, lost in books and papers, Richard had written modern Armenian history, compiled a comprehensive oral history of the Genocide, and directed much of the diaspora's intellectual activities. Now his face came to life.

"We did it!" he exclaimed. "We did it!"

He drew his students into an embrace and told them the news, which was history: By a vote of eighteen to seventeen on the afternoon of December 5, 1997, as a genocide quietly raged in faraway Rwanda, UCLA rejected a million dollars from the Turkish government.

IN THE OPENING WEEKS OF 1998 a great snowstorm laid siege to Yerevan and painted its churches and theaters and monuments in a blinding coat of white. The snow disguised the city from itself; one could not tell an enemy from a friend. All alone in the presidential mansion, Levon Ter-Petrosyan feared that his end was coming. Since the Copenhagen conference of December 1997, where Armenian delegates had been less than adamant in defending Mountainous Karabagh's right to self-determination, the president's own cabinet had lost faith in him. Defense Minister Vazgen Sargsyan, Interior Minister Serge Sargsyan, and Prime Minister Robert Kocharyan—the latter two recruits from Mountainous Karabagh—had been among the top military leaders of the war of liberation.

By February 1998, when the snow began to melt from Yerevan to reveal a pink and gold city, Levon Ter-Petrosyan had announced his resignation. Prime Minister Robert Kocharyan was now the acting president, and he was here to declare the end of the "dark and cold years," the first seven years of independence. Kocharyan was not a demagogue. Small and balding and shy, he had neither the charisma nor the stature of his predecessor. He was simply in the right place with the right ideas: a strong foreign policy for Mountainous Karabagh and international recognition of the Armenian Genocide.

In March 1998, when Kocharyan invited him to return to Armenian politics, Raffi did not argue over designations. He made only one request of the president: citizenship. The president said yes and Raffi accepted command of the Department of Information and Publications. He would work, in the next two weeks, to create "a level information field" for all candidates in the upcoming special presidential elections. But this, Raffi came to understand, was not so easy. For the state media, which had just been broadcasting the propaganda of Levon Ter-Petrosyan, were now, whether by instruction or out of an old habit of power worship, doing the very same thing for Robert Kocharyan. The front-runner himself shared in the blame. He had no concept of democratic ethics; he did not understand, for example, why Raffi said he couldn't join him on the campaign trail. In

any case, on the eve of the election, Robert Kocharyan was not about
to deny himself the advantages enjoyed by every incumbent leader in
the history of man.

After two rounds of voting on March 16 and March 30, 1998, Robert Kocharyan was elected president of the Republic of Armenia. One
of his first public acts was to release the ARF leaders from prison and
to restore the party's good standing in Yerevan. Citizens rejoiced, but
Raffi was already frustrated; he needed to see the president. Apparently the head of state television, a power broker close to Kocharyan,
had sent to the Department of Information and Publications several
irregular requests for wire transfers. Raffi had not approved the
transfers, and he was here to tell the president that if such requests
continued, he would have to resign. Kocharyan's response stunned
Raffi. "You have understood the situation very well," he said, and he
accepted Raffi's resignation.

Kocharyan, however, would not repeat Ter-Petrosyan's mistake.
He would not banish from his government a man who was too often called the "only clean politician" in Armenia, if for no other reason then because, in the local parlance, his "eye was full"—that is,
he came from prominence and education, and he was not in politics
for the money. So Kocharyan made Raffi a second offer. The foreign
ministry was taken, he said; Vartan Oskanian, one of Raffi's recruits
who had survived so much turbulence at the ministry, had just been
appointed. But Raffi could have the All-Armenian Fund, a department on a strictly humanitarian mission to build water pipelines and
electricity plants, support educational and cultural programs, and
pave a highway through the Lachin corridor connecting Armenia
and Mountainous Karabagh.

With tenuous faith Raffi accepted the new post, and moved into
yet another government building: the ministry of goodwill. His first
problem was that, through the winter of Armenia's political transformation, the diaspora's confidence in the republic had frozen, and

along with the confidence millions of dollars in the international bank accounts of the All-Armenian Fund. It was Raffi's first goal and immediate success to effect a national defrosting and to schedule major fund-raisers in the diaspora. These fund-raisers had not yet taken place, however, when Soviet symptoms reappeared. This time the requests for wire transfers—$50,000 to this account, $100,000 to the other—were coming from the presidential office. This time there was no higher authority to which he could appeal.

From Los Angeles, Raffi's parents and brother Armen advised patience. "Hang in there and work," Armenouhi said. And Raffi did work, but he refused to authorize the transfers, jealously guarding his signature and reminding himself that history could not be unsigned. Raffi was still without his citizenship. The president was referring him to the interior minister, Serge Sargsyan, who was referring him back to the president. Meanwhile, requests for wire transfers were continuing to come in, and Raffi began to fear that some sinister financial scandal was being planned for him. And still Armenouhi said: "Hang in there and work."

But now Raffi had changed. His response astounded Armenouhi. *"Guzes kogheru hed ashkhadink?"* he said. "Do you want us to work with thieves?"

In the fall of 1998 Raffi left the All-Armenian Fund. It had taken him one year to fall out with the first president of Armenia and six months to grow disillusioned with the second. The problem was not with the presidents at all, and Raffi knew now what his romanticism had long prevented him from knowing. The Soviet Union had collapsed—that was a fact—but the Armenian people were condemned, at least for the time being, to live in its debris: to breathe in and out the poison powder of a destroyed experiment in brotherhood, power, and corruption.

"I HAVE TO SAY THAT there has been no conflict and no problem," President Kocharyan was saying on state television. "There were, perhaps, different views, different approaches." I studied the man on the screen. He looked down as he spoke, his head tilted to the right. He did this often, and many months had gone by before I discovered that he had a mole on his right cheek. This was surprising, because one usually thinks he knows the face of a president. "Different approaches," he said. That's why my father had resigned.

We had, by now, moved out of our apartment. My mother was pregnant again and my father hadn't the heart to watch her walk up those ten flights of stairs—a tortuous climb familiar to Supreme Court justice Antonin Scalia who, with his bad knee, once made it for a special family dinner. So my father found a house fifteen minutes up a hill, just within the bounds of Yerevan. The trouble was that it was much too big for my father's tastes, which were loyal not so much to his childhood training in economy but to a newer spirituality of populism he had acquired by serving as the politician of principle in Armenia. This is why he no longer felt comfortable in fancy cars and taxis and expensive suits, and he never kept a bodyguard, which was the ultimate symbol of political stature.

The house had three stories, and it came with a German shepherd named Boy, a swimming pool, a ping-pong table, a garden, and walls surrounding it, which was something else my father didn't like. But the truth was that the house was not as big as he thought; we were, after all, five children. Armen Richard Hovannisian had appeared on the roster in November 1996. He was the only one of us not named for a city. But the concluding symbolism—the completion of Armenia— was obvious, and I knew then that my parents were finished having children. So my mother hadn't kept her promise, but the joke would be that five out of seven wasn't so bad.

The house had exactly one thing that worked for my father. The television room on the top floor opened up to a balcony, and from there he could see everything he wanted from life. Yerevan shone before him—"a sun-like city," the great Armenian poet Yeghishe Charents had called it. From its golden source at Republic Square, bright avenues beamed out to the opera house, the city reservoir, the soccer stadium, countless churches and monuments. To the right stood Mount Aragats and to the left the view that sold the house: the lesser and greater peaks of Mount Ararat. They would always be there for him, gigantic and omnipresent, as if they were part of the city—so incredibly close yet decisively on the other side of the closed border of Armenia and Turkey.

"Inchpes anhas parki champa / Es im Masis sarn em sirum." Raffi remembered the words of Charents. "Like the road to unreachable glory / I love my mountain Ararat."

I was almost a teenager, enjoying my final years in Armenia before I was sent to Los Angeles for high school and college, and spending my spare time on the streets of our hillside neighborhood. At five o'clock every day, the sun withdrawing, I would leave home and begin my walk along 15th Street, which was not really a street but rather a narrow asphalt pathway of bumps and potholes, lined on both sides by feeble stone-and-tin houses. Already our neighbors would have taken their seats on overturned Coca-Cola cases in front of their homes, chewing on sunflower seeds and peering into cups of Armenian coffee. I would yell out a *barev* in my best Eastern Armenian, because it was said that *barevn Asttsun e*, that greetings are for God, and even sworn enemies said *barev* to each other.

There were several sworn enemies in our neighborhood and a full ledger of unpaid debts, scandals, superstitions, suspicions, and betrayals. That was the price the men and women of 15th Street paid for being so close to one another, for the assurance that even though they were not employed they would never go hungry. I came to understand this Armenia through my friends, four boys of fifteen or sixteen years who had just finished school and were waiting, simply killing their days until they turned eighteen, when they would be drafted into two years of service in the army. I was not part of their world, but an honorary membership was issued to me, for many of those boys were kind and many others knew about my family.

Their world was a complete fiction, plagiarized from an old Soviet criminal culture in which men protected their neighborhoods, and *namus*, honor, was their most important virtue. Any slight to a man's honor—an awkward glance was enough—would lead to a confrontation or, more formally, a *bazaar*, where two groups of boys would meet to wage a verbal war. The *bazaar*, like any ordinary game of strategy, had its special tactics and traps and rules; if you took out a knife, for instance, you had to use it. To say these boys lacked refinement would not be enough, not even close, so I was surprised to see how delicately they could maneuver in and out of the most complex arguments, to defend the honor of their friend. That was what impressed me most: unconditional friendship.

This meant that my friends became devotees to me and my father's mission in the fatherland, but I knew always that they were, in manner and spirit, closer to my father's adversaries. The new government in Yerevan was linked to a group of powerful businessmen called "oligarchs," miniature versions of the power tycoons in Moscow, who invested in and ended up running the political game. One of them had the monopoly on gas, another the monopoly on sugar and flour, and all of them had nicknames, armies of bodyguards, and fleets of luxury cars escorting them ostentatiously through the city. These men commanded at once the fear, the loathing, and the respect of the Armenian people. I learned that lesson early on: the post-Soviet peoples were in total awe of powerful men.

Suddenly I realized that my family was very far from the breezy beaches of the Pacific Ocean. We were in a strange city of loyal neighbors, unlocked doors, mulberry and apricot trees, greed, jealousy, friendship, connections, vast wealth, and abject poverty—a city where people still had faith but were losing it, where the very men who had gained independence were abusing its lessons, where the memory of April 24, 1915, and the yearning for September 21, 1991, seemed to have vaporized, where Armenians were reverting to old ways, where the clean diasporan dream of a home free and complete, which had been deferred for decades, was exploding at last.

IN THE SUMMER OF 1998 Richard and his daughter, my aunt Ani, traveled for the first time to the Syrian deserts of Der Zor, the final destination of the Armenian caravans that had been led out of the Western Armenian homeland in 1915. Richard committed his memories to print:

> We now entered a wasteland, the image of the boundless desert that the name Der Zor has always conjured up. But this was not the desert of the Sahara. There were no blowing sands or shifting dunes, rather a hard, dry, baked land with occasional small patches of yellow or brown scrub grass. It is said that the deportee mothers taught their children the Armenian letters on the burning sands—but here, at least, no one could write on this hostile and unyielding surface.
>
> A hundred kilometers of envisioning thousands upon thousands of deportees moving slowly and aimlessly in this vast wilderness. It was a relief to come to the large city of Deir-el-Zor through which the green waters of the Euphrates River pass, headed for nearby Iraq and an eventual rendezvous with the Tigris River. . . .
>
> A candle, a chant, a prayer—and an imagination on the loose; the coolness and solitude shielding us from the sweltering reality above.
>
> Sweet watermelon, string cheese, lavash bread, local delicacies, Arabic coffee, before setting out again, now with the youthful priest, for an hour's ride northward in the direction of al-Hasakah and the Turkish frontier. The temperature at noon

soars to 58 degrees Centigrade (136 degrees Fahrenheit). In recent years, while the road was being widened at a village called Marka-deh, the hillside yielded up thousands of human bones—Armenian bones. This was apparently the scene of one of the several wholesale massacres in 1916 of those poor beings who somehow had managed to straggle all the way to the deserts of Deir-el-Zor from as far away as Erzerum (Garin). . . .

The government had granted 100 square meters of land to the Syrian Armenian community to build—not a memorial monument—but specifically a chapel on the site. It was consecrated as Holy Resurrection (Surp Harutiun) to signify not only the crucifixion but also the revival of the Armenian people. It was here that Ani and I had our most intimate and disturbing encounter with Der Zor.

The local village children, walking barefoot on the red hot ground and softened asphalt, quickly beckoned the long-robed Arab caretaker, who unlocked the chapel for yet another chant and another prayer. He then led us to the adjoining steep hill, dotted with the remains of small dugouts and shelters. At the very base of the hill, where bulldozers had pulverized the soil, my hand passed through the hot dirt and immediately brought forth fragments of human bones. The discovery was troubling yet strangely compelling at the same time. But then as we ascended the hill, our guide turned over stones and poked into the caves where much larger bone fragments appeared. He thrust them into Ani's hands, with the invitation to take them along. After all, every visitor here takes back a few bones as stark evidence of the colossal crime and as a remembrance of a personal pilgrimage.

Most of the bones we returned to the earth, but a few fragments we carried away from that place—haunted now by the searing questions of: Who are you? What did you look like in the flesh? From whom have we separated you? Have we disturbed

and desecrated a hallowed ground? And are we furthering the deniers' cause by removing piece by piece, fragment by fragment,
the physical evidence of the murder of a nation?

We no longer felt the withering heat—it was only right that the
sun should bear down on us mercilessly for a few hours, if only in
token symbolism of the days, months, and years that it tormented
the tormented—until they turned into dry bones.

ON THE EVENING OF OCTOBER 27, 1999, Raffi was on the balcony,
watching over Ararat, when he was summoned to the telephone in
his bedroom. It was the director of his research center, and Raffi assumed there were some outstanding questions about the planned
fifth-anniversary celebration of ACNIS. During the past few years
Raffi had built up the research center and slowly left it to its own
momentum. This is what he had done all his life, with the college Armenian clubs, the Armenian Bar Association, the ministry, his children: he breathed life into things, then retired to watch them flourish
without their founder. There was a private deistic pride in that logic,
and Raffi's devotees respected that. Only for consultations would he
be called, or else to receive some very catastrophic news.

The director was not calling for a consultation. A few hours earlier,
he said, five men in overcoats had walked through the gates of parliament on Baghramyan Boulevard. Whether they had been expected
or not was anyone's guess, but the men had not been screened or in-
terrogated by the security guards stationed there. They had crossed
the garden and ascended the steps of the majestic golden building, the
old headquarters of the Armenian Communist Party. Once inside
the main chamber, the men had reached into their overcoats and
produced Kalashnikov rifles. "We have come to avenge those who
have drunk the blood of our nation!" one of them had yelled.

Prime Minister Vazgen Sargsyan, Speaker of Parliament Karen

Demirchyan, Deputy Speaker Yuri Bakhshyan, and five other political leaders were killed.

On the morning of October 30 at Liberty Square, the courtyard of the opera house where once a democracy movement had erupted, seven caskets lay side by side. Tens of thousands of Armenians lined up to pay their final tributes to the murdered men and then to carry them to different cemeteries about the city. Most people followed Vazgen Sargsyan to Yerablur, the memorial park of military heroes, and Karen Demirchyan to the Komitas Pantheon, the resting place of Komitas, William Saroyan, Aram Khachaturian, Sergei Parajanov, and the giants of Armenian culture. Raffi and Armenouhi accompanied Yuri Bakhshyan to the city cemetery. His widow, the school principal Anahit Bakhshyan, was Armenouhi's friend.

For weeks the Armenians mourned in silence, but from their grief a startling theory began to evolve. The assassinations had been pinned on the terrorist leader, an ex-journalist named Nairi Hunanyan, but the public was not satisfied. The fact was that Prime Minister Sargsyan and Speaker Demirchyan had recently created in parliament an alliance for democratic reform, and they were the only men who commanded the resources and popularity to challenge the president one day. Of course, there was no actual evidence that Robert Kocharyan was complicit in this monstrous crime against the Armenian people, but it was clear that he emerged from the bloodbath with absolute power.

WHERE WAS HE?

Wearing shorts and an old T-shirt, Raffi was standing at the edge of the balcony, smoking a cigar. From this distant height, Yerevan appeared to be a miniature city—a different city from the one he had found ten years earlier. He had belonged to it then. Everything had been possible.

Now the oligarchs were in town, and every third-rate thug had a seat in the republic's parliament. Politics were funded by business, and business was protected by politics. The president had in his pocket every judge, prosecutor, and village mayor who wanted to keep his job. The rulers were multimillionaires, the lot of them, though they had incurred great debts to Moscow, to which they were rapidly selling the country's gold mines and electricity plants. They might have seemed powerful to their own people, but the Armenian rulers were actually mere vassals of the post-Soviet oligarchs surrounding the Kremlin, which had been transferred, after Boris Yeltsin's unexpected resignation in December 1999, to Vladimir Putin.

Armenian bones baked in Syrian deserts and Armenians still living defiled the national heritage, but somehow—nobody in the family quite understood how—Raffi's redemptive faith did not yield. It was almost as if he kept it in a special chamber of his heart, where nothing could complicate it or seduce it into the real world. Or perhaps it was that steep view of Mount Ararat, the behemoth next to the tiny city, that reminded Raffi always where he had come from and what he was doing on earth. Looking upon those mountains, an imperishable wonder in his eyes, he often recalled the poem of Avetik Isahakyan:

On the ancient peaks of Ararat
The century has come like a second,
And passed on.
The swords of innumerable lightnings
Have descended upon its diamond crest,
And passed on.
The eyes of generations dreading death
Have touched its luminous summit,
And passed on.
The turn is now yours for a moment.

You, too, look at its lofty brow,

And pass on. . .

This was Raffi's moment before Ararat. Disillusioned by the Armenian government but never disabused of the national creed, Raffi quietly carried on with his work. It was remarkable how unshaken he was. In February 2000, when the remains of General Antranig were unearthed from the Père Lachaise Cemetery in Paris and returned to Armenia, Raffi addressed the television camera with these words:

> With Antranig we welcome home also his disciples and soldiers, among them my grandfather Kaspar, who served in Antranig's first regiment. With their return, we rededicate our will and devotion to our state, our people, and to the fortification and integrity of our fatherland.

As Armenians were lining up at the embassies of the United States, Russia, France, Canada, and the United Kingdom to leave their decaying homeland, Raffi and Armenouhi were fortifying their lives in Yerevan. In April they opened a small children's center called Orran, meaning "cradle" or "haven"; on the streets of the capital a generation of starving child beggars had surfaced, and Armenouhi had made it her personal mission to return the children to decent lives. In a small apartment down the street from Raffi's research center, sixteen boys and girls daily gathered for meals, tutoring, therapy, and play.

Raffi and Armenouhi had chosen to stay in Armenia and to face the problems of contemporary humanity—the democratization of government and the welfare of society marked their division of labor—while the problems of the past, hidden on the other side of the mountain, threatened to die unresolved. In June 2000, Raffi's living link to the experience of the old Armenian homeland expired. Mami Khenguhi was laid to rest in Fresno, beside Babi Hovagim.

•   •   •

Raffi's many applications for citizenship were still floating about the bureaucracies of state, but none of them so far had landed on the desk of an official who had the authority or the courage to accept it once and for all. Russian and African athletes recruited by Armenia in Olympic seasons were issued citizenship overnight; Raffi had been kept in an empty line for nine years. But Raffi waited. And in the tenth year of his application, he was informed that his papers were ready. All that remained was for him to give up his United States citizenship.

The family had uniformly opposed the idea, so Raffi told no one except Armenouhi what he was about to do. Emerging from a sleepless night into the cool morning of April 23, 2001, Raffi showered, shaved, and put on a suit. Before the mirror in his bedroom, he combed his graying hair and mustache. Then he opened the top drawer of the dresser and retrieved his blue passport. Outside, his driver was waiting for him. In a boxy beige Zhiguli, they descended the hill toward the city center. On the way they picked up the two witnesses that would be required: Zori Balayan, a popular Armenian journalist, and Mesrob Ashjian, the gentle archbishop who had married Raffi and Armenouhi in Fresno.

The three men were dropped off at 18 Baghramyan Boulevard, a small gray building with a circular window opening toward the street—the most famous window of the entire republic. Vice Consul Gregory Morrison greeted Raffi outside. "You see these people?" he said, looking down the endless line of Armenians. "These are your people. All of them want to come to the United States." Raffi smiled. He followed the American inside. In the frame hanging on the wall of the embassy, George W. Bush had recently replaced Bill Clinton. Raffi was quiet through much of the briefing and the paperwork, though he did emerge from his silence to inquire if anybody had done this before him. The answer was no.

"You understand that once you give up your citizenship, you can never reclaim it?" Morrison asked, sliding the document toward Raffi. The vice consul, the journalist, the archbishop—they were all moved by the tragic beauty of this ceremony.

"Yes," Raffi said.

Raffi read the conditions of renunciation: "I hereby absolutely and entirely, without mental reservation, coercion or duress, renounce my United States nationality together with all rights and privileges and all duties of allegiance and fidelity thereunto pertaining." The embassy of the United States in Yerevan was silent when Raffi took his blue pen to the line beneath the print. He wrote his initials in clean Armenian cursive, but his hand did not stop where it was supposed to. In his decisive last gesture as a United States citizen, Raffi returned the pen to the beginning of the signature and encircled what he had just written: RKH.

The irreversible act was done, and now the vice consul asked if, for the record, Raffi wished to attach a written explanation. He did— just one sentence:

I am compelled to do so for the sole purpose of advancing the standards of liberty, democracy, and rule of law in the Republic of Armenia and in the absence there of a legal provision for dual citizenship.

Chapter Ten

THE ROAD TO
UNREACHABLE GLORY

On the morning of April 24, 2001, Raffi K. Hovannisian was a citizen of no country—a ghost in a suit, white roses clasped in his hands. On that day every year, the Armenians of Yerevan embarked together on a public pilgrimage to Tsitsernakaberd, the Fortress of Swallows, which was a monument and a flame at the top of a hill by the Hrazdan River. Perhaps they were meant to imagine the ancient ascent to Golgotha, but the Armenians were in possession of a more recent narrative of suffering. As he climbed toward the monument, Raffi imagined himself in 1915, among Kaspar, Hovagim, Khenguhi, and the caravans leaving the villages of Western Armenia for the deserts of a planned extinction.

At the top of the hill the cameras were waiting for Raffi; he had been spotted the previous morning at the embassy of the United States. Standing beside the stele that soared and sharpened into a clear sky, Raffi confirmed the rumors. "I expect that I will receive Armenian citizenship immediately," he said, "and that the president will secure for me a level field of public activity and safety." But what exactly did Raffi mean? Was he considering a return to national politics? Raffi would not answer directly—not today, not by this monument. "Proper Armenian politics are still in the future," he said. His face was careful not to smile.

The truth was that Raffi was already engaging the fantasies of a political comeback—fantasies that were only aggravated in the following months by Robert Kocharyan's refusal to sign the papers of his Armenian citizenship. The president had decided to punish Raffi, to keep him stateless and without a passport, and so unable to attend in July the unpredicted funeral of Uncle Ralph in Fresno. Only weeks later, when the scandal of the president's dishonor surfaced in the opposition newspapers, was a document of citizenship signed.

That September the World Trade Center fell in New York City and the great battle lines of a new century were drawn in the dust. But in their homeland, cut off from the Western world by the closed border with Turkey, Armenians were confronting their own problems. On October 27, 2001, two years after the assassinations in parliament, thousands in Yerevan were rallying for the removal of Robert Kocharyan. The president had fallen out of favor and out of grace. He refused to cross himself in church, and by now everyone knew about it. On national television, when the Catholicos of All Armenians had extended a crucifix to presidential lips, Kocharyan had turned his head forcefully. In a nation that prided itself on being the first to officially accept Christianity in A.D. 301, this was sacrilege.

But the president had outgrown his dependence on the popular will. The ideological support of the Armenian Revolutionary Federation, the allegiance of the Republican Party, the patronage of the oligarchs, the blessings of President Vladimir Putin—they were all his. Soon his government would shut down A1+, the country's only opposition television channel, and Kocharyan's power over the Armenian mind would be complete. It was against this backdrop in December 2001 that Raffi launched the National Citizens' Initiative, a nonprofit organization aimed at accomplishing a democratic reawakening in Yerevan, and released, through his research center, two landmark publications: a daily newspaper called *Orran*, the first attempt at objective journalism in the republic, and a monthly magazine called *Hayatsk Yerevanits*, or *View from Yerevan*, the first journal of politics and culture.

Only so much could be achieved within the boundaries of civil society, however. One had to get dirty if he wanted to move mountains—and Raffi did. In 2002 he founded Heritage. "A national-liberal party," he called it, though that sounded ridiculous in a land where a patriotic foreign policy had never before been paired with the principles of classical liberal economics. But that was Heritage, a collection of conflicting minds—nationalists disenchanted with Robert Kocharyan and liberals disenchanted with Levon Ter-Petrosyan. They were teachers, doctors, professors, lawyers, and musicians; only out of necessity had they taken the night shift as politicians.

With the support of Siroon Hovannisian and Kirk Kerkorian's charitable foundation, ACNIS had moved by 2002 into a three-story building off Baghramyan Boulevard. This had opened up Raffi's offices on the backside of the Armenia Hotel, and Heritage had moved in. It was there, on the site of the original Armenian parliament of 1918, that the founding members of the party met in the fall of 2002 to make their first major decision. In the upcoming presidential elections, Heritage would nominate Raffi K. Hovannisian.

ON JANUARY 8, 2003, SIX weeks before Election Day, a hundred Armenians crowded into a cold room with wooden chairs and a fading Armenian flag. No one would have imagined that this was a courtroom, except that a man with gray hair and a black robe was now tapping his pen on his desk to announce the opening of trial. The questions were simple. First, had Raffi Hovannisian illegally been denied Armenian citizenship from the date of his original application? Second, did Raffi Hovannisian have a valid claim to retroactive citizenship beginning in 1991? Third, did Raffi Hovannisian fulfill, therefore, the ten-year citizenship requirement to stand for president?

From the back of the room, Raffi and Vartiter examined the spectacle: the severe judge, the cheering fans, the journalists, and then the fifteen muscular men who seemed to have been cast in the wrong film. Raffi recognized them. They were the men of the Armenian national wrestling and boxing teams, but today they had been called out of their gyms to perform a special service for the president. They sat in the front row, all of them wearing black, their eyes shifty and frightening.

Having made her way to the front of the room, Vartiter now stood politely before the wrestlers. "May I have a seat?" she asked. The wrestlers laughed at the sight of this small, graying woman. They knew who she was, but they did not know what she was capable of. "Go away," they said. And here, as the people watched, Vartiter flashed her remarkable smile, which was more like a wound on her face. "No matter," she said, eyeing an especially massive wrestler. "He, too, is my son." And then she sat on his lap.

The man squirmed violently as his teammates laughed at him. They were not trained for this situation.

The judge was tense, the crowd boisterous. The lawyers were yelling at each other, and the judge was tapping his pen against the desk. He was interjecting constantly, getting personal, even questioning the existence of Raffi's applications for citizenship. The illusion of justice was disintegrating, and a verdict was imminent. The judge called a fifteen-minute recess. He said that he had forgotten a document in his chambers, but the Armenians knew what that meant: he needed to make a phone call.

During the break, Raffi walked about the room. He shook hands one by one—that was what he did everywhere—and thanked his supporters for such a wonderful showing. He approached the wrestlers, too. That was something else he did, greet his adversaries. There was pride and poetry in that. He shook their hands and offered them a few words. "You're obviously free to do what you want," he said, "but maybe instead of intimidating your own people, you should be at practice." And of course the men were not trained for this situation, either. They merely listened as Raffi told them that one day they would raise the Armenian flag and bring glory to the Armenian people.

Soon the judge returned. He held a piece of paper in his hand, and whispers fluttered across the room. The paper was blank.

THEIR CANDIDATE DISQUALIFIED FROM THE presidential race, the leaders of Heritage met in January 2003 to explore the opposition field and issue an endorsement. Stepan Demirchyan was the major contender. He was the son of Kocharyan's 1998 challenger, the late Karen Demirchyan, and he was trailed by a long list of candidates including Vazgen Manukyan, Levon Ter-Petrosyan's 1996 challenger, and Aram Sargsyan, the brother of the slain prime minister Vazgen Sargsyan. They were all honorable men, but each of them appeared to carry complexes of entitlement or revenge, and it was not always clear who was in the race for the right reasons.

In the end, Heritage endorsed Stepan Demirchyan, helping him to achieve, on Election Day, 28 percent of the vote and a spot in the second-round runoff against Robert Kocharyan. Demirchyan was not an obvious president. He did not have the intellectual experience of Manukyan, the oratorical skills of Sargsyan, or the moral authority of Hovannisian, but from February to March 2003 he had their support. As a war coalition led by the United States was preparing to invade Saddam Hussein's Iraq and the part-Armenian tennis champion Andre Agassi was battling for his eighth Grand Slam title, the leaders of the Armenian opposition in Yerevan were also agitating. Before enormous crowds, they were sharing the microphone and the people were chanting their names.

The totalitarian machine triumphed. In the aftermath of a routine election marred by ballot stuffing and violence, Kocharyan collected 67 percent of the vote and a second term as president of the Republic of Armenia. Meanwhile, Stepan Demirchyan stood before a demonstration of a hundred thousand citizens and told his people to go home and wait for the next election.

IN FRESNO, GRANDMA SIROON WAS saying strange things. "What are you doing over there?" she was asking Raffi. "I heard they're giving you problems." Siroon was sitting on the golden sofa in the piano parlor, surrounded by yarn and playing cards in the dark house she once had shared with Kaspar. She had long ago learned to live without her husband; she was almost ninety-five years old, her matriarchal mission fulfilled and made official by a Mother of the Year Award from the City of Fresno. She was strong and ready in her faith, a constant pilgrim and matron of the Holy Trinity Armenian Apostolic Church. But her health was fast deteriorating, and the death of her second son had destroyed her spirits once and for all.

"I heard you're not popular anymore," Grandma Siroon was saying to Raffi.

From unprecedented return and proud beginnings at the foreign ministry in 1991, Raffi had enjoyed all measures of devotion from his family. Uncle Ralph and Cousin David, especially, had invested serious money in Raffi's research institution and Armenouhi's center for children and the elderly. Ralph junior and the full company of cousins had come through on important days. But for the first time Grandma, the supreme authority, was casting her royal doubt on the fundamental decisions of her grandson's life. Had Raffi chosen the losing side of the struggle in Armenia? Had he been wrong to return? Had Mami Khenguhi been right to predict, so many years ago, that the Soviet Armenians would eat Raffi's head?

It was curious to consider where Raffi might have ended up. He had been the undisputed leader of his old friends, and by now all of his friends were facing middle age with power and wealth. Zaven Sinanian and Greg Keosian had been appointed to the judicial bench in California. Ruben Keoseyan had been hired as the executive editor of *La Opinión*, the largest Spanish-language daily in the United States. Raffi's pals, second- and third-generation Americans, were now doctors, poets, actors, and businessmen. His brothers, Armen and Garo, were thriving lawyers, and his sister, Ani, was always in demand as a producer of television shows and documentaries.

As to what his generation could expect one day to become, Raffi had only to look to his father's contemporaries, first- and second-generation Americans, who had been appointed to federal benches, elected to the United States Congress, named professors, and earned millions in business and real estate. They had won Oscars and Presidential Awards for Freedom and made the bestseller lists. Vartan Gregorian, the young man who had struggled to teach Armenian to Richard at the Jemaran in Beirut, had served as the president of the New York Public Library, Brown University, and the Carnegie Corporation. Those who had stayed loyal to the American dream had been rewarded by it.

But Raffi had interpreted the American dream in his own way. He had refused the conventional glories. And as his reward, he had become, in some faraway land, a chanted name of an impoverished opposition.

ONE BY ONE SIROON'S GRANDCHILDREN and great-grandchildren approached the open casket. Some of them cried. A few whispered parting secrets in her ear and left quietly. Her surviving sons came last: John, Richard, and Vernon. I had never seen my grandfather the way he was that day. He staggered toward the casket and kneeled before his mother. He put his hand to hers, as he had done sixty years earlier, when mother and son would do the Monday wash together. After a few minutes he stood up and turned around, and for the first time I saw my grandfather's tears. From the back of the room I moved to embrace him. But our arms interlocked awkwardly. They had never been able to communicate well.

In October 2005 Siroon Hovannisian was laid to rest alongside Soghomon Tehlirian, Hovagim and Khenguhi Kotcholosian, and thousands of Western Armenian refugees in the Masis section of the Ararat Cemetery in Fresno. She was buried next to Kaspar Hovannisian, and she would share his epitaph: "If such great wrongs our sons forget . . ."

IN EARLY NOVEMBER A THOUSAND Armenians packed into two lecture halls at the Court of Sciences at the University of California, Los Angeles. The professor was pleased by the turnout—his conferences typically drew a crowd of three or four hundred—but he was not, a few weeks after the death of his mother, quite ready for the show. The special event had attracted every possible element of the Armenian community of Los Angeles—founded by the survivors of the Turkish massacres in 1915, but subsequently replenished by Armenian refugees who had fled Germany and Russia in the 1940s, the civil war of Lebanon in the 1970s, the Islamic Revolution of Iran in 1979, and the independence of Armenia in 1991. How depressing it was that by the break of the new millennium most Armenians in Los Angeles were refugees not of foreign terror but of their own national independence.

Only the Genocide could command the attention of this complicated diaspora. Now, for the first time in the United States, three Turkish professors would talk about it. Not all of them used the word *genocide*, but the professors had studied the events of 1915 and concluded, within the framework of their own fields—sociology, history, and literature—that they amounted to something total and catastrophic. Suffice it to say that Fatma Müge Göçek, Taner Akçam, and Elif Şafak were not heroes for the Republic of Turkey. Akçam, who had publicized self-incriminating documents kept by Turkey in its state archives, and Şafak, who had woven her novels with infidel thoughts, would soon be prosecuted in Turkey for "insulting Turkishness," a violation of Article 301 of its criminal code.

Sometimes history happens and nobody knows it. But sitting in that auditorium of disparate Armenians, I knew that a movement was beginning. Finally, an alliance of Armenian and Turkish intellectuals was preparing to confront the original sin of modern history.

"THE ARMENIAN PEOPLE'S MARATHON OF freedom does not start here at this hour, but comes to us from a rich, brave, and complete legacy of struggle." With those words Raffi opened on the afternoon of November 25, 2005, a continuous rally, sleep-in, celebration, and hunger strike in Yerevan—a popular boycott of the upcoming referendum that had been proposed by President Robert Kocharyan. The new constitution had its share of defects—the invention of a new presidential privilege, for example, to declare emergency rule—but Raffi did not lose himself in details. For the next three days at Liberty Square, he presided over a comprehensive protest against the government, Armenia's first movement of civil disobedience.

The OSCE was not even invited to observe the vote on November 27, so the authorities had no need for humility: turnout was pegged at 65 percent, to match that of the presidential races, and the constitution passed with an affirmative vote of 95 percent. The airwaves were free of scandal, but a hundred thousand Armenians needed only to follow their wrath and instinct to Liberty Square and the Matenadaran. At the top of the hill, the leaders of the opposition were once again standing by Raffi, and together they were inciting public sentiments. But something was different about Raffi. The people never before had seen such pure loathing reflected in his eyes or heard such violence in his voice. Raffi had never been so frightening as he was now, and he was looking not to his people but directly at the video camera of the state television. He peered straight into its lens, at the president beyond, and roared:

> From this moment on we reject your sermons on democratic principles. . . . The presidency of Mountainous Karabagh, and its independence, you turned into frauds. Our centuries-long national dream, our yearning, the creed of our national unity, you tried to turn into frauds. The Armenian laws and rights you turned into frauds. All elections, local and national, you turned into frauds. The branches of government—executive, legislative, judicial— you turned into frauds. The presidency of the Republic of Armenia, by your own behavior, disposition, deed, and example, you turned into a fraud. You have turned yourselves into frauds. But we, standing together, the people united, and those who will come tomorrow and the day after and eternally, will not allow you to turn our homeland, Armenia, into a fraud.

The state television cameraman kneeled sweating, and the citizens stood in disbelief, as if they had just witnessed a miracle of metamorphosis—a diplomat turned into a public prosecutor. Amid whistling and applause, a chant was reborn—"Raf-fi! Raf-fi! Raf-fi!"— but Raffi could not bear to hear his name. He felt the slippery winter earth under him. He remembered that once upon a time he had been among that crowd, an anonymous diasporan lawyer with a video camera in his hands. He knew that these very same people at this very place had chanted "Levon!" and then "Robert!" and would continue to chant the names of different men. Raffi did not want to be one of them. His voice thundered above the people: *"Hayastan!*

Hayastan! Hayastan!" And soon everybody was chanting together that single word, so simple that it was almost embarrassing: "Armenia! Armenia! Armenia!"

ON WEDNESDAY, NOVEMBER 30, 2005, Raffi was dropped off at Zvartnots International Airport in Yerevan. Clothes and papers stuffed into his black bag, he checked in at the Austrian Airlines counter and passed easily through security. On the other side of the X-ray machines he was stopped. The agent from the National Security Service, formerly the KGB, asked Raffi to open his bag. He found the document of interest. It was a version of the constitution, the one Heritage had drafted as an alternative to the presidential version just passed.

"What is this?" the agent asked, continuing the search. "Where are you taking this?" He knew that Raffi was headed to Kiev, Ukraine, where he would meet with Czech president Vaclav Havel and United States senator John McCain.

But the agent now discovered a second document, a single sheet of paper, and he was mortified. He examined it for a moment, absorbing its simple and shocking words. He called another agent, this one from customs, and whispered something to him. Raffi looked nervously at the gate. No one was there; the plane was boarded. The agents glanced helplessly at each other, and Raffi decided to relieve them of their dilemma. He took the paper from the agents and tore it to pieces. "They are all in my head," Raffi said. "When I am ready, I will make them public." He buckled his bag and rushed toward the gate.

A voice followed him. *"Menk eli ktesnvenk.* We shall meet again."

ON DECEMBER 9, 2005, RAFFI was at the top of the hill, peering upon the Armenians. He retrieved a document from his coat pocket and held it out near the microphone. He began: "To Acting President Robert Kocharyan from Citizen R. K. Hovannisian." As Raffi read the letter to the public, his words were trailed by furious breaths of winter frost.

> Do you consider Armenia an independent, sovereign republic?
>
> Do you consider Mountainous Karabagh an independent, sovereign republic?
>
> Of which country or countries are you a citizen?
>
> Does the answer to the previous question have anything to do with your decision to leave Mountainous Karabagh and come to Yerevan?
>
> During your tenure in the government of Mountainous Karabagh and Armenia, outside of the actions of war, have you killed anyone, or caused his murder, or have known about his murder, or have witnessed his murder?

The Armenians cheered and whistled through the reading. There were twenty-one questions in all, but to those men and women who first heard them on the hill of the Matenadaran, they were not questions. Raffi was confronting Robert Kocharyan with a final record of accusations: murder, theft, and a forgery of the national will. At the end, lifting his eyes from the letter, Raffi spoke to the president directly: "If you have any will left in you, if you are a man, come alone. Come without arms and answer my people's questions." Then Raffi descended the hill. Followed by a thousand chants of *"Hayastan!"* he walked down to Baghramyan Boulevard and laid down his questions at the closed gates of the Armenian presidency.

In the days that followed, thousands of citizens, intellectuals, politicians, and artists signed under Raffi's impudent words, while the presidential spokesman declared, in his official capacity, that Hovannisian's letter "might be a secret code written by a professional spy."

In rain and snow, public rallies continued. Raffi soaked proudly, his shout resonating through a sadistic winter: "There is no question without answer, no secret that will not be known."

The authorities waited for the New Year to answer Raffi's twenty-one questions. In February 2006, in its prime-time news broadcast, state television accused Armenouhi of using American money to sponsor Raffi's rallies in Yerevan. The director of state television, whose request for wire transfers Raffi had years ago denied at the Department of Information and Publications, personally appeared to defend the broadcast. He said that he had presented only 30 percent of the information he had on Raffi.

Each visit to Zvartnots International Airport, meanwhile, became a comedy of inquisition. The customs officials were searching for en-crypted messages not only in Raffi's papers but now in the school notebooks and textbooks of his children. On one occasion, having received a paper cut from Shushi's Armenian history textbook, an agent awkwardly held out his bleeding finger as Raffi wrapped it with a Band-Aid. They grinned at each other—an apology and an absolution—and carried on with their lives.

Until Raffi's recent crash into Armenian politics, the presidency had viewed the republic's first foreign minister as a generally harm-less figure, a personification of principled opposition who had always embarrassed but never really threatened them. But Raffi was finally emancipated from the conventions of Western etiquette. He was dan-gerous now. He had citizenship, a party, and an unpredictable temper. So in March 2006 the authorities locked down, without judicial sanc-tion, the headquarters of the Heritage Party. A few days later, shortly after midnight of March 8, unidentified agents entered the building and, after cracking the main computer's password, extracted data on the party's membership and planned activities.

Neither the police nor the prosecutor's office carried out a thor-ough investigation. They conspired, instead, to terrorize Heritage into extinction. Across the republic, regional party leaders were threatened and blackmailed, while rank-and-file members suffered sudden unemployment. A team of spies was assigned by the National Security Service to follow Raffi's movements. And the television stations, public and private, were ordered not to broadast news or images associated with the Hovannisian family. There was no official announcement, but it was clear that the Armenian government had identified its public enemy number one.

AT THE BRUSSELS FORUM, THE annual conference of the international political elite, an untitled former something of Armenia was carrying on as if he were the president himself. In April 2006 Raffi was making advances toward prime ministers and presidents, and filling their ears with fighting words: *genocide, dispossession, self-determination.* There was one man in particular Raffi wanted to talk to. He recognized the white hair at the other end of the reception hall and gravitated toward it.

"Senator!" he shouted, as if to an old friend.

John McCain smiled warmly through the end of Raffi's confusing introduction. "We love Armenia," he said. "But that Karabagh—what a horrible place! You guys gotta do something about that." Montenegro and Kosovo were campaigning for independence, and the world's leaders were in a panic.

"That's our land of liberty!" Raffi hit back. "We have to get you some good information!"

Raffi was not about to let this one go. It was moments like this, he knew, on which whole histories had turned. He lived for them. And so, as champagne glasses clanked around him, Raffi went to work. He explained to the senator that Mountainous Karabagh had been the crown jewel of the Armenian homeland from time immemorial; it had been confiscated and transferred to Soviet Azerbaijan only in the twentieth century, and this by none other than the bloodiest of all Communist dictators. He knew how to tickle his colleague.

"But don't say it's a horrible place," Raffi told McCain. "Some people a few hundred years ago talked about the United States as a horrible place."

So what if he wasn't the president or even the foreign minister? For the past fifteen years Raffi had been running a private, one-man ministry of dreams, ceaselessly promoting at European summits the independence of Mountainous Karabagh, the international recognition of the Armenian Genocide, and a historic solution to the Armenian-Turkish crisis. The bullying in Yerevan had not frightened Raffi off his path.

Quietly, though, my father was hurting. Sometimes for weeks, he would not leave the house. Never a steady sleeper, he would rise frequently in the dark to visit the computer, where the Armenian websites were being refreshed with the latest gossip surrounding his whereabouts. The warm days he would spend on the balcony and the cold days in the bedroom, half asleep on a bed full of papers, his eyes closed and looking inward to old fantasies and ambitions, eroded in time. For a half hour Shushi might come in for an after-school chat, or Armen, the youngest, might charge in for a quick game of backgammon. But soon they would leave, and Raffi would return to his solitude.

When it occurred to me that my father no longer had any true friends beyond family, I was filled with pure pity for him—and this was such a strange feeling to have about the commanding figure of my life. He deserved to be understood, I thought, and more than just once or twice a year, when his brother Armen joined him on the balcony, or his cousin David, or a long-lost pal. But even with the closest people, my father seemed never to confess or confide or put his soul out to dry, as I did with my friends. He spoke in an almost coded political language—even in casual conversation, he strived for good phrases, and I hated that—which was the effect of two decades in diplomacy, but also of a need to disguise some inner turmoil. That was my theory.

My mother was closest to my father—which was also a bizarre discovery to make—although they did keep a decorous relationship for their children. We knew they loved each other deeply, but we also knew that their love was too deep, in a way, for it did not easily suffer the clichés and gestures of lesser relationships. The only time we could expect to see some action was when my father got into a grouchy mood and my mother planted kisses on him, called him "Winnie the Pooh," and tried to wring a smile from him, which she inevitably did. Or sometimes on the couch, when they were watching the news together, my mother would rest her legs on my father's lap.

The domestic, youthful aspect of my mother was something few people ever witnessed on the outside. By now Armenouhi was a household name in Yerevan. The Junior Achievement of Armenia programs in economic and civic education had been integrated into all Armenian schools. Orran, meanwhile, had become the sanctuary of hundreds of impoverished families and the choice charity of Krikor Krikorian and a long list of diasporan philanthropists. So Armenouhi enjoyed a celebrity truly independent of her husband, and she was constantly in demand for embassy dinners, charity balls, magazine covers, and movie premieres. She worked the crowd alone, gracefully explaining why her husband had not been able to come. Often he had been trapped in one of his meditative moods. Just as often he had not been invited.

From time to time, on break from college in Los Angeles, I would show up at our Yerevan balcony and find my father where I had left him. A cigar would be burning in the ashtray and music playing from an old boom box. Except I no longer recognized these songs; they were not the Armenian revolutionary anthems of my childhood. There was no drumbeat in them, or battle cry. And then I knew that my father had changed. His face remained, in Yerevan, the raging symbol of resistance, but I knew that his heart quietly had aged, mellowed, and retired to the *ergir*, the villages of Western Armenia. He did not need inspiration, as he once had, but rather a kind of atonement, which he found in the old folk songs—peaceful and melodic—that had been sung beyond the mountains for centuries, long before the revolution had become necessary:

> *Dzarin vra nush g'ella,*
> *Vartin vra push g'ella.*
> *Bak me das ne, hima dur—*
> *Vaghva mna, ush g'ella.*

> There are almonds on the tree,
> There are thorns on the rose.
> If you'll kiss me, kiss me now—
> It will be too late tomorrow.

ON THE OTHER SIDE OF Ararat, Richard and Vartiter were following Professor Fatma Müge Göçek through the hot hills and golden plains of Western Armenia, which Richard had studied for decades but never before seen with his own eyes. There always had been fears over his safety; the Turkish government was no great fan of the pioneer scholar of the Armenian Genocide. But Richard had harbored more private fears. He had actually been afraid of what he would see in the historic homeland. Those bustling homes of Bazmashen, his father's village, or the giant cabbages of Keserig, his mother's village—he had not wanted them to be untrue. He feared that Kharpert would lose its fantastic proportions.

Yet here he was, seventy-three years old in the summer of 2006, wearing khaki pants and tennis shoes, on an overdue pilgrimage into the past he had written of. In every corner history was coming to life, then dying again, right before his eyes. Richard was looking at the empty Kemakh Gorge, but he was seeing the endless caravans that had been pressed along the Euphrates and slaughtered there in 1915. He was peering at the blue lake of Dzovk, but he was peering in terror, because he knew what the American consul Leslie Davis had witnessed there almost a century earlier: thousands of dead, floating Armenian bodies.

Most visitors do not see the ghosts, however. They find a few broken homes in Bazmashen, and a garden of ordinary cabbages in Keserig. They see stables where churches used to be, and mosques everywhere, the exhibits of an Islamic revival. They knock at the door of a stone house in Tsitogh, a village of Garin, and a Turkish woman opens the door. She invites the strangers in for a *tahn*, a cool yogurt drink, and she tells them that this was her father's house, and they believe it and she believes it, for no one there has ever heard of Hovagim Kotcholosian.

It is not their fault; the visitors have no way of knowing. They see Kurds everywhere, millions of Kurds, and every so often they remark on the sorrowful hazel eyes of a boy. They pause, perhaps raise a brow, and move on, never to know that they have just seen an Armenian, or the descendant of an Armenian who was saved from the massacres by a "good Turk" or a "good Kurd." It is not their fault, for there is nothing to suggest that Armenians lived here before they were annihilated in 1915 and the Turks and Kurds moved into their empty homes and churches. What a gift of God these abandoned cities must have seemed to them!

But history had played tricks on the Kurds, too. It had cajoled them into a wartime conspiracy with the Young Turks against the Greeks, Assyrians, and Armenians, and even charmed some elements into an early faith in Mustafa Kemal's Turkic paradise. But then Kemal betrayed the Kurds, impounding their rights and obliterating their hope for Kurdistan, a homeland of their own. So when the descendants of these Kurds met the descendants of their Armenian victims, they confided their bitterness to them. The Turkish Ministry of the Interior was worried enough about an Armenian-Kurdish partnership that it instructed its agents to follow Richard and Vartiter.

There was little possibility of partnership, however, because there still remained a deep distrust between many Armenians and Kurds. "I know why you are here," a Kurdish landlord said to Richard. "But I will burn this building before I give it to you." The Kurds believed that the Armenians had come to reclaim their old homes, or else to excavate the treasures reportedly buried there by their parents or grandparents in 1915. That is why those two Turkish words, *altin* and *para*, greeted the Armenians at every village. "Gold" and "money," the locals were saying.

At the end of the journey, Richard and Vartiter made their way to Istanbul. Hrant Dink was waiting for them. Handsome as ever, his hair graying and disheveled, the Armenian editor of the weekly newspaper *Agos* rose from his desk. He was overjoyed to see the professor, and the professor was pleased by the reception of this brave intellectual warrior. Yet it was obvious that fear, genuine fear, had insinuated itself into Hrant. The death threats had not stopped and the Turkish prosecutor was preparing to charge him for the third time with a violation of Article 301. Evil was lurking all around him, Hrant said, and Richard knew that the struggle was undoing the man.

IN JANUARY 2007, WHEN A seventeen-year-old Turkish nationalist shouted *"Giavur!"* and murdered Hrant Dink in Istanbul, I was in the corner room of my grandparents' home in Los Angeles, packing into cardboard boxes my college papers, the evidence of the punditry I had practiced as an undergraduate at UCLA. I was parting with the newspapers and placards and essays, and with the dusty blue examination book I had tried to forget, because I had done there what no one in generations of my family could have done: cheat in my own grandfather's Armenian history course. I had been terrified that I would disappoint him, and then I had, and I was happy now to be leaving all the trappings of a difficult relationship.

My father and mother were waiting for me in Yerevan, and I wanted to be with them. I missed Armenia. I missed my brothers and sister and friends, and the endless nights we would spend walking the streets of our moon-charmed capital. But there was another, less innocent reason I had been yearning for Yerevan. Parliamentary elections had been called for May 2007, and my father was eligible to run. I had six months before a summer's internship in Washington, and I planned to spend them in his service. The fact was that I was desperate to see my father in action—I could not bear to watch him waste himself in silence—and I was possessed by the hope that I might awaken him.

Fortunately, when I arrived in Yerevan, my father was out of hibernation, and the leaders of Heritage were already discussing the possibility of participating in their first formal test of popularity. I took a seat at my father's table and examined the men and women assembled there: a musician, a physicist, a fitness instructor, a professor of religion. There was Anahit Bakhshyan, the school principal and widow of the assassinated parliamentary Deputy Speaker, and Zaruhi Postanjyan, the restless human rights lawyer and worst nightmare of the Armenian police. They were purists, all of them, with absolutely no experience in government. But that, my father believed, was precisely their advantage.

We were chattering through the night about my father's fate, delighting in our own predictions of his victory, but the man himself was quiet. We did not know, until he began to speak, that Raffi was harboring serious doubts. The Heritage Party had no money, he said, and no republic-wide structure. The headquarters in Yerevan were still under lockdown, while regional offices were unstaffed. If the party were to compete in the coming elections, it would have to stake its campaign on one name alone, and that name had been banned from public airwaves for more than a year. Was it worth it, then—the question had to be asked, and Raffi was not pleased that he was the one asking it—to invest a twenty-year fortune of public trust into a fanatical war against a wealthy, powerful, and indomitable regime?

The room fell silent. The illusion was cracked. The consensus began to sway. A few of the board members recalibrated their optimism. I did, too, fully embarrassed that I had not been wiser than the others. *Turn out the lights*, I thought, *the party's over*. And just then, in his calmest voice, my father said that we were about to make history. All this time he had only wanted us to be deliberate. He had instilled in us the proper doubt, made us understand that we should not be so arrogant, proved to us that he could invade our minds. And then he had revealed that we could influence his.

There were 131 seats in the National Assembly of Armenia, and most of these seats were filled through national elections, in which citizens would vote for a single party list. Once the votes had been tabulated, the seats would be allocated to the parties in proportion to their percentages. The minimum for victory was 5 percent, which translated into six members of parliament. Of course, Raffi had greater aspirations than this; he was hoping to achieve not only a majority in the National Assembly but also a total reconstitution of Armenian politics. But if this were to happen, Raffi knew, the opposition parties would first have to unite.

Stepan Demirchyan bowed out gracefully almost as soon as the opposition talks began. His party recognized him as the legitimately elected president of 2003, and it would not allow him to share the parliamentary list equally with other parties. The problem was that Vazgen Manukyan was a denied president, too—he from the 1996 race against Levon Ter-Petrosyan—while Aram Sargsyan, though he could not claim to be a president, was proving to be a most eccentric political strategist. One evening he brought to the negotiation table a leader of the Armenian National Movement, the long-forgotten party of Levon Ter-Petrosyan.

That my father included me in these closed negotiations was plainly ridiculous, but there I was, sitting among four party leaders, watching sparks of envy and vanity blow across the room. It was heartbreaking to see my father speak in such romantic terms. "This is our chance with history," he was saying to practiced politicians who saved such phrases for the people. For them the only question was the list and who among them should top it.

Much to my horror, my father never once suggested himself to his colleagues, seeking instead to develop formulas on which all parties might agree. One of these was a balancing act between the upcoming parliamentary elections of 2007 and the presidential elections of 2008. He who coveted the first spot on the parliamentary list would go on to play only a supporting role in the opposition's presidential campaign. The one who held the second place would be rewarded for his modesty with the title of Speaker of the National Assembly, the one in third place with the title of Prime Minister. The fourth place on the parliamentary list, he who would not even show on this year's paper ballot, would stand as the united opposition's candidate for President of the Republic of Armenia. In this way, Raffi said, the last would become the first.

The idea flopped like the others, and my father tendered his final, most creative offer on February 25. It was a list titled *"Kaghakatsiakan Hayastan"*—"Civic Armenia"—and my father had chosen as its leader Rafael Ghazaryan, an ailing physicist and universally admired sage of the Karabagh Committee. Vazgen Manukyan was second on the list, Aram Sargsyan third, and what followed was a series of artists, writers, politicians, and academicians, which reflected a thorough re-imagining of Armenia's political order. Raffi had put himself in sixth place, but apparently even that was not enough to appease the ambitions of everyone. Ultimately, the parties of Vazgen Manukyan and Levon Ter-Petrosyan dropped out of the race, while the parties of Stepan Demirchyan, Aram Sargsyan, and Raffi Hovannisian submitted separate lists to the Central Election Commission.

In addition to the three principal forces of opposition, ten parties had registered for the election. The Republican Party, directed by Serge Sargsyan, Kocharyan's prime minister, was by far the most powerful, while Prosperous Armenia was the wealthiest. It had just been established by Gagik Tsarukyan, an oversized arm-wrestling champion turned billionaire beer magnate—and also Kocharyan's ally. The Armenian Revolutionary Federation was the only traditional party to enter the race, and it could expect, on account of its historic name—and its loyalty to Kocharyan—a modest representation in parliament. But nothing would delight so many citizens more than the campaign of Tigran Karapetyan, a bespectacled conspiracy theorist who would spend the next few weeks inviting desperate villagers to sing on the talk shows of his very own television channel, and then reward them with toasters and microwaves.

And that is how it all began. Somewhere near the intersection of high drama and comic absurdity—locked out of party headquarters, banned from the airwaves, intimidated by the police, and budgeted down to the crust of his personal savings—Raffi launched the underdog campaign of his life. He would not look back. With the slogan "Faith and Fatherland" he would lead us into the chaos, knowing full well that we might emerge on the other side without much left of either.

NESTLED AMONG VOLUNTEERS AND BEWILDERED hitchhikers on a campaign bus called "Toward Victory," I was looking out the window and getting nervous, because we were no longer in Yerevan and all the good feelings that had been circulating there among the intellectual population. I admired my father, so cheery and unstoppable in the front of the bus, singing nationalist songs and telling stories and lecturing about the countryside: the sweet apricots of these verdant groves or the battle that had been fought in those distant fields. Sometimes he would tell the bus driver to turn onto an unmarked dirt road because the last time he was here, five years ago, he had not taken it, and he had been thinking about the road ever since.

In the shade of a tin shack, seven men in faded suits and newsboy caps were sitting on a bench, playing backgammon. This was the village entrance, and these were the village elders.

"*Voghjuyn, hayrenakitsner!*" my father yelled out. "Hello, compatriots!"

The men rose, squinting. "What are you doing here?" they exclaimed, rubbing the doubt from their eyes. "We thought you had left!"

For years now, the villagers had not seen my father on television, and they had just assumed that he had done the reasonable thing and left the damned country for good. Now they were smiling. They poured out shots of mulberry vodka and drank to my father's victory. And then, suddenly, they turned serious, as Armenian men have the habit of doing. They spoke of their troubles: the bad harvest, the contaminated water, the corrupt mayor. My father listened, nodding helplessly, his eyes wet with sorrow. And then he told the men that very soon things would change. But they could not lose faith. They just could not lose faith.

"Are you masters of this land?" my father asked.

The villagers answered: "Yes, we are."

The scene was not so poetic in the more isolated villages of Armenia. Here we had no chance. The regional governor, a Republican, had brought a water pipeline into the village, or the Hummers of Prosperous Armenia had, just the other day, delivered a hundred sacks of potatoes. *"Duk inch ek mez talu?"* the villagers asked. "What will *you* give us?" And we could only give them our orange pamphlets, although we knew very well that words could not fill an empty stomach:

> Authority is born of popular will, not administrative fraud.
> Bribery is a crime, not a strategy.
> Victory is for the strong and the worthy, not the powerful and
> the wealthy.

There was not an Armenian town, village, or tent unthreatened by Republican power or untouched by Prosperous money, but my father seemed not to care. He was darting into pastry shops with pretty women in them and losing himself in labyrinthine fruit bazaars—and he was always smiling. He was probably the first politician to be found smiling in these parts, where it was a weakness to smile, or to walk without bodyguards, or to dress in old suits. Here people did not vote for underdogs. Yet my father was smiling and walking without bodyguards and wearing his old suits, trying desperately to prove to the Armenians that true power is not in the boasting of it. One by one, he was charming the stale Soviet ghost out of these people—realizing, in his own way, the paradox of St. Paul: "When I am weak, then am I strong."

Indeed, those who saw Raffi on the campaign trail in the spring of 2007 could never claim to have witnessed a weak man. They were filled with awe and wonder to see him barge into the offices of Prosperous Armenia and wish his best to the goons stationed there, or march into the mass rallies of the Republicans, where entire schools and villages had been forcibly bused in to create a good turnout. Raffi would walk through the people and smile and shake hands, and very soon he would be washed in ovations. From enemy crowds, an unlikely chant would begin: "Raf-fi! Raf-fi! Raf-fi!" And it was clear that these were not enemy crowds.

• • •

ON THE EVENING OF MAY 12, 2007, Election Day, I left my father at a bus stop on Baghramyan Boulevard and crossed the street to the statue of Martiros Saryan, where the Yerevan artist-salesmen were griping about a slow day of sales. I hastened to the gray building just beyond and ran up a flight of stairs to Heritage's newly rented offices. Party volunteers were already huddled around an old television, and the count was about to begin. Our hearts suspended, we watched as a precinct manager reached into a plastic box and retrieved the first ballot of the National Assembly Elections of 2007.

"Heritage," he announced, and we yelled and jumped like madmen. But the precinct manager had already reached into the box again, needing to correct his mistake. He read the second ballot: Heritage. Then the third: Heritage. And then, suddenly, the feed was changed to another precinct, and soon to another. But the results did not change. Heritage was winning everywhere. Within the hour, all feeds had been cut, and American soap operas and basketball games were saturating the airwaves. I got my father on the phone.

"They're going to steal it from us!" I yelled into the receiver.

"What do you mean?" he said. I had woken him up.

I told my father what was happening, but he was not angry. He was not even surprised. His voice was warm and unworried over the phone.

"What should I do?" I asked.

"Don't worry about it," he said.

Immediately we called an emergency press conference. A few newspaper reporters turned up at the office an hour later, and our press secretary began to brief them. That was when the doorbell rang. We had posted observers at about half of the two thousand precincts, and the first of them had arrived to report her results.

"First place!" she shouted.

And just then, a second observer appeared behind her. "First place!" he shouted. All through the night, the results arrived from hundreds of precincts: First place, second place, third place, first again, first, first, first, second, first. We were up all night, receiving our observers, toasting them, and celebrating the coming rebirth of our fatherland. We were sure, we were very sure, that in the morning Armenia would be a different place.

THE CENTRAL ELECTION COMMISSION ISSUED the official results the following day: Republican Party, 34 percent; Prosperous Armenia, 15 percent; Armenian Revolutionary Federation, 13 percent; Rule of Law, 7 percent; Heritage, 6 percent. Heritage had done very well in about a thousand precincts, the election officials explained—the thousand where they had posted observers. At the other thousand, though, the party had not done so well. In fact, 30 percent of those precincts had reported exactly zero votes for the Heritage Party.

We had been given 6 percent—a mockery—and in the heat of an unjust moment, some of us said that we should reject the results and refuse to take our seven seats in the National Assembly. But too many people had believed in us. Too many people were calling this a victory. The winning parties were already forming a governing coalition in parliament, and the burden of representing the opposition—the disenfranchised majority, we believed, of the Armenian people—was falling upon Heritage alone.

Seven seats could change nothing, but the four men and three women who took them in the spring of 2007 pretended with all their might that they could. From the podium of the National Assembly, Raffi and his colleagues realized a passionate vindication of their vows. They spoke for the first time about election fraud, corruption, and conflict of interest. Of course their ideas were lost on a chamber of empty seats; the oligarch-parliamentarians were not present unless a vote had been scheduled. But the cameras of state television, which were required by law to record parliamentary activities, kept rolling, channeling our protests into living rooms across the republic.

In the summer after its victory, Heritage committed its first grave mistake. A parliamentary seat belonging to the fifteenth electoral district in the outskirts of Armenia had been vacated, and Raffi decided he would compete. If he won, then he could transfer his present seat in parliament to the next candidate on the Heritage list. But in this district there was no chance of victory. For weeks the authorities unleashed their powers upon its villages, and on the day of elections scored a landslide victory against Heritage. For Raffi this was a bitter lesson in the capacity of state and the vulnerability of rural citizenry— but perhaps also a relatively cheap and cautionary lesson in the politics of hubris.

The electoral carnage in the fifteenth district had little effect on the morale of the party in Yerevan. Throughout the summer, the parliamentary members of Heritage challenged the government on its abuses of eminent domain. Through a series of filibusters in parliament, they successfully defeated a bill that would ban Radio Liberty, the major radio program favorable to civil society, from the public airwaves. They sought to overturn Article 301 of the Armenian constitution—the cousin of the infamous Article 301 in Turkey, which had served as the basis most recently to prosecute in Istanbul the novelist Orhan Pamuk, the winner of the 2006 Nobel Prize for Literature. And they introduced to the National Assembly floor a resolution that would recognize the independence of Mountainous Karabagh. The coalition parties rejected the bill.

The truth was that in nine years of Kocharyan's "nationalist" presidency, the Armenians had been losing their foreign policy case. In Strasbourg, France, the headquarters of the Council of Europe, Turkish and Azerbaijani delegates had conspired to crush the Armenian Question once and for all, while the Armenian delegates, with their thick accents and insecurities, had failed to formulate a success-ful counterattack. Mountainous Karabagh was considered no longer a model of self-determination, as it had been during the first foreign ministry, but rather Azerbaijani land occupied by Armenia. Turkey was no longer condemned as a state of denial but celebrated as a qual-ified aspirant to European values.

In October 2007 Raffi arrived in Strasbourg to change that. He was a member of Armenia's delegation to the Parliamentary Assembly of the Council of Europe, where the legislatures of all the continent's countries merged into a common parliament. Raffi proved himself as an internationalist—in his opening speech, he invoked John Donne to rally Europe to action in Darfur: "Do not ask for whom the bell tolls. It tolls for thee"—but his sense of justice was actually animated by the historic disfigurement of his own nation. He was making his old de-mands: Turkey's repentance for the Genocide and Azerbaijan's recogni-tion of an independent Mountainous Karabagh. Most urgently, he was pushing a commission on European cultural heritage to investigate the destruction in December 2005 of Armenian *khachkars*, or cross-stones, in Julfa, Nakhichevan, Armenian land now part of Azerbaijan.

Raffi's style of nationalist diplomacy was instantly familiar to vet-eran characters of the Council of Europe, who recalled his previous incarnation as foreign minister. It had been fifteen years, but in their eyes Raffi had not changed. He was still walking up to Turkish and Azerbaijani colleagues, hoping to find the honest and courageous among them. He was still roaring fire from the podium. He was still rising, matriculating into the governing bureau and leadership of the European People's Party, quickly rediscovering his role as a firebrand of Europe.

ON OCTOBER 26, 2007, HISTORY was preparing to repeat itself at Liberty Square. In 1988, he had stood there to command the movement for Armenian independence, and now Levon Ter-Petrosyan was standing there again, back from a decade of self-imposed exile in his black stone Yerevan mansion, his hair still brown-gold at the age of sixty-two. He had come "to obey the will of the people," which was of course that he return to Armenian politics and seek to overthrow the oligarchic regime. Presidential elections were coming up in February 2008, and Robert Kocharyan had decided on a successor: his prime minister, Serge Sargsyan.

To be clear, Ter-Petrosyan was not asking for the forgiveness of his people, nor was he basking in an emerging popularity he knew to be complicated. Time seemed to have humbled him, and many people believed that his only wish was to clear his name in history. Ter-Petrosyan was saying the right things—that he was only offering himself as an instrument for change, that he would keep the presidency for two years and then leave—and he was gathering around him many opposition leaders who were willing to digest their disbelief for one good shot at a better government. History was being kind to Levon Ter-Petrosyan. It was returning to his ears the pleasing chants of a vanished movement: "Le-von! Le-von! Le-von!"

Barred once again from entering the presidential contest—he would not be officially eligible until 2011—Raffi was expected to make an endorsement. There were three plausible choices: Levon Ter-Petrosyan, first president of Armenia; Vazgen Manukyan, Ter-Petrosyan's early challenger; and Vahan Hovhannisyan, the candidate for the Armenian Revolutionary Federation. The ARF still kept close ties with the Kocharyan-Sargsyan government, but at least now it was running its own candidate and even, behind closed doors, considering Raffi's proposal for a new national-liberal alliance of the ARF, Manukyan, and Ter-Petrosyan.

There was, it turned out, too much history and ideology to overcome. The talks failed, and soon individual candidates appealed to Heritage for the key endorsement. They did not know that Heritage no longer belonged to its leader, that Raffi had been slowly turning over his powers to other party members. Without any publicity, he would soon do the unprecedented and the unfathomable, which was to leave the chairmanship of his own party. He wanted Heritage to achieve an identity and standing independent of him—and it had. But Raffi could not have predicted that on February 11, 2008, the board of his party would carefully listen to his opinion—which was that the party should issue an open endorsement of all opposition candidates—and then defy it in favor of an exclusive endorsement of Levon Ter-Petrosyan.

On February 20, in a nine-way presidential race, Serge Sargsyan collected in the usual manner an absolute majority of the public vote. The authorities had not risked a second round—but, in fact, they had risked much more. Levon Ter-Petrosyan condemned the fraudulent elections and invited the people to Liberty Square. On the first day twenty-five thousand protestors gathered. On the second day it was fifty thousand. On the ninth day, a hundred thousand. A momentum was building. Prosecutors, oligarchs, and deputy ministers were defecting from the government and turning up at the demonstrations. Armenians were aching for a revolution again, and again turning to the leadership of Levon Ter-Petrosyan.

But Ter-Petrosyan was reformed now. That was what the people believed, anyway, even though he did slip up once and begin, from the platform, a chant of his own name.

ON THE EVENING OF MARCH 1, 2008, after previewing the electoral precincts of Moscow and then St. Petersburg, Raffi retired to his hotel on the Neva River. A delegate of an observation group deployed by the Council of Europe, he had witnessed in Russia what Armenia was fast becoming. Commissioned by state power, Dmitry Medvedev was about to inherit the Russian presidency from Vladimir Putin. An important liberal challenger, the half-Armenian world chess champion Garry Kasparov, had already dropped out of the race.

But it was an altogether different story, developing on the television screen at the lobby of the hotel, that alarmed Raffi. Apparently, at seven-thirty that morning Armenian police had invaded the tents pitched at Liberty Square, where they had beaten thousands with truncheons and electric prods and arrested more than a hundred protestors. The people had dispersed, but by noon they had assembled again, this time at the square by the French Embassy. By 6:30 p.m. a hundred thousand protestors were shouting in the streets; three thousand riot police and a thousand soldiers carrying AK-47 and M-16 rifles had surrounded them. The radical opposition leaders had been arrested, and Levon Ter-Petrosyan was nowhere to be found.

That was the latest news, and Raffi knew that Armenia was in the greatest political crisis of its history. He retrieved his luggage and rushed to the airport.

When Raffi arrived in Yerevan on the morning of March 2, the capital was silent. Armenian soldiers stood at every intersection, while civilians hid in their homes. The outgoing president, Robert Kocharyan, had declared a state of emergency in Armenia. All public demonstrations had been banned. Levon Ter-Petrosyan was under house arrest. Ten citizens were dead and hundreds locked up in cellars of the state police and the National Security Service. Countless others would be tortured and forced to bear false testimony about an opposition coup.

At the National Assembly, a loyal majority quickly approved the president's emergency rule and then, defying the objections of Heritage, proceeded to strip several of its own members, including a powerful tycoon who had defected to Ter-Petrosyan's camp, of their parliamentary immunity. They would be charged by the prosecutor-general with colluding in an attempted overthrow of the government. And so, ignored in his own parliament, Raffi left for the parliament of Europe. In Strasbourg, he appeared before his Western colleagues to challenge not only Azerbaijan and Turkey but now also his own government.

By the summer of 2008, an epiphany had dawned on Raffi: the Council of Europe, that highest forum of his young diplomatic ambitions, was something of a sham. Azerbaijan was blocking the Council's rapporteur from investigating the destroyed Armenian historical sites within its borders, and Europe did nothing. Turkey was trying its own Nobel laureates for speaking about the killings of Armenians, Greeks, Kurds, Assyrians, and Jews in the Ottoman Empire, and Europe did nothing. Armenia was falsifying elections and refusing to try its political prisoners, and Europe did nothing. For generations, through a century of genocide and injustice, Europe had convened, deliberated, and done nothing.

On the afternoon of June 25 Raffi stood for the last time at the podium of Europe's parliamentary assembly. "There is no shame in accepting the truth," he said. For Azerbaijan: "The right of Mountainous Karabagh to live in liberty on its ancestral lands, owning up to the barbaric attack on the Armenian, thus European, heritage at Julfa, Nakhichevan." For Turkey: "The philosophy of state, as well as the exclusivist legacy of the Armenian Genocide and the great Armenian dispossession of 1915." For Georgia: a history of repeated injuries to the minority communities of Armenians and Azerbaijanis. For Armenia: a catastrophic failure of human rights and democracy. For Europe: a record of inadequate reactions to the suffering of peoples.

> I do not know about the Assembly and its criteria, but it is evident that for the time being the Republic of Armenia and the Council of Europe do not deserve each other. Hence, I wish you success in your future deliberations, your voting and your monitoring, but I hereby suspend my participation in the affairs of the Assembly until such time as Armenia meets standards—its own and Europe's—

and Europe rises to the realization of its own values, rights, and benchmarks.

With those words Raffi walked out of the Council of Europe, the leadership of the European People's Party, and the world of wine and cheap talk called diplomacy.

RICHARD HAD SPENT ALMOST A half century at the helm of Armenian studies. He had written the original history of the first Republic of Armenia, compiled a comprehensive oral history of the Genocide, and established the Armenian Educational Foundation Chair in Modern Armenian History at UCLA. He had tormented his Ph.D. students, then watched them grow into their own offices at the University of Michigan, Boston University, and other towers of American academia. It was almost impossible to conceive how much he had traveled in life, how far he had gotten from that daydreaming boy in Kaspar's vineyard, how hard he had worked, what it had taken—from him and very few others—to fill that empty space between Armageddon and Armistice Day.

In the past fifty years Richard had earned the graces of the American intelligentsia and broken into the Soviet establishment. And now the independent homeland's top honors were his, a presidential medal and honorary doctorates from the state universities of Yerevan and Stepanakert. A public school had been named after him. Armenian journalists no longer asked him for history lessons but for prophecies about the new Republic of Armenia, as if a lifetime's study of the past had given Richard special powers over the future.

Vartiter was Richard's only friend and judge—and she was enough. His children, married and prospering, were his pride, his fourteen grandchildren his cheer and posterity. Richard knew he had been lucky, and maybe that is why he seemed more and more peaceful, deliberately and sometimes even explicitly kind to people. The severe, professorial expressions were slowly retiring from his face, as they had from his father's, and time was returning him to the roots. Of course, the professor hid the most obvious evidence of this—the yellow Mr. Goodbar chocolates—in his top desk drawer.

Yet Richard was still worrying about his son's resigning spirit. Raffi had achieved every office he had sought, and given up every office he had achieved. The Armenian Youth Federation, three law firms, the Armenian Bar Association, the Armenian Assembly of America, the foreign ministry, the All-Armenian Fund, the Council of Europe—Raffi had walked out of them, one by one. He was so jealously obsessed with his principles that he could not see that his principles were of no use if they were not committed to the service of some power. Only on rare occasions, and only in public, did Richard reveal admiration for his son. Asked by a reporter if he would ever return to Armenia, Richard sank into his chair and came up with a touching answer: "I am not as patient and forgiving as Raffi."

Indeed, Raffi's return to Armenia was an interminable test of patience and mercy. It was not that he never felt disillusioned, but that he beat disillusionment daily, privately. And that is why he was withdrawing again, even from Heritage, his own creation. Freedom was its great virtue, but then total freedom, like a world without gravity, threatened always to disintegrate. Party leaders divided their affections according to the usual dichotomies—"liberal" and "nationalist," Levon Ter-Petrosyan and the Armenian Revolutionary Federation. Their diversity had been their power, as it was the source of a potential unraveling.

"Bickering is starting within your team," Armenouhi wrote to her husband. "You need to be there to bring everyone together—encouraging and setting the tone." These were the thoughts of the entire family, but what we did not realize about our father was that he could smile for only so long—that it was a painful thing to smile when the country of his dreams was falling apart. We resented him for his sessions in solitude, but we did not understand that they were ultimately not a resignation but a rehabilitation of his spirit.

On the outside, of course, nobody knew that a conflict was even taking place. In parliament or at conventions of the Heritage Party, Raffi was as fierce and passionate as ever. A tricolor pin fastened to his suit, his voice booming in a jam-packed government hall in July 2008, Raffi was addressing a convention of Yerevan's political leaders, intellectuals, and citizens. "Azerbaijan will have to accept its responsibility for the Armenian cross-stones, and will come to accept that it has not lost Mountainous Karabagh, because it never had it," he said. "Turkey will accept that the foundations of its Kemalist republic were set upon the ashes of the Armenian homeland." And then, staring into the eyes of the audience—the past president, the current prime minister, his wife, his children—he burst out in glorious anger. "Shame on us!" he yelled. "Shame on us!" For everyone in that room had collaborated, through word, deed, or criminal silence, in the corruption of the Republic of Armenia.

Raffi waited through the silence, waited for the damnation to overcome us completely, and then, as he had done all his life, he rescued us from it. His voice grew fair. He spoke with pain and then with hope, and then he began to convince us—and to convince himself—that the history of the past hundred years was about to reach the hour of judgment and salvation. "Armenia's centuries-long quest must end in triumph," he said, "for one and all, citizen and country, and for our timeless yearning." Raffi paused again, one last time. He surveyed our faces—which were the faces of the millions who had been marched to oblivion in 1915—before whispering, almost breathing, a parting confession.

"*Inchpes anhas parki champa*," he said. "Like the road to unreachable glory."

EPILOGUE

For three weeks every winter, my father returned to his father's home in Los Angeles, and on Christmas morning the family returned together to the great San Joaquin Valley of California. We left behind city houses and city lives, and journeyed by caravan northward on the Golden State Freeway, over the mountains to Highway 99, and into a native landscape of farms and orchards and vineyards—"the strange, weed-infested, junky, wonderful, senseless yet beautiful world" of William Saroyan.

Somewhere in the back of the van, trapped between younger cousins, I retreated into my own world, pretending not to hear my grandfather's voice: "Garin, do you know what kind of tree that is?" He was sitting in the passenger's seat, next to my father, a complicated nostalgia filling him up—sometimes spilling over into strange questions about trees or clouds or black widow spiders—on this pilgrimage to Fresno, the home of his mother and our matriarch.

"*Ge knana*," my father said, but he knew very well I was not sleeping.

Every year, on our way to Grandma's, my father took us on the same desperate tour into the family past. He showed us again that exhausted Tulare town: the old school, the old barbershop, the old boarded-up house rotting near a vineyard. In Fresno he showed us the cemetery with the statue of an eagle slaying a snake and a gravestone with a forgotten epitaph, and then the red church where he was married, the swamp where a school used to be, and a cottage nearby. He told us about the people who had once lived there, and we told him, in the kindest way we could, that we did not care.

And then the van stopped. Every year the van stopped in the middle of the same street, at the same peeling house with a porch and overhang—3312 Lowe Avenue, the house of another family— and every year my father said the same thing: "You don't have to come out." And we did not. We watched from the van as he breached a side gate and disappeared into the forbidden garden beyond. And nothing ever changed. Every year we watched him leave, and every year we laughed at the sight of his return: our father, a mischievous smile spread upon his face, running back with a dozen oranges in his arms.

In the van, finally on our way to Christmas, we peeled the stolen oranges and devoured them. They were sour and delicious.

IN THE SUMMER OF 2008 I settled into my grandfather's pool house, where the family kept its archives in Los Angeles, and opened the first box. I remember thinking how simple it was all going to be, and then finding inside the dust of decades and the corpses of white spiders. They were covering a pile of letters other men had written to my grandmother. I was overcome by such a funny melancholy as I read of those unfinished romances, passions burned out, professions of eternal this or that which had failed to last even a half century.

By summer's end I had turned over hundreds of boxes. Memories were emancipated and I was in possession of my characters: three powerful men who defied the great forces of modern history. I was fascinated not with their national significance but with their intuitions of individualism. Obviously I had read too deep into my father's poem, composed in the first grade:

> Sam tried to fish.
> Sam wanted to fish.
> Sam lived on the farm.

My family story was about three men who left—that was my guiding insight. My great-grandfather left the ruins of his homeland. My grandfather left his father's farm. My father left the wonders of an American life. The family story, I believed, was about prodigal sons, which is to say men who ruled over their own destinies.

I learned too late that Kaspar, Richard, and Raffi were not free men. They had liberated themselves not from responsibility but from expectation, only to become more perfect slaves. They followed each other through history, leaving but returning in enigmatic ways. I discovered my fathers in the mythology of the Armenian flag. Red: blood. Blue: sky. Orange: the fertile earth. The family story of destruction, remembrance, and return had long been prophesied in our national tricolor.

At first I resented the determinism, but resentment evolved in strange directions. As I began to write the life of my father, I recognized a logic and foresaw the end of our story. Snowflakes had been falling upon a mountain and my father was to be the snowflake that set off the avalanche. That is how I came to recall the Yerevan afternoon, a decade earlier, when I had recited to my father the words of Winston Churchill: "History will be kind to me, for I intend to write it." He had whispered a few words to himself that day, but I had not understood.

"I intend to make it," my father had said.

AT 9:32 A.M. ON MONDAY, January 14, 2008, my father and I were waiting in line at a post office in Los Angeles. It was a good time for our first interview. I took out my recorder, and my father looked at it with suspicion. He knew I was preparing to exploit him. "Posterity scares me," he said. Speaking was such an ordeal for my father. It was as if each word was mined from a subterranean soul and each idea made a journey through some kind of hell before it could be released to the world.

A few hours later, in the car, I confronted my father. "Why do you reach deep to talk?" I asked. He paused for a moment; he was reaching deep again. And then he spoke: "I have the sense that I am always on the record."

Once my father overcame his initial doubts about our interviews, our conversations grew long and exhilarating. On the balcony of our house in Yerevan, we spoke for hours about his memories, his fears, his visions of glory and death. He reconstructed for me, play by play, the night he and the pals excommunicated a friend on charges of inferior love, and did not allow himself to say the obvious, which was that he regretted doing it.

My father did not want to appear to be sanitizing himself. He knew I wanted to find more stories like that one, to show him to be "complex," as real people are supposed to be. He understood that I had problems with his purity, and I did. One time, probably feeling guilty after an interview about his high school days, my father wrote to me in a panic to say that he had once been caught lifting a burrito from the cafeteria.

MORE THAN A YEAR AFTER the election bloodshed of spring 2008, just when the movement to return Levon Ter-Petrosyan to power was dying on the streets of Yerevan, President Serge Sargsyan declared an amnesty for the political prisoners languishing in the capital's jail cells. Neither the assassination of political leaders on October 27, 1999, nor the killing of citizens on March 1, 2008, which were the inaugural events of the Kocharyan and Sargsyan presidencies, would be investigated or explained.

International economies disintegrated in 2009, but the Armenian president was spared an economic catastrophe. From Moscow and Los Angeles, hundreds of thousands of Armenians continued to send money to their relatives in the homeland, while Kirk Kerkorian, Gerard Cafesjian, Garo Armen, and the diasporan philanthropists sustained humanitarian and state projects. Their generosity was boundless; they did not allow their patriotism to be complicated by the politics of the times.

The rival factions of the Armenian American community—represented in Washington by the Armenian National Committee of America and the Armenian Assembly of America—competed still, but they competed less over ideas than over credit. In a remarkable collaboration in 2004, the Armenian lawyers Mark Geragos and Vartkes Yeghiayan together scored a $20 million settlement with the New York Life Insurance Company to resolve thousands of policies issued to Armenians living in the Ottoman Empire before 1915.

Yet the community's recurrent effort to pass an Armenian Genocide resolution in the United States Congress and to secure a statement of recognition from successive American presidents—George H. W. Bush, Bill Clinton, George W. Bush—had failed again and again and again. But hope was not lost. Presidential elections were imminent, and one candidate in particular had impressed the Armenians. On the campaign trail, Barack Obama had promised to reaffirm officially the record on the Armenian Genocide.

In Yerevan, many Armenians came to accept the rule of President Serge Sargsyan, and even allowed themselves the consolation that he was better than his predecessor. He did not make cynical outbursts as Kocharyan had. He smiled at people and shook their hands. And his popularity did profit, in the first year of his presidency, from Armenia's first-place victory at the Chess Olympiad and six Olympic medals in wrestling, boxing, and weight lifting. Armenians commanded either the mind or the body, but not both at the same time, and not as a team.

Even so, the Armenian citizens did not forgive their president; they drove him to seek legitimacy elsewhere. So in the summer of 2008, Serge Sargsyan invited his Turkish counterpart, Abdullah Gul, to a breakthrough soccer match in Yerevan. It was the first step, he hoped, toward normalizing Armenian-Turkish relations, lifting the border blockade imposed by Turkey, and realizing a triumph of diplomacy. To great international acclaim, President Gul arrived in Yerevan in September 2008, cheered his team to a 2–0 victory, and promptly returned to Ankara.

The following spring, the Armenian and Turkish foreign ministries announced that they had agreed on a plan of good relations, which allowed President Barack Obama, in his anticipated April 24 address, to refer to the events of 1915 not by the desired designation but by an Armenian alternative: *Medz Yeghern*, meaning "great calamity." The diasporan writer and public activist Harut Sassounian explained that the president had accepted the "Turkish line that third countries should not acknowledge the Armenian Genocide, while Armenia and Turkey were trying to normalize their relations." By the end of the year, the Armenian and Turkish foreign ministers had signed "the protocols," a deal to establish diplomatic relations.

As the protocols were submitted for improbable ratification to courts and parliaments in Yerevan and Ankara, President Sargsyan glowed in international stardom. But his people knew what he had done. In return for Turkey's basic assurances of an open border, Sargsyan had made two incredible concessions: first, an agreement to launch a commission that would explore the "events" of Armenian-Turkish history; second, an official recognition of Armenia's modern border with Turkey. To many nationalists, this meant: first, a readiness to negotiate over the reality of the Genocide, and second, the end of Armenia's legal rights to its historic homeland.

As countless thousands marched in the diaspora to protest the protocols, the Armenian Revolutionary Federation in Yerevan dissolved a decade-long alliance with the ruling authorities—breaking, finally, its parliamentary partnership with the Republican Party and the Prosperous Armenia Party. It was not clear whether the dissolution was final—whether the party would one day join a historic coalition to uproot the oligarchic regime—but for the time being it had entered the opposition. Before extraordinary crowds, leaders of the ARF, the Heritage Party, the Hunchakian Party, and the Ramgavar Party—once great rivals—were together rallying against a government that was about to announce the official surrender of Western Armenia.

At the National Assembly, Raffi's temper was burning. The prime minister was in parliament, and he had remarked, in the course of a cumbersome defense of the protocols, that the modern Armenian-Turkish border—the direct result of the Armenian Genocide and great national dispossession of 1915—was, in fact, the only border his government recognized. Raffi's views were known to the Armenians, and circulated in newspapers worldwide, but no one in that parliamentary chamber quite understood how personal it really was for him.

"Your answer means a resignation," he called out at the prime minister, "from our homeland and your authority!"

Raffi was still the iconic member of parliament and the commanding authority of Heritage, but he no longer kept an official title. He did not long for the high offices, and that was why, perhaps, so many people thought that he deserved one. All around him, they talked about a decisive wave of demonstrations should the protocols be passed. They talked about 2012, the next parliamentary elections, when Heritage would seek to fortify its role in a new National Assembly. But most often they talked about 2013, the presidential elections, when Raffi would finally be eligible to compete—would be expected to compete—in what might become a spectacular two-way contest: the most popular repatriate citizen against the most powerful incumbent president in the history of this Republic of Armenia.

MY FATHER'S DISENGAGEMENT FROM THE diplomatic code was evident as early as 2005, when he made his first call for civil disobedience against the Yerevan government. But I did not appreciate the depth of his actual disenchantment until the autumn of 2008, when I accompanied him to a conference sponsored by Tufts University and held in the resort town of Talloires, France. I confess that I suffered that September morning, listening to my father speak in hot and vacant words. I did not like how easy it had become for him, pairing his Armenian patriotism with diplomatic banalities and receiving constant admiration.

My skepticism was shared, apparently, by one other person in the room. He was a political scientist, and also an invited speaker. In the question and answer session that concluded the morning meeting, he confronted my father with the very simple accusation that he had offered no actual solutions to anything. "As far as I'm concerned," he said, "you haven't earned your lunch." I looked at my father, front and center, certain that he would be hurt, and hoping with all my hope that he would dismantle the man.

"Good time to start a diet," my father said with a smile.

At lunch my father and I shared a table with five international students who told him how wonderful he was and asked him how he had made it, whom he looked up to, and what he considered to be the most important quality of leadership. "A politician always has to bear in mind that, at some point in his life, his career will end," my father said. "He must always be ready for life after politics."

That afternoon, painless questions continued to find painful answers, but I no longer listened. For the first time in my life, as I gazed out the window at magnificent Lake Annecy, I was swept up in the most devastating doubt over the fate of my father.

"Vorun ge khosis?" MY MOTHER said. *"Genigt em."*

My father had been justifying to her one of his political decisions. He had been speaking romantically, drawing deep again—maybe he had mentioned Ararat, I don't remember—and my mother had replied: "Whom are you talking to? I'm your wife." She had accused him of being false, and my father had fallen silent. I knew that must have hurt him more than anything else.

The truth is that we admired the man in different ways, but we did not always believe him. His persona seemed to us an excellent, unbroken act, wherein he played a higher version of himself. But my father did not correct our impressions. Instead, he proceeded to do what strangers have always done. He returned quietly to himself.

I knew of my father's inner life only vaguely. I had noticed his attachment to old things—his black diplomat's bag, a torn and faded pair of shorts, a broken silver hairbrush. I had seen his eyes glow during the Armenian circle dance. I knew that he deeply craved culture; there was scarcely a play, concert, or art show that he missed. I knew also that my father lived with the conviction that his life mattered, that he was living it not only for himself but for others who were not able to, that he was a character in an Armenian fairytale someone had already written or was writing: "There was and there was not . . ."

My father felt himself strangely accountable to his author, and I do believe he tried to please him. After visiting the chosen graves at a cemetery, he would invariably take the spare white roses to the farthest reaches of the lawn and deliver them to the forgotten and the flowerless—the unvisited ghosts. He lived symbolically. He liked to sit in the back row, and when he was traveling on state business, he always stayed in the cheapest hotels, though he was aware his frugality would be known to none except a lone accountant at the National Assembly.

My father loved Armenia, but he loved it less for what it was than what it had been or could become. For him nostalgia and yearning were the same thing: a village table set with yogurt, honey, and *lavash* bread; the confluence of the Arax and Akhurian rivers, the liquid border of Armenia and Turkey where his sons Daron and Armen Richard had been baptized; the royal Republic Square and the enlightened opera house; and of course the blue and immovable Ararat, mountains of God. They stood just beyond his balcony, the way some returning dove had seen them thousands of years before.

IN THE SUMMER OF 2009 I asked my father to write poems again, because I believed in poetry and because I hoped that I might know my father in them. I had uncovered a younger generation of his poems, written twenty years earlier, before his return to Armenia. They had been romantic and simple.

Upon Return

Food
We will grow. Homes
We will build. Our
Women and children
We will protect with
Blood

I thought my father would refuse. I thought that by now politics would have choked the poet out of him. So I was surprised to receive,

within the month, the first of my father's new poems. It was called
"Upon Return II," and it was very different from the first one. He was
writing no longer about an immaculate homeland but about "old freedom's flag, fallen and forlorn . . . upon ancient peaks always twin."

> Where all crests resolve
> There is no other side
> Neither hearth nor fields of green
> And curtains close on yesternight.
> Souls without number dreading death
> But giving life without return
> For liberty of another
> Kind and place and time.
> Party long says poet to the young
> But never again like us.

The following week, my father sent me another poem, this one
composed in Armenian. *"Kgam heto, antsyalits araj, apagayits andin,"*
he wrote. *"Heto kgam vor chlinem arajine."* I had not known that my
father was capable of such lines. I had come to believe that he was
a man of high purpose, the culmination of the family story and the
national history—the snowflake that would set off the avalanche. Yet
there he was, my father, standing at the peak of his powers, crying
out: "I will come later—before the past, beyond the future. / I will
come later, so that I am not the first."

I had believed that history was inevitable. I had found in my family narrative all the evidence of a dramatic, triumphant epic, never
realizing that it had all the trappings of a tragedy, too—the possibility of a sudden and meaningless finish. I never considered, in all the
years I had known my father, that he might not have wanted to be the
last snowflake, but rather the snowflake before that: the one proudly,
but secretly, responsible for another's avalanche.

The summer ended with "Man of the Mount," a poetic biography of a flying man—"a pattern of quilt," my father called him, "and a love of sky."

> He came to give heart
> a boy in ambush
> president of another plateau
> Rewards to reap
> from years in years
> of grapevines and grandmothers
> From the valley of hell
> once heaven
> he soared up and away
> Leaving as trail
> the now bitter fruit
> of a sweet place
> once called home

It was that single phrase—"up and away"—that broke me, because it was so light and cheery and comically superheroic, yet I understood that my father was writing about his end. Only later did he tell me that he was writing about his own father.

By the close of this poetic season, my father's thoughts no longer rhymed. They had no punctuation. His fears were bare, and I had cried reading about them for the first time. But I knew that they were only fears, not prophecies, and I believed that my father was merely cleansing himself of them. I was consoled to find on his desk a loose page from an old calendar, a scrap of William Shakespeare's wisdom: "All the world's a stage, and all the men and women merely players. They have their exits and their entrances; and one man in his time plays many parts."

I no longer knew what part my father was meant to play, and

maybe my father did not know, either. Maybe we both had lost, somewhere on this road of endless return, a sense of destiny. But my father seemed not to need that sense anymore. Too many people had invested in him, and I knew he would do it all for them. The evidence of this I also found on my father's desk. It was a letter from Babi Kaspar. "We keep the hope that one day you will raise the Armenian tricolor on Ararat," he had written to Raffi in 1970, the year of his death. "Through the work of your generation, we will once again achieve the Great Armenia."

And so I came not to mind my father's occasional introversion. I knew that he wasn't going anywhere, only sinking deeper and deeper into himself, preparing his soul for the coming fight, and surfacing always with a smile, which was his love of life and the faith to move mountains.

I MOURNED MY WORDS AS I wrote them, because I knew they were unjust. I had seen how a twist of thought or phrase could corrupt the innocence of a human feeling or the truth of a moment in time. I had faith in words, yet I knew that words were disenfranchised of the past they dreamed to tell. And as I wrote of great men, I came to believe that writing history was really an act of mortifying the past. I was resurrecting the dead only to give them their final shapes, then to kill them for eternity.

I do not know what will become of us, Garin, Daron, Van, Shushi, and Armen Richard—if we will live up to our names, or find new names, ones that aren't obsessed with posterity or the past. I do not know if the Armenian spirit in us will wane and die, as it has a bad habit of doing in this wonderful dispersion. I do not know if we are to become the real prodigal sons, wasting a fortune of inherited memories to pursue our own phantoms of happiness. I do not know what we will do now that the mythology is complete:

fatherland lost, remembered, regained. There is no fourth color to the Armenian flag.

And so, at the end of our story, a kind of repentance for committed and uncommitted sins, I am left only with an epitaph: "If such great wrongs our sons forget . . ." I hope you have read softly, because each word was a coffin, each sentence a grave, and the book a cemetery for a civilization that was—and was not.

NOTES

I began in Bazmashen, and I was fortunate to find in the family
archives an extensive recorded interview of Kaspar Hovannisian
conducted in the summer of 1970 by Richard G. Hovannisian. I heard
my great-grandfather's story in the original voice. Two other interviews, kept in the archives of the oral history collection at the University of California, Los Angeles, were helpful in reconstructing village
life and the experience of 1915. The interviewees were Garabed Der
Sarkissian and Khatchkhatun Kazarian, natives of Bazmashen. I also
conducted extensive interviews with my grandfather Richard and his
brothers John and Vernon Hovannisian.

For the history of Bazmashen, I turned to Vartan Khosrovian's
Bazmasheni Badmutiune: Kiughi Gianken (Newton Upper Falls,
MA: n.p., 1930) and Abdal Gulej Boghosian's *Bazmasheni Entar-
tsag Badmutiune: Ir Himnargutiunen Minchev Verchin Orere* (Boston:
Baikar, 1930). For the regional context: Richard G. Hovannisian's
Armenian Tsopk/Kharpert (Costa Mesa, CA: Mazda, 2002), espe-
cially Christopher J. Walker's chapter "Kharpert in 1915–16" and
Barbara J. Merguerian's chapter "Kharpert: The View from the
United States Consulate"; Leslie Davis's report to the director of
the Consular Service on February 9, 1918, which the Armenian

Genocide Documentation Project of the Gomidas Institute has made available to the public.

An understanding of the early revolutionary movement, which I offered as a flashback, I gained from Louise Nalbandian's *The Armenian Revolutionary Movement: The Development of Armenian Political Parties through the Nineteenth Century* (Berkeley and Los Angeles: University of California Press, 1963). I also found the article "Mobs Killed More than 3,000; No Effort Made by Police and Rioters Murdered from House to House" (August 28, 1896), published without a byline, in the *New York Times.*

Kaspar escaped the inferno, and I followed him. For the geography and history of Alexandropol, or Giumri, I consulted Vazgen Harutyunyan's *Giumrin ev Giumretsinere* (Giumri: Dpir, 1998). For the geography and history of Garin (Erzerum): Richard G. Hovannisian's *Armenian Karin/Erzerum* (Costa Mesa, CA: Mazda, 2003), especially Christina Maranci's chapter "The Architecture of the Karin/Erzerum Region," Pamela Young's "The Sanasarian Varzharan: Making a People into a Nation," Simon Payaslian's "The Death of Armenian Karin/Erzerum," and Richard G. Hovannisian's "The Competition for Erzerum, 1914–1921."

The stand in Garin was a dramatic moment in family and national history, and I heard it recounted in the many voices of my family. But I did depend—for the timeline, the events, and the details of General Antranig's life—on Antranig Chalabian's *General Andranik and the Armenian Revolutionary Movement* (n.p., 1988), A. N. Mnatsakanyan's and H.Gh. Hakobyan's *Zoravar Andranik* (Moscow: Vernatun, 1991), and Vartiter Kotcholosian Hovannisian's *Dzitogh: An Historical-Ethnographic Study of the Village of Dzitogh in the Plain of Karin (Erzerum) on the Armenian Plateau* (Beirut: Hamazkaïne Press, 1972).

Kaspar's immigration records I found at the National Archives building in Washington, D.C. I was taken by Tulare, and I collected memories of the farming community not only from my grandfather and his brothers but also from Charlotte Asadoorian and Abraham Kazarian of Tulare. I was lucky to look through photographs kept by Varsenig Hovannisian and to listen to an interview of my great-grandmother Siroon Hovannisian conducted by Gia Hovannisian for the UCLA oral history project.

In his office, my grandfather spoke to me about a delicate childhood, which elaborated on his published account in Samuel Totten and Steven Leonard Jacobs's *Pioneers of Genocide Studies* (New Brunswick, NJ: Transaction, 2002). My understanding of Tulare itself was enriched by conversations with Linda Ruminer at the Tulare Historical Museum and Marilyn Hanson at the Tulare Public Library Genealogy Room. Looking through the microfilm of the *Tulare Advance-Register* kept there, I developed a sense of Old Tulare. I found a more formal history in Derryl and Wanda Dumermuth's *Tulare: Legends and Trivia from A to Z* (Visalia, CA: Jostens, 2004), where I also found the poem "Little Town."

For the account of Soghomon Tehlirian's assassination of Talaat, I read Jacques Derogy's *Resistance and Revenge: The Armenian Assassination of the Turkish Leaders Responsible for the 1915 Massacres and Deportations* (New Brunswick, NJ: Transaction, 1986) and Samantha Power's *A Problem from Hell: America in the Age of Genocide* (New York: Harper Perennial, 2003). For details of Ghevont Tourian's murder: Michael Stern's "The Murder of the New York Archbishop," published in the July 1935 edition of the *Master Detective*, and Sarkis Atamian's *The Armenian Community: The Historical Development of a Social and Ideological Conflict* (New York: Philosophical Library, 1955).

My grandfather's departure from his father's farm was, and remains, one of the great mysteries of the story—one that my grandmother, Vartiter Kotcholosian Hovannisian, tried honestly and at length to explain to me. Her sister, Nazeli Kotcholosian Messerlian, was herself in possession of great insights. So were Hrayr Kabakian, whom I interviewed by telephone, and Vartan Gregorian, whom I interviewed in his New York office. I profited from reading the letters exchanged between my grandfather and grandmother; the diary my grandfather kept from July 22, 1955, to August 15, 1956; and "Reflections on Academic Dialogue: Impediments and Prospects," my grandfather's remarks from the 2006 symposium of the National Association of Armenian Studies and Research.

I also decided to travel to the source of my grandfather's great education. With my father and mother in the summer of 2008, I visited Beirut for the first time. With Carlo Keusseian always at my side, I followed my grandfather's footsteps. Benjamin Bouchakdjian opened many doors, and Dikran Jinbashian welcomed me to the Hamazgayin Nishan Palanjian Jemaran—a treasury. In the archives of Simon Vratzian, Yervant Pamboukian helped me find the letters my grandfather had written to the prime minister beginning in 1955. Alice Kazandjian offered me stories and pictures of the Jemaran. Peter Karageozian was too kind to a stranger; he guided me patiently through a week of reporting.

In Beirut I conducted two formal interviews: the first with Hovsep Eskidjian, who attended the Jemaran in 1955–56, and the second with Antoine Keheyan, known as "Sir," who was Vratzian's confidant and my grandfather's companion through many Jemaran nights. I also visited the headquarters of the newspaper *Aztag*. Its editor, Shahan Kandaharian, invited me to search the newspaper archives and was helpful, many months later, when I wrote to him for more answers. Nazaret "Nazo" Boulghourjian was always supportive. His Holiness Aram I, Catholicos of the Holy See of Cilicia, was most generous with his time and wisdom.

My grandmother delighted me with stories of her strange romance in 1956, and guided me into my father's first years, which were also the last years of my great-grandfather Kaspar. The past was alive in my father's siblings, Armen K. Hovannisian, Ani K. Hovannisian, and Garo K. Hovannisian; cousins John Hovannisian Jr., David

Hovannisian, Ralph Hovannisian Jr., and Florence Parnagian, who is Grandma Siroon's living incarnation; uncle and aunt Vartkes and Nazeli Messerlian; and my father himself.

Hagop and Marilyn Arshagouni were most helpful in recalling events of family and diaspora history, especially the unveiling of the Montebello Genocide Memorial. The minutes of the meetings of the Armenian Monument Council, which are kept in their home in Northridge, California, were valuable to my research. So were back issues of *Hairenik*, archived at the library of the University of California, Los Angeles. A journal of recollections, dedicated to Vartiter, was my source for Richard's trip to Armenia in 1959.

My father's adolescence and involvement in the Armenian Youth Federation I reconstructed with much help from his siblings, cousins, and friends. I interviewed Moushig Andonian, Armen Chalian, Greg Keosian, and Hrair Messerlian. Conversations with Raffi Ghazarian and Vahe Messerlian were also helpful. For details of the Hovannisian family trip to Soviet Armenia in 1972, I relied on my father's journal and the memories of Marian Hovannisian.

For my grandfather's role in the Armenian Assembly of America, and the history of that organization, I drew on original paperwork kept by my grandfather and discussions with Mihran Agbabian, Sona Hamalian, Robert Aram Kaloosdian, Ken Khachigian, and Van Krikorian. I interviewed Hirair Hovnanian at his home in Yerevan. At the Armenian National Committee of America, meanwhile, Aram Suren Hamparian was always kind, and quick, to respond.

I found the details of Monte Melkonian's life in Markar Melkonian's *My Brother's Road: An American's Fateful Journey to Armenia* (London: I. B. Tauris, 2004); the theories of Stanford Shaw in Stanford Shaw and Ezel Kural Shaw's *History of the Ottoman Empire and Modern Turkey* (Cambridge: Cambridge University Press, 1977); the account of the Tel Aviv conference in Richard G. Hovannisian's chapter "Confronting the Armenian Genocide" in Totten and Jacobs's *Pioneers of*

Genocide Studies; the events of the July 1982 trip to Western Armenia in the journals of Raffi and Armen Hovannisian; and various details of diaspora history in Michael Bobelian's *Children of Armenia* (New York: Simon & Schuster, 2009).

For details of Ruben Keoseyan's final meeting with the pals, I relied on my father's recollections, the notes he had kept during that meeting, and an interview conducted by phone with Ruben Keoseyan. To reconstruct my father's intellectual and romantic adventures on the East Coast, I depended on interviews with my mother, Armenouhi Khatchikian Hovannisian, and my father's friends Gregor Koobatian, Mark Momjian, and Ara Tramblian. To reconstruct the courtship, *khoskgab*, engagement, and wedding of my father and mother, I was assisted by Takouhi Khatchikian, Harout Barseghian, Alvard Barseghian, Vasken Artinian, and Karine Artinian.

The earthquake of December 7, 1988, was a turning point in the family story. For details of international coverage, I consulted and quoted from Bill Keller's "Amid the Rubble, Armenians Express Rage at Gorbachev" (December 12, 1988), "From Soviet Quake, Echoes Widen" (December 18, 1988), and "Sakharov Visits the Caucasus in the Quest for Ethnic Peace" (December 29, 1988), all published in the *New York Times*, and David Remnick's "Soviet Relief Plane Crashes, Killing 78"; "Gorbachev Blasts 'Political Adventurists'" (December 11, 1988) and "In Spitak, 'We Have No More Tears Left'; A Week After the Quake, Numbed Survivors Still Comb Ruins of Devastated Town" (December 15, 1988), both published in the *Washington Post*.

For details of Jeb Bush's visit to Armenia, I turned to John-Thor Dahlburg's "Bush's Son Visits Quake Victims; Injured Armenian Children Receive Candy, Teddy Bears" (December 26, 1988), published in the *Washington Post*. A phone interview with David Remnick and a discussion with Ann Cooper, in her office at the Columbia University Graduate School of Journalism, were invaluable. They shared with me their personal stories and historical views. Michael Shapiro,

my professor, was kind not only to arrange those discussions but to inspire me to pursue new trails of research.

My father moved permanently to Armenia in 1990, and I was fortunate to gain the perspectives of many women and men who observed him in action there. I spoke with Karine Hovsepyan, the woman he lifted from Mountainous Karabagh in May 1991. I read the notes of Congressman Wayne Owens titled "Notes on the Trip to Jordan, Israel and Armenia," which reported on my father's activities on Armenian Independence Day, September 21, 1991. I interviewed Gerard Libaridian, Matthew Der Manuelian, Raffi Sarrafian, Zaven Sinanian, and Christian Ter-Stepanian, who were there for the creation of state and ministry.

The paper trails were long, and I followed them. I read and quoted from the Summary of Conclusions of the Helsinki Additional Meeting of the CSCE on March 24, 1992; the minutes of the September 10, 1992, Istanbul meeting of the Committee of Ministers of the Council of Europe; *The Politics of Diplomacy: Revolution, War and Peace 1989–1992* (New York: G. P. Putnam's Sons, 1995), written by James A. Baker III with Thomas M. DeFrank; Esther B. Fein's "11 Armenians Leave Prison, Find Celebrity" (August 27, 1989), published in the *New York Times*; Daniel Sneider's "Nationalist Vision Draws Diaspora" (May 29, 1991), published in the *Christian Science Monitor*; Carey Goldberg's "Armenian Office Has an American Accent" (September 22, 1992), published in the *Los Angeles Times*; and hundreds of ministry documents kept in the personal archives of my father and of Zaven Sinanian.

The years after my father's resignation I remember especially well. Even so, I confirmed the key events, quotations, and figures through interviews I conducted for that purpose, or else by reference to reports of the international press. Gregory Avedikian's "President Der Bedrosian and the Political Crisis in Armenia" (December 12, 1992) I found in kept issues of the *Armenian Reporter*. I made some translations of poetry in consultation with the work of Diana Der-Hovanessian. Levon Ter-Petrosyan's quotation regarding the priorities of national politics I drew from Simon Payaslian's *The History of Armenia* (New York: Palgrave Macmillan, 2007). The quotation originated in the March 1994 issue of *AIM* magazine, pages 32–35, from an interview by Salpi Haroutinian Ghazarian.

I had heard the name of Stanford Shaw many times in my childhood, but I learned of the great battle against the Turkish history chair at UCLA through a thick file of papers, including a private memorandum my grandfather drafted in the days of that debate. The story was much improved by details provided by Ardashes Kassakhian and Pedro Zarokian, who were two of the many student activists who carried out an information campaign on the dangers of such a chair.

Armenian politics are fragile, and I tried to tread softly. Where possible, I checked memories against international reports: "Armenia: After the 1996 Presidential Elections" issued by the United Nations High Commissioner on Refugees on March 1, 1997; "Armenian Presidential Elections: September 24, 1996—Final Report" issued by the Office for Democratic Institutions and Human Rights of the OSCE on September 24, 1996; "Republic of Armenia Presidential Election March 16 and 30, 1998: Final Report" issued by the Office for Democratic Institutions and Human Rights of the OSCE on April 9, 1998; and "Presidential Election 19 February and 5 March 2003: Final Report" issued by the Office of Democratic Institutions and Human Rights of the Organization for the Security and Cooperation of Europe on April 28, 2003. Conversations with Anahit Bakhshyan and Gevorg Kalenchian were helpful, as were official election data Kalenchian shared with me at the Yerevan headquarters of the Heritage Party.

For the journey of Richard and Vartiter into Western Armenia in the summer of 2006, my first source was the lecture "Changing Land-

——∞——

LANGUAGE AND TRANSLITERATION

The modern Armenian language has developed two literary dialects—Western Armenian and Eastern Armenian—and separate conventions for transliterating these into English. Both have been used as appropriate to the narrative.

—∞∞∞—

ACKNOWLEDGMENTS

T he idea was conceived in Room 801 of the Columbia University Graduate School of Journalism—the realm, in the spring of 2008, of Samuel G. Freedman: professor, writer, and guardian of good things. This work is the result of his wisdom and devotion.

I owe these pages to the kindness of strangers. At the Scovil Galen Ghosh Literary Agency, Anna Ghosh had the imagination to see through untested words, and the courage to stand up for them. Elisabeth Dyssegaard received me with such wise and hopeful hands. And George Quraishi, an exceptional editor, along with Barry Harbaugh, guided me to the end with dedication and style.

I am thankful for the Lynton Award for Book Writing and the Fulbright Fellowship in Creative Writing; the good counsel of Kelly McMasters, Alice Mandell, Liel Leibovitz, and Matthew Miller; the guidance and friendship of Hakop Barseghian and Katherine Eastland; and the many revelations of the magnificent Michael Shapiro.

The better part of my life is unwritten. I have known Grandma Siroon and Mami Khenguhi, and I am lucky to have them reanimated in so many cousins, uncles, and aunts. I depend on my brothers—Daron, Van, and Armen Richard—more than they know. They are my pride, my strength, and my vitality, as Shushi is our sensation of beauty. My mother, Armenouhi, is my one idea of eternal grace—the inspiration and ambition of all my words.

I discovered literature and liberty in Stephen D. Cox. He is the original faith and everlasting teacher.

I end upon a few pilgrim souls: Artashes Khurshudyan—*mon camarade* in the night; Molly Trabue Kordares—my lady of the harbor; Ruben Melikyan—the mythologist and the myth; and Alec Mouhibian—the endless influence, my many-splendored friend. Sorry, I borrowed of you more than I can return.